SWAMI VIVEKANANDA

ON HIMSELF

Advaita Ashrama
(PUBLICATION DEPARTMENT)
5 DEHI ENTALLY ROAD · KOLKATA 700 014

Published by
Swami Muktidananda
Adhyaksha, Advaita Ashrama
Mayavati, Champawat, Uttarakhand, Himalayas
from its Publication Department, Kolkata
Email: mail@advaitaashrama.org
Website: www.advaitaashrama.org

© *All Rights Reserved*
First Edition, 1963
Second Enlarged Edition, May 2006
Thirteenth Reprint, August 2017
3M3C

ISBN 978-81-7505-280-2

Typeset in Storm Type Baskerville Ten

Printed in India at
Gipidi Box Co.
Kolkata · 700 014

CONTENTS

Preface to the Second Edition • v
Preface to the First Edition • vi
1. Birth and Boyhood • 1
2. Discipleship • 9
3. Sri Ramakrishna, My Master • 45
4. The Baranagore Math & Days of Wandering • 73
5. The Divine Call & The Parliament of Religions • 111
6. March of Events • 133
7. Return to India • 234
8. The Plan of Work • 271
9. Second Visit to the West • 293
10. "I Believe . . ." • 325
11. The Last Days • 333
Endnotes • 353

PREFACE TO THE SECOND EDITION

MORE THAN FORTY YEARS have passed since the first edition of *Swami Vivekananda on Himself* was published in 1963. The original publisher, Swami Sambuddhananda, was general secretary of the Swami Vivekananda Centenary committee, which was dissolved after its work was completed.

Since that time, much new material about Swami Vivekananda has appeared in print. Revised editions of the two volumes of the *Life of Swami Vivekananda* by His Eastern and Western Disciples were released in 1979 and 1981. *Swami Vivekananda in the West: New Discoveries* in 6 volumes, by Marie Louise Burke, was completed in 1987. The ninth volume of the *Complete Works of Swami Vivekananda* was published in 1997. In this second edition much new material has been incorporated from these sources, and every entry has been carefully referenced and revised where necessary, by Brahmachari Nirmala Chaitanya.

We are sure that students and devotees of Swami Vivekananda, through these pages, will gain new inspiration from and fresh insight into the personality that is Swami Vivekananda.

Kolkata   PUBLISHER
May 2006

PREFACE TO THE FIRST EDITION

SWAMI VIVEKANANDA WAS born in Calcutta on the 12th of January, 1863, and peacefully passed away on July 4, 1902, in the monastery at Belur Math near Calcutta. After remaining an unknown figure for nearly thirty years of his life he emerged as a World Teacher in the true sense of the term and blessed innumerable souls all over the globe.

It was on January 27, 1900 during his second visit to America that Swami Vivekananda delivered to the Shakespeare Club of Pasadena, California, somewhat reluctantly, a touching account of "My Life and Mission." In it the Swami naturally gave out very little of his great and eventful life. Fortunately for us, however, we are able to gather a fund of information about his life and work in the East and the West from the large number of his letters to his disciples, friends, and admirers in both the Hemispheres, as also from a few other very reliable sources.

In fact the present book is a documentation of selected notes and utterances of Swamiji about himself and his work collected from the books mentioned below. These are arranged chronologically so as to form what may be called a near autobiography of the great saint. And for this very important work we are much indebted to a swami of the Ramakrishna Order, who prefers to remain anonymous. The original manuscript prepared by him was the product of patient labour for a long period, and it was passed on to a senior swami of

PREFACE TO THE FIRST EDITION

the Bombay Ashrama, who jointly with Prof. Charu Chandra Chatterjee went through the manuscript, weighing and judging the passages, collating and comparing them with the sourcebooks, removing a passage here, or replacing a passage there. As a result of these changes, the book seemed to take a definite shape, and Prof. Chatterjee was then asked to prepare a press copy exercising all editorial power so that it might become a good readable and presentable volume when it came out of the press.

Prof. Chatterjee was very ably assisted by Smt. S. Bhargava M. A., who was entrusted with the heavy and responsible work of maintaining proper reference of the books and passages from which the materials of the manuscript were culled, as also noting the dates of Swamiji's letters included in the manuscript. It is thus intended to be an authentic record for future guidance.

We are indebted to these Swamis and friends for the commendable work they did with devotion and care and also to the proprietor of the Saxon Press without whose active cooperation it would have been very difficult for us to bring out the present volume.

The excerpts are from the following:

1. *The Complete Works of Swami Vivekananda*, in 8 volumes.
2. *The Gospel of Sri Ramakrishna*.
3. *Sri Ramakrishna, The Great Master*.
4. *The Master as I Saw Him* . .
5. *The Life of Swami Vivekananda* by His Eastern and Western Disciples.
6. *New Discoveries: Swami Vivekananda in America*.

SWAMI VIVEKANANDA ON HIMSELF

This selected compilation, which includes Swamiji's own words about his beloved Guru Sri Ramakrishna, we believe, will be a highly valuable and handy document and will remain a source of inspiration to the coming generation.

PUBLISHER

CHAPTER ONE

BIRTH AND BOYHOOD

For the salvation of his own soul, and for the good and happiness of the many, the Sannyasin is born in the world. To sacrifice his life for others, to alleviate the misery of millions rending the air with their cries, to wipe away the tears from the eyes of the widow, to console the heart of the bereaved mother, to provide the ignorant and depressed masses with the ways and means for the struggle for existence, and enable them to stand on their own feet, to preach broadcast the teachings of the Shastras to one and all without distinction for their material and spiritual welfare, to rouse the sleeping lion of Brahman in the hearts of all beings by the diffusion of the light of knowledge—for this the Sannyasin is born in the world!... it is for the consummation of this purpose in life that we have taken birth, and we shall lay down our lives for it.[1]

My father and mother fasted and prayed, for years and years, so that I would be born.[2]

I know that before I was born, my mother would fast and pray and do hundreds of things which I could not even do for five minutes. She did that for two years. I believe that whatever religious culture I have, I owe to that. It was consciously that my mother brought me into the world to be what I am. Whatever good impulse I have was given to me by my mother—and consciously, not unconsciously.[3]

The love which my mother gave to me has made me what I am, and I owe a debt to her that I can never repay.[4]

How many times I have seen my mother going to take her first meal when it was two o'clock. We took ours at ten and she at two because she had so many things to attend to. [For example], someone knocks at the door and says, "Guest," and there is no food except what was for my mother. She would give that to him willingly and then wait for her own. That was her life and she liked it. And that is why we worship mothers as gods.[5]

I have such a memory. When I was only two years old, I used to play with my syce at being a Vairagi, clothed in ashes and Kaupina. And if a Sadhu came to beg, they would lock me in, upstairs, to prevent my giving too much away. I felt that I also was this, and that for some mischief I had had to be sent away from Shiva. No doubt my family increased this feeling, for when I was naughty they would say "Dear, dear! So many austerities, yet Shiva sent us this demon after all, instead of a good soul!" Or when I was very rebellious they would empty a can of water over me, saying "Shiva! Shiva!" And then I was all right, always. Even now, when I feel mischievous, that word keeps me straight.[6]

When I was a little boy at school, I had a fight with another schoolfellow about some sweetmeats, and he being the stronger boy snatched them from my hand. I remember the feeling I had; I thought that boy was the most wicked boy ever born, and that as soon as I grew strong enough I would punish him; there was no punishment sufficient for his wickedness. We have both grown up now, and we are fast friends. This world is full of babies to whom eating and drinking, and all these little cakes are everything. They will dream of these

BIRTH AND BOYHOOD

cakes, and their idea of future life is where these cakes will be plentiful.[7]

What I saw and felt when going through the forest [on the way to Raipur]* has for ever remained firmly imprinted in my memory, particularly a certain event of one day. We had to travel by the foot of the Vindhya mountains that day. The peaks of the ranges on both sides of the road rose very high in the sky; various kinds of trees and creepers bending under the weight of fruits and flowers produced wonderful beauty on the mountainsides. Birds of various colours, flying from tree to tree, filled the quarters with sweet notes. I saw all these and felt an extraordinary peace in my mind. The slow-moving bullock-carts arrived at a place where two mountain peaks, coming forward as though in love, locked themselves in an embrace over the narrow forest path. Observing carefully below the meeting-points I saw that there was a very big cleft from the crest to the foot of the mountain on one side of the path; and filling that cleft, there was hanging in it an enormous honeycomb, the result of the bees' labour for ages. Filled with wonder, as I was pondering over the beginning and the end of that kingdom of bees, my mind became so much absorbed in the thought of the infinite power of God, the controller of the three worlds, that I completely lost my consciousness of the external world for some time. I do not remember how long I was lying in the bullock-cart in that condition. When I regained normal consciousness, I found that we had crossed that place and come far away. As I was

---

* In the year 1877, when Vivekananda (then Naren) was about fourteen years old, his father went to Raipur in the Central Provinces (Madhya Pradesh). He arranged that his family should follow him later on led by Naren. It was a journey partly by bullock cart via Allahabad and Jabalpur through dense forests and over unfrequented roads, for the railways were in those days constructed only up to Nagpur.

alone in the cart, no one could know anything about it.[8]

We cannot deny that there is much misery in [the world]; to go out and help others is, therefore, the best thing we can do, although in the long run, we shall find that helping others is only helping ourselves. As a boy I had some white mice. They were kept in a little box in which there were little wheels, and when the mice tried to cross the wheels, the wheels turned and turned, and the mice never got anywhere. So it is with the world and our helping it. The only help is that we get moral exercise.[9]

When [my teacher] came to our house, I brought my English and Bengali books to him, and showing him the particular books and the portions in them that were to be learnt as lessons for the day, I laid myself down or sat quietly. The teacher repeated twice or thrice the spelling, pronunciation, meaning etc., of the words of those portions of those books, as if he was himself learning the lesson, and went away. That was sufficient for me to learn them.[10]

A little arithmetic, some Sanskrit grammar, a little of language and accounts—these are taught in the primary school. A little book on ethics, taught by an old man, we learnt by heart, and I remember one of the lessons:

"For the good of a village, a man ought to give up his family; for the good of a country, he ought to give up his village; for the good of humanity, he may give up his country; for the good of the world, everything."

Such verses are there in the books. We get them by heart, and they are explained by teacher and pupil.[11]

This was the first verse that I was taught in my life, the first day I went to school: "He indeed is a learned man who looks upon all women as his mother, who looks upon every man's property as so much dust, and looks upon every being as his own soul."[12]

Even while I was a student at Calcutta, I was of a religious temperament. I was critical even at that time of my life; mere words would not satisfy me.[13]

I used to see all my life a wonderful point of light between my eyebrows, as soon as I shut my eyes in order to go to sleep, and I used to observe attentively its various changes. So that it might be convenient to see it, I used to lie on my bed in the way people bow down touching the ground with their foreheads. The extraordinary point kept changing its colours and increasing in size, became gradually converted into the form of a ball, and bursting at last, covered my body from head to foot with white liquid light. As soon as that happened, I lost consciousness and fell asleep. I believed that all people went to sleep that way. I was long under that impression. When I grew up and began to practise meditation, that point of light used to come before me as soon as I closed my eyes, and then I concentrated my mind on it. In those days I daily practised meditation with a few friends according to the instruction of Maharshi Devendranath. We talked among ourselves about the nature of visions and experiences that each of us had. At that time I came to know from what they said that they never had the vision of such a light and that none of them went to sleep in that way.[14]

From my boyhood I have been a dare-devil; otherwise could I have attempted to make a tour round the world, almost without a penny in my pocket?[15]

While at school, one night I was meditating within closed doors and had a fairly deep concentration of mind. How long I meditated in that way, I cannot say. It was over, and I still kept my seat, when from the southern wall of that room a luminous figure stepped out and stood in front of me. There was a wonderful radiance on its visage, yet there seemed to be no play of emotion on it. It was the figure of a Sannyasin absolutely calm, shaven-headed, and staff and Kamandalu [a Sannyasin's water pitcher] in hand. He gazed at me for some time and seemed as if he would address me. I too gazed at him in speechless wonder. Then a kind of fright seized me, I opened the door, and hurried out of the room. Then it struck me that it was foolish of me to run away like that, that perhaps he might say something to me. But I have never met that figure since. Many a time and often I have thought that if again I saw him, I would no more be afraid but would speak to him. But I met him no more.... I could find no clue to its solution. I now think it was the Lord Buddha whom I saw.[16]

From my very boyhood, whenever I came in contact with a particular object, man or place, it would sometimes appear to me as if I had been acquainted with it beforehand. But all my efforts to recollect [the particulars] were unsuccessful, and yet the impression persisted. I will give you an instance: One day I was discussing various topics with my friends at a particular place. Suddenly something was said, which at once reminded me that in some time past in this very house I had talked with these friends on that very subject and that the discussion had even taken the same turn. Later on I thought that it might be due to the law of transmigration. But soon I decided that such definite conclusions on the subject were not reasonable. Now I believe that before I was born I must have had visions somehow, of those subjects and people with whom I would have to come in contact in my present birth. Such memories have come every now and then throughout my life.[17]

Just two or three days before the Entrance examination I found that I hardly knew anything of geometry. So I began to study the subject, keeping awake the whole night, and in twenty-four hours I mastered the four books of geometry.[18]

I studied hard for twelve years and became a graduate of Calcutta University.[19]

It so happened that I could understand an author without reading his book line by line. I could get the meaning by just reading the first and the last line of a paragraph. As this power developed I found it unnecessary to read even the paragraphs. I could follow by reading only the first and last lines of a page. Further, where the author introduced discussions to explain a matter and it took him four or five or even more pages to clear the subject, I could grasp the whole trend of his arguments by only reading the first few lines.[20]

As soon as I went to bed, two ideals appeared before me every night ever since I had reached my youth. One vision presented me as a person of endless wealth and property, innumerable servants and dependants, high rank and dignity, great pomp and power. I thought that I was seated at the head of those who were called big men in the world. I felt I certainly had the power to achieve this end. Again, the next moment, I felt as if I had given up everything of the world and was leading a life of renunciation, putting on a loincloth, eating whatever was available without effort, spending nights under trees, and depending solely on God's will. I felt I could live the life of the Rishis and the Munis if I wanted. These two opposite pictures, according to which I could mould my life, thus arose in my mind. But the latter would grip the mind in the end. I thought that it was in this way alone that man could attain real bliss, and that I should follow this path and not the other. Brooding on the happiness of such a life, my mind would then merge in the contemplation of God and I would fall asleep. It is a matter of astonishment that this happened every night, for a long time.[21]

I never terrified children by speaking of hobgoblins as I was afraid of uttering a falsehood, and scolded all whom I saw doing it. As the result of English education and my frequenting the Brahmo Samaj, the devotion to verbal expression of truth increased so much then.[22]

At the beginning of this century [19th] it was almost feared that religion was at an end. Under the tremendous sledge-hammer blows of scientific research, old superstitions were crumbling away like masses of porcelain. Those to whom religion meant only a bundle of creeds and meaningless ceremonials were in despair; they were at their wit's end. Everything was slipping between their fingers. For a time it seemed inevitable that the surging tide of agnosticism and materialism would sweep all before it.... When I was a boy, this scepticism reached me, and it seemed for a time as if I must give up all hope of religion. But fortunately for me I studied the Christian religion, the Mohammedan, the Buddhistic, and others, and what was my surprise to find that the same foundation principles taught by my religion were also taught by all religions. It appealed to me this way. What is the truth? I asked.[23]

When I was a boy here, in this city of Calcutta, I used to go from place to place in search of religion, and everywhere I asked the lecturer after hearing very big lectures, "Have you seen God?" The man was taken aback at the idea of seeing God; and the only man who told me, "I have," was Ramakrishna Paramahamsa, and not only so, but he said, "I will put you in the way of seeing Him too."[24]

Swami Vivekananda's Ancestral Home, Calcutta

I used to play with my syce at being a Vairagi, clothed in ashes and Kaupina. And if a Sadhu came to beg, they would lock me in, upstairs, to prevent my giving too much away.

Bhuvanesvari Devi (1841–1911)

The love which my mother gave to me has made me what I am, and I owe a debt to her that I can never repay.

Sri Ramakrishna, Dakshineswar, 1884

I crept near him and asked him the question which I had asked so often: "Have you seen God, sir?" "Yes, I see Him just as I see you here, only in a much intenser sense."

Narendranath, Cossipore, 1886

Two or three days before Sri Ramakrishna's passing away, She whom he used to call "Kali" entered this body.

Dakshineswar Kali Temple

The Panchavati at Dakshineswar

After all . . . I am only the boy who used to listen with rapt wonderment to the wonderful words of Ramakrishna under the Banyan at Dakshineswar.

CHAPTER TWO

DISCIPLESHIP

I was born in Bengal and became a monk and a celibate by choice. At my birth my father had a horoscope taken of my life, but would never tell me what it was. Some years ago when I visited my home, my father having died, I came across the chart among some papers in my mother's possession and saw from it that I was destined to become a wanderer on the face of the earth.[1]

I had a deep interest in religion and philosophy from my childhood, and our books teach renunciation as the highest ideal to which man can aspire. It only needed the meeting with a great teacher—Ramakrishna Paramahamsa—to kindle in me the final determination to follow the path he himself had trod, as in him I found my highest ideal realised.[2]

In the Order to which I belong we are called Sannyasins. The word means "a man who has renounced." This is a very, very, very ancient Order. Even Buddha, who was 560 years before Christ, belonged to that Order.... So ancient! You find it mentioned away back in the Vedas, the oldest book in the world....

The Order is not a church, and the people who join the Order are not priests. There is an absolute difference between the priests and the Sannyasins.... The Sannyasins do not possess property, and they do not marry. Beyond that there is no organisation. The only bond that is there is the bond between the teacher and the taught—and that is peculiar to India. The teacher is not a man who comes just to teach me, and I pay him so much, and there it ends. In India it is really like an adoption. The teacher is more than my own father, and I am truly his child, his son in every respect. I owe him obedience and reverence first, before my own father even; because, they say, the father gave me this body, but [the teacher] showed me the way to salvation, he is greater than father. And we carry this love, this respect for our teacher all our lives.... Sometimes the teacher will be a young man and the disciple a very old man....

Now, I happened to get an old man to teach me, and he was very peculiar. He did not go much for intellectual scholarship, scarcely studied books; but when he was a boy he was seized with the tremendous idea of getting truth direct. First he tried by studying his own religion. Then he got the idea that he must get the truth of other religions; and with that idea he joined all the sects, one after another. For the time being he did exactly what they told him to do—lived with the devotees of these different sects in turn, until interpenetrated with the particular ideal of that sect. After a few years he would go to another sect. When he had gone through with all that, he came to the conclusion that they were all good. He had no criticism to offer to any one; they are all so many paths leading to the same goal. And then he said, "That is a glorious thing, that there should be so many paths, because if there were only one path, perhaps it would suit only an individual man. The more the number of paths, the more the chance for every one of us to know the truth. If I cannot be taught in one language, I will try another," and so on. Thus his benediction was for every religion.[3]

People came by thousands to see this wonderful man who spoke in a patois, every word of which was forceful and instinct with light.... This man came to live near Calcutta, the capital of India, the most important university town in our country, which was sending out sceptics and materialists by the hundreds every year. Yet many of these university men—sceptics and agnostics—used to come and listen to him. I heard of this man, and I went to hear him. He looked just like an ordinary man, with nothing remarkable about him.[4]

[*Question: You must remember vividly your first visit to him.*] Yes. It was at the temple garden at Dakshineswar, in his own room. That day I sang two songs.... He went into Samadhi. He said to Ram Babu, "Who is this boy? How well he sings!" He asked me to come again.[5]

Well, I sang the song; but shortly after, he suddenly rose, and taking me by the hand, led me to the northern veranda, shutting the door behind him. It was locked from the outside; so we were alone. I thought that he would give me some private instructions; but to my utter surprise he began to shed profuse tears of joy as he held my hand, and, addressing me most tenderly as one long familiar to him, said, "Ah, you come so late! How could you be so unkind as to keep me waiting so long! My ears are well-nigh burnt by listening to the profane talk of worldly people. Oh, how I yearn to unburden my mind to one who can appreciate my innermost experience!" Thus he went on amid sobs. The next moment he stood before me with folded hands and began to address me, "Lord, I know you are that ancient sage, Nara, the Incarnation of Narayana, born on earth to remove the miseries of mankind," and so on.

I was altogether taken aback by his conduct. "Who is this man whom I have come to see," I thought, "he must be stark mad! Why, I am just the son of Vishwanath Datta, and yet he dares to address me thus!" But I kept quiet, allowing him to go on. Presently he went back to his room, and bringing some sweets, sugar candy, and butter, began to feed me with his own hands. In vain did I say again and again, "Please give the sweets to me, I shall share them with my friends!" He simply said, "They may have some afterwards," and desisted only after I had eaten all. Then he seized me by the hand and said, "Promise that you will come alone to me at an early date." At his importunity I had to say "yes" and returned with him to my friends.[6]

I sat and watched him. There was nothing wrong in his words, movements or behaviour towards others. Rather, from his spiritual words and ecstatic states he seemed to be a man of genuine renunciation; and there was a marked consistency between his words and life. He used the most simple language, and I thought, "Can this man be a great teacher?" I crept near him and asked him the question which I had asked so often: "Have you seen God, sir?" "Yes, I see Him just as I see you here, only in a much intenser sense." "God can be realized," he went on; "one can see and talk to Him as I am seeing and talking to you. But who cares? People shed torrents of tears for their wife and children, for wealth or property, but who does so for the sake of God? If one weeps sincerely for Him, He surely manifests Himself." That impressed me at once. For the first time I found a man who dared to say that he had seen God, that religion was a reality to be felt, to be sensed in an infinitely more intense way than we can sense the world. As I heard these things from his lips, I could not but believe that he was saying them not like an ordinary preacher, but from the depths of his own realizations. But I could not reconcile his words with his strange conduct with me. So I concluded that he must be a monomaniac. Yet I could not help acknowledging the magnitude of his renunciation. "He may be a madman," I thought, "but only the

DISCIPLESHIP

fortunate few can have such renunciation. Even if insane, this man is the holiest of the holy, a true saint, and for that alone he deserves the reverent homage of mankind!" With such conflicting thoughts I bowed before him and begged leave to return to Calcutta.[7]

[*Question: Where did you see him next?*] At Rajmohan's house. The third visit was at Dakshineswar again. During that visit he went into Samadhi and began to praise me as if I were God. He said to me, "O Narayana, you have assumed this body for my sake.... I asked the Divine Mother, "Mother, unless I enjoy the company of some genuine devotees completely free from 'woman and gold', how shall I live on earth?" Then he said to me, "You came to me at night, woke me up, and said, 'Here I am!'" But I did not know anything of this. I was sound asleep in our Calcutta house.[8]

I did not realize then that the temple garden of Dakshineswar was so far from Calcutta, since on the previous occasion I had gone there in a carriage. The road seemed to me so long as to be almost endless. However, I reached the garden somehow and went straight to Sri Ramakrishna's room. I found him sitting alone on the small bedstead. He was glad to see me, and calling me affectionately to his side, made me sit beside him on the bed. But the next moment I found him overcome with a sort of emotion. Muttering something to himself, with his eyes fixed on me, he slowly drew near me. I thought he might do something queer as on the previous occasion. But in the twinkling of an eye he placed his right foot on my body. The touch at once gave rise to a novel experience within me. With my eyes open I saw that the walls, and everything in the room, whirled rapidly and vanished into naught, and the whole universe together with my individuality was about to merge in an all-encompassing mysterious void! I was terribly frightened and thought that I was facing death, for the loss of individuality meant nothing short of that. Unable to control myself I cried out, "What is it that you are doing to me! I have my parents at home!" He laughed aloud at this and stroking my chest said, "All right, let it rest now. Everything will come in time!" The wonder of it was that no sooner had he said this than that strange experience of mine vanished. I was myself again and found everything within and without the room as it had been before.

All this happened in less time than it takes me to narrate it, but it revolutionized my mind. Amazed, I wondered what it could possibly be. It came and went at the mere wish of this amazing man! I began to question whether it was mesmerism or hypnotism. But that was not likely, for these acted only on weak minds, and I prided myself on having just the reverse. I had not as yet surrendered myself to the stronger personality of the man. Rather I had taken him to be a monomaniac. So to what might this sudden transformation of mine be due? I could not come to any conclusion. It was an enigma, I thought, which I had better not attempt to solve. I was determined, however, to be on my guard and not to give him another chance to exert a similar influence over me.

The next moment I thought, how can a man who shatters to pieces a resolute and strong mind like mine be dismissed as a lunatic? Yet that was just the conclusion at which one would arrive from his effusiveness on our first meeting—unless he were an Incarnation of God, which was indeed a far cry. So I was in a dilemma about the real nature of my experience as well as about the truth of this wonderful man, who was obviously as pure and simple as a child. My rationalistic mind received an unpleasant rebuff at this failure in judging the true state of things. But I was determined to fathom the mystery somehow.

Thoughts like these occupied my mind during the whole of that day. But he became quite another man after that incident, and as on the previous occasion, treated me with great kindness and cordiality. His behaviour towards me was like that of a man who meets an old friend or relative after long separation. He seemed not to be satisfied with entertaining and taking all possible care of me. This remarkably loving treatment drew me all the more to him. At last, finding that the day was coming to a close, I asked leave to go. He seemed very dejected at this and gave me permission only after I had promised to come again at my earliest convenience.[9]

One day in the temple-garden at Dakshineswar Sri Ramakrishna touched me over the heart, and first of all I began to see that the houses—rooms, doors, windows, verandas—the trees, the sun, the moon—all were flying off, shattering to pieces as it were—reduced to atoms and molecules—and ultimately became merged in the Akasha. Gradually again, the Akasha also vanished, and after that, my consciousness of the ego with it; what happened next I do not recollect. I was at first frightened. Coming back from that state, again I began to see the houses, doors, windows, verandas, and other things. On another occasion, I had exactly the same realisation by the side of a lake in America.... A derangement of the brain! How can you call it so, when it comes neither as the result of delirium from any disease, nor of intoxication from drinking, nor as an illusion produced by various sorts of queer breathing exercises—but when it comes to a normal man in full possession of his health and wits? Then again, this experience is in perfect harmony with the Vedas. It also coincides with the words of realisation of the inspired Rishis and Acharyas of old. Do you take me, at last, to be a crack-brained man?... Know [that] this knowledge of Oneness is what the Shastras speak of as realisation of Brahman, by knowing which one gets rid of fear, and the shackles of birth and death break for ever. Having once realised that Supreme Bliss, one is no more overwhelmed by the pleasure and pain of this world....

That Supreme Bliss fully exists in all, from Brahma down to the blade of grass. You are also that undivided Brahman.... Being again and again entangled in the intricate maze of delusion and hard hit by sorrows and afflictions, the eye will turn of itself to one's own real nature, the Inner Self. It is owing to the presence of this desire for bliss in the heart, that man, getting hard shocks one after another, turns his eye inwards—to his own Self. A time is sure to come to everyone, without exception, when he will do so—to one it may be in this life, to another, after thousands of incarnations.[10]

Seeing that the Master gave no thought to himself on account of me, I did not hesitate on occasion to use harsh words about his blind love for me. I used to warn him, saying that if he constantly thought of me, he would become like me, even as King Bharata of the old legend, who so doted upon his pet deer that even at the time of death he was unable to think of anything else, and as a result, was born as a deer in his next life. At these words, the Master, so simple was he, became very nervous, and said, "What you say is quite true. What is to become of me, for I cannot bear to be separated from you?" Dejected, he went to the Kali temple. In a few minutes he returned smiling and said, "You rogue, I shall not listen to you any more. Mother says that I love you because I see the Lord in you, and the day I no longer do so, I shall not be able to bear even the sight of you." With this short but emphatic statement he dismissed once for all everything that I had ever said to him on the subject.[11]

One day he said to me, "You can see Krishna in your heart if

DISCIPLESHIP

you want." I replied, "I don't believe in Krishna or any such nonsense!"[12]

Once I said to him, "The forms of God and things like that, which you see in your visions, are all figments of your imagination." He had so much faith in my words that he went to the Divine Mother in the temple and told Her what I had said to him. He asked Her, "Are these hallucinations, then?" Afterwards he said to me, "Mother told me that all these are real"....

[Again], he said to me, "When you sing, He who dwells here (touching his heart), like a snake, hisses as it were, and then, spreading his hood, quietly holds himself steady and listens to your music."[13]

We [Sri Ramakrishna and I] talked of our revealed book, the Vedas, of your Bible, of the Koran, and of revealed books in general. At the close of our talk, this good man asked me to go to the table and take up a book; it was a book which, among other things, contained a forecast of the rainfall during the year. The sage said, "Read that." And I read out the quantity of rain that was to fall. He said, "Now take the book and squeeze it." I did so and he said, "Why, my boy, not a drop of water comes out. Until the water comes out, it is all book, book. So until your religion makes you realise God, it is useless. He who only studies books for religion reminds one of the fable of the ass which carried a heavy load of sugar on its back, but did not know the sweetness of it."[14]

I did not believe in anything.... At first I did not accept most of what the Master said. One day he asked me, "Then why do you come here?" I replied, "I come here to see you, not to listen to you".... He was very much pleased.[15]

One day when I was alone with him he said something to

me. Nobody else was present.... He said, "It is not possible for me to exercise occult powers; but I shall do so through you. What do you say?" "No," I replied, "you can't do that."

I used to laugh at his words.... I told him that his visions of God were all hallucinations of his mind.

He said to me, "I used to climb to the roof of the Kuthi and cry, 'O devotees, where are you all? Come to me, O devotees! I am about to die. I shall certainly die if I do not see you.' And the Divine Mother told me, 'The devotees will come.' You see, everything is turning out to be true." What else could I say? I kept quiet.[16]

I used to follow my own whims in everything I did. The Master never interfered.... I became a member of the Sadharan Brahmo Samaj.... The Master knew that women attended the meetings of the Brahmo Samaj. A man cannot meditate with women sitting in front of him; therefore he criticized the meditation of the Brahmo Samaj. But he didn't object to my going there. But one day he said to me, "Don't tell Rakhal about your being a member of the Brahmo Samaj, or he too will feel like becoming one."[17]

When I found that the Master did not bestow that kind of grace on [my friends] which he had done on me by accepting me and instructing me in spiritual matters, I used to press him to bestow it also on them too. On account of boyish flippancy I was ready on many occasions to argue with him on this point. I said, "Why, Sir? God can never be so partial as to bestow His grace on some and not on others. Why should you then not accept them as you have done me? Is it not certain that one can attain spiritual realisation by one's effort also, just as one can become a learned scholar if one puts forth sufficient effort?" The Master replied, "What can I do, my child? Mother shows me that there is the beastly mental attitude of a bull in them. They cannot realize spirituality in this life. What can I do? And what is it you say? Can anyone become in this life what he wishes to be, by mere will and effort?" But, who lent an ear to the Master's word then? I said, "What do you say, sir? Can't one become what one wishes to be, if one wills and makes an effort? Surely one can. I cannot believe what you say about it." At this also the Master said the same thing, "Whether you believe it or not, Mother shows me that." I never accepted then what he said. But, as time passed on, more and more did I understand from experience that what the Master said was right and what I had thought was wrong.[18]

As soon as I went to Dakshineswar, the Master gave me those books which he forbade others to read. Among other books, a copy of the *Ashtavakra Samhita* was in his room. When the Master found anyone reading that book, he would forbid him and would give him instead such books as *Mukti and How to Attain It*, the *Bhagavad Gita*, or some Purana. But, scarcely had I gone to him, when he took out that book and asked me to read it. Or, he would ask me to read some part of the *Adhyatma Ramayana* which is full of non-dualistic ideas. I would reply, sometimes bluntly, "What is the use of reading this book? It is a sin even to think, 'I am God.' The book teaches this blasphemy. It should be burnt." The Master would smile and say, "Do I ask you to read it for yourself? I ask you to read a little to me. Please do it. In that case, you will not have to think that you are God." So I had to read a little for him at his request.[19]

The magic touch of the Master [one] day immediately brought a wonderful change over my mind. I was astounded to find that really there was nothing in the universe but God! I saw it quite clearly, but kept silent to see whether the impression would last; but it did not abate in the course of the day. I returned home, but there too, everything I saw appeared to be Brahman. I sat down to take my meal, but found that everything—the food, the plate, the person who served, and even myself—was nothing but That. I ate a morsel or two and sat still. I was startled by my mother's words, "Why do you sit still? Finish your meal," and then began to eat again. But all the while, whether eating or lying down, or going to college, I had the same experience and felt myself always in a sort of trance. While walking in the streets, I noticed cabs plying, but I did not feel inclined to move out of the way. I felt that the cabs and myself were of one stuff. There was no sensation in my limbs, which seemed to be becoming paralysed. I did not relish eating, and felt as if somebody else were eating. Sometimes I lay down during a meal; after a few minutes I got up and again began to eat. The result would be that on some days I would take too much, but it did no harm. My mother became alarmed and said that there must be something wrong with me. She was afraid that I might not live long. When there was a slight change in this state, the world began to appear dream-like. While walking in Cornwallis Square, I would strike my head against the iron railings to see if they were real or only a dream. This state of things continued for some days. When I became normal again, I realized that I must have had a glimpse of the Advaita state. Then it struck me that the words of the scriptures were not false. Thenceforth I could not deny the conclusions of the Advaita philosophy.[20]

For the first time I had found a man who dared to say that he saw God, that religion was a reality to be felt, to be sensed in an infinitely more intense way than we can sense the world. I began to go to that man, day after day, and I actually saw that religion could be given. One touch, one glance, can change a whole life. I had read about Buddha and Christ and Mohammed, about all those different luminaries of ancient times, how they would stand up and say, "Be thou whole," and the man became whole. I now found it to be true, and when I myself saw this man, all scepticism was brushed aside. It could be done; and my Master used to say, "Religion can be given and taken more tangibly, more really than anything else in the world"....

The second idea that I learnt from my Master, and which is perhaps the most vital, is the wonderful truth that the religions of the world are not contradictory or antagonistic. They are but various phases of one eternal religion. That one eternal religion is applied to different planes of existence, is applied to the opinions of various minds and various races.[21]

Devotion as taught by Narada, he used to preach to the masses, those who were incapable of any higher training. He used generally to teach dualism. As a rule, he never taught Advaitism. But he taught it to me. I had been a dualist before.[22]

[Sri Ramakrishna] once told me that not one in twenty millions in this world believed in God. I asked him why, and he told me, "Suppose there is a thief in this room, and he gets to know that there is a mass of gold in the next room, and only a very thin partition between the two rooms; what will be the condition of that thief?" I answered, "He will not be able to sleep at all; his brain will be actively thinking of some means of getting at the gold, and he will think of nothing else." Then he replied, "Do you believe that a man could believe in God and not go mad to get Him? If a man sincerely believes that there is that immense, infinite mine of bliss, and that it can be reached, would not that man go mad in his struggle to reach it?"[23]

One day at that time I spent a night with the Master at

Dakshineswar. I was sitting quiet for some time under the Panchavati, when the Master suddenly came there and catching hold of my hand, said smiling, "Your intellect and learning will be examined today. You have passed two and a half examinations only; a teacher who has passed three and a half* has come today. Come, let me see how you fare in conversation with him." Willy-nilly, I had to go with the Master. When I reached his room and was introduced to M., I began to talk with him on various subjects. Having thus engaged us in a talk, the Master sat silent and went on listening to our words and observing us. Afterwards, when Sri M. took leave and went away, he said, "What matters it, even if he has passed those examinations? The teacher is womanish in character—shy. He cannot talk with emphasis." Thus pitting me against others, the Master used to enjoy the fun of it.[24]

[*Shortly after meeting the Master*] I might not have gained anything else by this practice of religion; but it is certain that I have gained control over my terrible anger by his grace. Formerly I used to lose all control over myself in rage and be seized with repentance afterwards. But now if anyone does me a great harm or even beats me severely, I don't become so very angry.[25]

One day, during one of my early visits, the Master in an ecstatic mood said to me, "You have come!" "How amazing!" I said to myself. "It is as if he had known me a long time." Then he said to me, "Do you ever see light?" I replied, "Yes, sir. Before I fall asleep I feel something like a light revolving near my forehead"....

    I used to see it frequently. In Jadu Mallick's garden house

---

* Narendra was then studying for his B.A. Examination while Sri M. had passed that examination and was studying law (B.L.). The Master put these facts in that way.

the Master one day touched me and muttered something to himself. I became unconscious. The effect of the touch lingered with me a month, like an intoxication.

When he heard that a proposal had been made about my marriage, he wept, holding the feet of the image of Kali. With tears in his eyes he prayed to the Divine Mother, "O Mother, please upset the whole thing! Don't let Narendra be drowned."[26]

One day when the Master came to my study and was giving me the instruction to observe lifelong continence, my grandmother overheard everything and informed my parents of it. They began making great efforts from that day to get me married lest I should become a monk by moving with a Sadhu. But of what avail was all that? All their efforts against the strong will of the Master failed. Even when everything was settled, the marriage negotiations broke off in a few cases on account of the difference of opinion between the two parties about trifling things.[27]

It is impossible to give others any idea of the ineffable joy we derived from the presence of the Master. It is really beyond our understanding how he could train us, without our knowing it, through fun and play, and thus mould our spiritual life. As the master wrestler proceeds with great caution and restraint with the beginner, now overpowering him in the struggle with great difficulty as it were, again allowing himself to be defeated to strengthen the pupil's self-confidence—in exactly the same manner did Sri Ramakrishna handle us. Realizing that the Atman, the source of infinite strength, exists in every individual, pigmy though he might be, he was able to see the potential giant in all. He could clearly discern the latent spiritual power which would in the fullness of time manifest itself. Holding up that bright picture to view, he would speak highly of us and encourage us. Again he would warn us lest we should obstruct this future consummation by becoming entangled in worldly desires, and moreover, he would keep us under control by carefully observing even the minute details of our life. All this was done silently and unobtrusively. That was the secret of his training of the disciples and of his moulding of their lives.

Once I felt that I could not practise deep concentration during meditation. I told him of it and sought his advice and direction. He told me his personal experiences in the matter and gave me instructions. I remember that as I sat down to meditate during the early hours of the morning, my mind would be disturbed and diverted by the shrill note of the whistle of a neighbouring jute mill. I told him about it, and he advised me to concentrate my mind on the sound of the whistle itself. I followed his advice and derived much benefit from it.

On another occasion I felt difficulty in totally forgetting my body during meditation and concentrating the mind wholly on the ideal. I went to him for counsel, and he gave me the very instruction which he himself had received from Tota Puri while practising Samadhi according to Vedantic disciplines. He sharply pressed between my eyebrows with his fingernail and said, "Now concentrate your mind on this painful sensation!" I found I could concentrate easily on that sensation as long as I liked, and during that period I completely let go the consciousness of the other parts of my body, not to speak of their causing any distraction hindering my meditation.

The solitude of the Panchavati, associated with the various spiritual realizations of the Master, was also the most suitable place for our meditation. Besides meditation and spiritual exercises, we used to spend a good deal of time there in sheer fun and merry-making. Sri Ramakrishna also joined in with us, and by taking part enhanced our innocent pleasure. We used to run and skip about, climb on the trees, swing from the creepers, and at times hold merry picnics. On the first day that we picnicked the Master noticed that I myself had cooked the food, and he partook of it. I knew that he could not take food unless it was cooked by Brahmins, and therefore I had arranged for his meal at the Kali temple. But he said, "It won't be wrong for me to take food from such a pure soul as yourself." In spite of my repeated remonstrations, he enjoyed the food I had cooked that day.[28]

After my father's death my mother and my brothers were starving. When the Master met Annada Guha one day, he said to him, "Narendra's father has died. His family is in a state of great privation. It would be good if his friends helped him now with money." After Annada had left I scolded him. I said, "Why did you say all those things to him?" Thus rebuked, he wept and said, "Alas! for your sake I could beg from door to door." He tamed us by his love.[29]

Even before the period of mourning [after my father's death] was over I had to go about in search of a job. Starving and barefooted, I wandered from office to office under the scorching noonday sun with an application in hand, one or two intimate friends who sympathized with me in my misfortunes accompanying me sometimes. But everywhere the door was slammed in my face. This first contact with the reality of life convinced me that unselfish sympathy was a rarity in the world—there was no place in it for the weak, the poor, and the destitute. I noticed that those who only a few days ago would have been proud to have helped me in any way, now turned their face against me, though they had enough and to spare. Seeing all this, the world sometimes seemed to me to be the handiwork of the devil. One day, weary and footsore, I sat down in the shade of the Ochterlony Monument [the present Shahid Minar] on the Maidan. A friend or two were with me that day or maybe met me there by chance. One of them, I remember distinctly, sang by way of consoling me, "Here blows the wind, the breath of Brahman, His grace palpable!... " It was like a terrible blow on my head. I remembered the helpless condition of my mother and brothers, and exclaimed in bitter anguish and despondency, "Will you please stop that song? Such fancies may be pleasing to those who are born with a silver spoon in their mouth and have no starving relatives at home. Yes, there was a time when I too thought like that. But today, before the hard facts of life, it sounds like grim mockery."

My friend must have been wounded. How could he fathom the dire misery that had forced these words out of my mouth? Sometimes when I found that there were not provisions enough for the family and my purse was empty, I would pretend to my mother that I had an invitation to dine out and remain practically without food. Out of self-respect I could not disclose the facts to others. My rich friends sometimes requested me to go to their homes or gardens and sing. I had to comply when I could not avoid doing so. I did not feel inclined to express my woes before them, nor did they try themselves to find out my difficulties. A few among them sometimes used to ask me, "Why do you look so pale and weak today?" Only one of them came to know about my poverty, and now and then, unknown to me, sent anonymous help to my mother, by which act of kindness he has put me under a deep debt of gratitude.

Some of my old friends who earned their livelihood by unfair means asked me to join them. A few among them, who had been compelled to follow this dubious way of life by sudden turns of fortune as in my case, really felt sympathy for me. There were other troubles also. Various temptations came my way. A rich woman sent me an ugly proposal to end my days of penury, which I sternly rejected with scorn. Another woman also made similar overtures to me. I said to her, "You have wasted your life seeking the pleasures of the flesh. The dark shadows of death are before you. Have you done anything to face that? Give up all these filthy desires and remember God!"

In spite of all these troubles, however, I never lost faith in the existence of God or in His divine mercy. Every morning, taking His name, I got up and went out in search of a job. One day my mother overheard me and said bitterly, "Hush, you fool! you have been crying yourself hoarse for God from your childhood, and what has He done for you?" I was stung to the quick. Doubt crossed my mind. "Does God really exist?" I thought, "and if so, does He really hear the fervent prayer of man? Then why is there no response to my passionate appeals? Why is there so much woe in His benign kingdom? Why does Satan rule in the realm of the merciful God?" Pandit Ishwarchandra Vidyasagar's words—"If God is good and gracious, why then do millions of people die for want of a few morsels of food at times of famine?"—rang in my ears with bitter irony. I was exceedingly annoyed with God. That was also the most opportune moment for doubt to creep into my heart.

It was ever against my nature to do anything secretly. On the contrary it was a habit with me from my boyhood not to hide even my thoughts from others through fear or anything else. So it was quite natural for me now to proceed to prove to the world that God was a myth, or that, even if He existed, to call upon Him was fruitless. Soon the report gained currency that I was an atheist and did not scruple to drink or even frequent houses of ill fame. This unmerited calumny hardened my heart still more. I openly declared that in this miserable world there was nothing reprehensible in a man who, seeking for a brief respite, should resort to anything; not only that, but that if I was once convinced of the efficacy of such a course, I should not, through fear of anybody, shrink from following it.

A garbled report of the matter soon reached the ears of the Master and his devotees in Calcutta. Some of these came to me for first-hand knowledge of the situation and hinted that they believed some of the rumours at least. A sense of wounded pride filled my heart on finding that they could think me so low. In an exasperated mood I gave them to understand plainly that it was cowardice to believe in God through fear of hell and argued with them as to His existence or non-existence, quoting several Western philosophers in support. The result was that they took leave of me convinced that I was hopelessly lost—and I was glad. When I thought that perhaps Sri Ramakrishna also would believe that, I was deeply wounded at heart. "Never mind," I said to myself, "if the good or bad opinion of a man rests upon such flimsy foundations, I don't care." And I was amazed to hear later that the Master had, at first, received the report coldly, without expressing an opinion one way or the other. But when one of his favourite disciples, Bhavanath, said to him with tears in his eyes, "Sir, I could not even dream that Narendra could stoop so low," he was furious and said, "Hush, you fool! The Mother has told me that it can never be so. I shan't be able to look at you if you speak to me like that again."

But notwithstanding these forced atheistic views, the vivid memory of the divine visions I had experienced since my boyhood, and especially since my contact with Sri Ramakrishna, would lead me to think that God must exist and that there must be some way to realize Him. Otherwise life would be meaningless. In the midst of all these troubles and tribulations

DISCIPLESHIP

I must find that way. Days passed and the mind continued to waver between doubt and certainty. My pecuniary needs also remained just the same.

The summer was over, and the rains set in. The search for a job still went on. One evening, after a whole day's fast and exposure to rain I was returning home with tired limbs and a jaded mind; overpowered with exhaustion and unable to move a step forward, I sank down on the outer plinth of a house by the roadside.

I can't say whether I was insensible for a time or not. Various thoughts crowded in on my mind, and I was too weak to drive them off and fix my attention on anything in particular. Suddenly I felt as if by some divine power the coverings of my soul were being removed one after another. All my former doubts regarding the coexistence of divine justice and mercy, and the presence of misery in the creation of a Blissful Providence, were automatically solved. By a deep introspection I found the meaning of it all and was satisfied. As I proceeded homewards I found there was no trace of fatigue in the body, and the mind was refreshed with wonderful strength and peace. The night was well-nigh over.

Thenceforth I became deaf to the praise and blame of worldly people. I was convinced that I was not born like ordinary people to earn money and maintain a family, much less strive for sense-pleasures. I began secretly to prepare myself to renounce the world like my grandfather. I fixed a day for the purpose and was glad to hear that the Master was to come to Calcutta that very day. "It is lucky," I thought, "I shall leave the world with the blessing of my Guru." As soon as I met the Master, he pressed me hard to spend that night with him at Dakshineswar. I made various excuses, but to no purpose. I had to accompany him. There was not much talk in the carriage. Reaching Dakshineswar I was seated for some time in his room along with others, when he went into a trance. Presently he drew near me and, touching me with great tenderness, began to sing a song, with tears in his eyes:

"I am afraid to speak, and am afraid not to speak. The doubt arises in my mind, lest I should lose you—Ah! my Rai, lest I should lose you."

I had suppressed my feelings for so long, but now they overflowed in tears. The meaning of the Master's singing the song was apparent—he knew of my intentions. The audience marvelled at this exchange of feeling between us. When the Master regained his normal mood, some of them asked him the reason for it. He replied with a smile, "Oh, it was something between him and me." Then at night he dismissed the others and calling me to his side said, "I know you have come for the Mother's work, and won't be able to live a worldly life; but for my sake, stay in the world as long as I live." Saying this he burst into tears again. The next day, with his permission, I returned home. A thousand thoughts about the maintenance of the family assailed me. I began to look about again for a living. By working in an attorney's office and translating a few books, I got just enough to live on—from hand to mouth, not permanent. There was no fixed income to maintain my mother and brothers.

One day the idea struck me that God listened to Sri Ramakrishna's prayers; so why should I not ask him to pray for me for the removal of my pecuniary needs—a favour the Master would never deny me? I hurried to Dakshineswar and insisted on his making the appeal on behalf of my starving family. He said, "My boy, I can't make such demands. But why don't you go and ask the Mother yourself? All your sufferings are due to your disregard of Her." I said, "I do not know the Mother; you please speak to Her on my behalf. You must." He replied tenderly, "My dear boy, I have done so again and again. But

DISCIPLESHIP

you do not accept Her, so She does not grant my prayer. All right, it is Tuesday—go to the Kali temple tonight, prostrate yourself before the Mother, and ask of Her any boon you like. It shall be granted. She is Knowledge Absolute, the Inscrutable Power of Brahman. By Her mere will She has given birth to this world. Everything is in Her power to give." I believed every word and eagerly waited for the night. About nine o'clock the Master asked me to go to the temple. As I went, I was filled with a divine intoxication. My feet were unsteady. My heart was leaping in anticipation of the joy of beholding the living Goddess and hearing Her words. I was full of the idea. Reaching the temple, as I cast my eyes on the image, I actually found that the Divine Mother was living and conscious, the perennial fountain of Divine Love and Beauty. I was caught in a surging wave of devotion and love. In an ecstasy of joy I prostrated myself again and again before the Mother and prayed, "Mother, give me discrimination! Give me renunciation! Give me knowledge and devotion! Grant that I may have the uninterrupted vision of Thee!" A serene peace reigned in my soul. The world was forgotten. Only the Divine Mother shone within my heart.

As soon as I returned, the Master asked me if I had prayed to the Mother for the removal of my worldly needs. I was startled at this question and said, "No sir, I forgot all about it. But is there any remedy now?" "Go again," said he, "and tell Her about your needs." I again set out for the temple, but at the sight of the Mother again forgot my mission, bowed to Her repeatedly and prayed only for love and devotion. The Master asked me if I had done it the second time. I told him what had happened. He said, "How thoughtless! Couldn't you restrain yourself enough to say those few words? Well, try once more and make that prayer to Her. Quick!" I went for the third time, but on entering the temple a terrible shame overpowered me.

I thought, "What a trifle I have come to pray to the Mother about! It is like asking a gracious king for a few vegetables! What a fool I am!" In shame and remorse I bowed to Her respectfully and said, "Mother, I want nothing but knowledge and devotion." Coming out of the temple I understood that all this was due to the Master's will. Otherwise how could I fail in my object no less than three times? I came to him and said, "Sir, it is you who have cast a charm over my mind and made me forgetful. Now please grant me the boon that my people at home may no longer suffer the pinch of poverty." He said, "Such a prayer never comes to my lips. I asked you to pray for yourself; but you couldn't do it. It seems that you are not destined to enjoy worldly happiness. Well, I can't help it." But I wouldn't let him go. I insisted on his granting that prayer. At last he said, "All right, your people at home will never be in want of plain food and clothing."[30]

How many times he prayed to the Divine Mother for my sake! After my father's death, when I had no food at home and my mother and sisters and brothers were starving too, the Master prayed to the Divine Mother to give me money.... But I didn't get any money. The Master told me what the Divine Mother had said to him: "He will get simple food and clothing. He will eat rice and dal."

He loved me so much! But whenever an impure idea crept into my mind he at once knew about it. While going around with Annada, sometime I found myself in the company of evil people. On those occasions the Master could not eat any food from my hands. He could raise his hand only a little, and could not bring it to his mouth. On one such occasion, while he was ill, he brought his hand very close to his mouth, but it did not go in. He said to me, "You are not yet ready."[31]

Sri Ramakrishna was the only person who, ever since he met

DISCIPLESHIP

me, believed in me uniformly throughout—even my mother and brothers did not do so. It was his unflinching trust in me and love that bound me to him for ever. He alone knew how to love another. Worldly people only make a show of love for selfish ends.[32]

How I used to hate Kali and all Her ways! That was the ground of my six years' fight—that I would not accept Her. But I had to accept Her at last. Ramakrishna Paramahamsa dedicated me to Her, and now I believe that She guides me in every little thing I do, and does with me what She will! ... Yet I fought so long! I loved him, you see, and that was what held me. I saw his marvellous purity ... I felt his wonderful love ... His greatness had not dawned on me then. All that came afterwards, when I had given in. At that time I thought him a brain-sick baby, always seeing visions and the rest. I hated it. And then I too had to accept Her!

No, the thing that made me do it is a secret that will die with me. I had great misfortunes at that time ... It was an opportunity ... She made a slave of me. Those were the very words—"a slave of you." And Ramakrishna Paramahamsa made me over to Her ... Strange! He lived only two years after doing that, and most of the time he was suffering. Not more than six months did he keep his own health and brightness.[33]

Let none regret that they were difficult to convince! I fought my Master for six years with the result that I know every inch of the way! Every inch of the way![34]

You see my devotion is the dog's devotion. I have been wrong so often and he has always been right, and now I trust his judgement blindly.[35]

Shyampukur, 27 October 1885 · We think of [Sri Ramakrishna] as a person who is like God. Do you know ... what it is like?

There is a point between the vegetable creation and the animal creation where it is very difficult to determine whether a particular thing is a vegetable or an animal. Likewise, there is a stage between the man-world and the God-world where it is extremely hard to say whether a person is a man or God.... I don't say that he is God. What I am saying is that he is a godlike man.... We offer worship to him bordering on divine worship.[36]

Cossipore, 4 January 1886 · I have been thinking of going there [to Dakshineswar] today.... I intend to light a fire under the bel-tree and meditate.... I shall feel greatly relieved if I find a medicine that will make me forget all I have studied.[37]

Cossipore, 4 January 1886 · I was meditating here last Saturday when suddenly I felt a peculiar sensation in my heart.... Probably it was [the awakening of the Kundalini]. I clearly perceived the Ida and the Pingala nerves. I asked Hazra to feel my chest. Yesterday I saw [Sri Ramakrishna] upstairs and told him about it. I said to him, "All the others have had their realization; please give me some. All have succeeded; shall I alone remain unsatisfied?" ... He said, "Why don't you settle your family affairs first and then come to me? You will get everything. What do you want?" I replied, "It is my desire to remain absorbed in Samadhi continually for three or four days, only once in a while coming down to the sense plane to eat a little food." Thereupon he said to me, "You are a very small-minded person. There is a state higher even than that. 'All that exists art Thou'—it is you who sing that song ... Settle your family affairs and then come to me. You will attain a state higher than Samadhi." I went home this morning. My people scolded me, saying, "Why do you wander about like a vagabond? Your law examination is near at hand and you are not paying any attention to your studies. You wander about aimlessly".... [*Question: did your mother say anything?*] No. She was very eager to feed me. She gave me venison. I ate a little, though I didn't feel like eating meat....

I went to my study at my grandmother's. As I tried to read I was seized with a great fear, as if studying were a terrible thing. My heart struggled within me. I burst into tears: I never wept so bitterly in my life. I left my books and ran away. I ran along the streets. My shoes slipped from my feet—I didn't know where. I ran past a haystack and got hay all over me. I kept on running along the road to Cossipore....

Since reading the *Vivekachudamani* I have felt very much depressed. In it Shankaracharya says that only through great tapasya and good fortune does one acquire these three things: a human birth, the desire for liberation, and refuge with a great soul. I said to myself, "I have surely gained all these three. As a result of great tapasya I have been born a human being; through great tapasya, again, I have the desire for liberation; and through great tapasya I have secured the companionship of such a great soul".... I have no more taste for the world. I do not relish the company of those who live in the world—of course, with the exception of one or two devotees.[38]

Cossipore, 21 April 1886 · Has anybody seen God as I see that tree?... [Sri Ramakrishna's experience] may be his hallucination....

I want truth. The other day I had a great argument with Sri Ramakrishna himself.... He said to me, "Some people call me God." I replied, "Let a thousand people call you God, but I shall certainly not call you God as long as I do not know it to be true." He said, "Whatever many people say is indeed truth; that is Dharma." Thereupon I replied, "Let others proclaim a thing as truth, but I shall certainly not listen to them unless I myself realize it as truth."[39]

Cossipore, 23 April 1886 · How amazing it is! One learns hardly anything though one reads books for many years. How can a man realize God by practising Sadhana for two or three days? Is it so easy to realize God?... I have no peace.[40]

Baranagore, 25 March 1887 [*Referring to his experience of Nirvikalpa Samadhi at Cossipore*] · In that experience I felt that I had no body. I could see only my face. The Master was in the upstairs room. I had that experience downstairs. I was weeping. I said, "What has happened to me?" The elder Gopal went to the Master's room and said, "Narendra is crying." When I saw the Master he said to me, "Now you have known. But I am going to keep the key with me." I said to him, "What is it that happened to me?" Turning to the devotees, he said: "He will not keep his body if he knows who he is. But I have put a veil over his eyes."[41]

One day in the Cossipore garden, I had expressed my prayer to Sri Ramakrishna with great earnestness. Then in the evening, at the hour of meditation, I lost the consciousness of the body, and felt that it was absolutely non-existent. I felt that the sun, moon, space, time, ether, and all had been reduced to a homogeneous mass and then melted far away into the unknown; the body-consciousness had almost vanished, and I had nearly merged in the Supreme. But I had just a trace of the feeling of ego, so I could again return to the world of relativity from the Samadhi. In this state of Samadhi all the difference between "I" and "Brahman" goes away; everything is reduced into unity, like the waters of the infinite ocean—water everywhere, nothing else exists—language and thought, all fail there. Then only is the state "beyond mind and speech" realised in its actuality....

After that experience, even after trying repeatedly, I failed to bring back the state of Samadhi. On informing Sri Ramakrishna about it, he said, "If you remain day and night in that state, the work of the Divine Mother will not be accomplished; therefore you won't be able to induce that state again; when your work is finished, it will come again"....

Sri Ramakrishna used to say that the Avataras alone can descend to the ordinary plane from that state of Samadhi, for the good of the world. Ordinary Jivas do not; immersed in that state, they remain alive for a period of twenty-one days; after that, their body drops like a sere leaf from the tree of Samsara.[42]

All philosophy and scriptures have come from the plane of relative knowledge of subject and object. But no thought or language of the human mind can fully express the Reality which lies beyond the plane of relative knowledge! Science, philosophy, etc. are only partial truths. So they can never be adequate channels of expression for the transcendent Reality. Hence viewed from the transcendent standpoint, everything appears to be unreal—religious creeds, and works, I and thou, and the universe—everything is unreal! Then only it is perceived: "I am the only reality; I am the all-pervading Atman, and I am the proof of my own existence." Where is the room for a separate proof to establish the reality of my existence? I am, as the scriptures say, "*Nityam asmat prasiddham*—always known to myself as the eternal subject."* I have seen that state, realised it.[43]

At Cossipore [Sri Ramakrishna] transmitted his power to me.... One day, while meditating, I asked Kali [Swami Abhedananda] to hold my hand. Kali said to me, "When I touched your body I felt something like an electric shock coming to my body"....

---
* *Vivekachudamani*, 409

[*One day Sri Ramakrishna wrote on a piece of paper, "Naren will teach people."*] But I said to him, "I won't do any such thing." Thereupon he said, "Your very bones will do it."[44]

Now, all the ideas that I preach are only an attempt to echo [Sri Ramakrishna's] ideas. Nothing is mine originally except the wicked ones, everything I say which is false and wicked. But every word that I have ever uttered which is true and good is simply an attempt to echo his voice....

Well, there at his feet I conceived these ideas—there with some other young men. I was just a boy. I went there when I was about sixteen. Some of the other boys were still younger, some a little older—about a dozen or more. And together we conceived that this ideal had to be spread. And not only spread, but made practical. That is to say, we must show the spirituality of the Hindus, the mercifulness of the Buddhists, the activity of the Christians, the brotherhood of the Mohammedans, by our practical lives. "We shall start a universal religion now and here," we said, "we will not wait."

Our teacher was an old man who would never touch a coin with his hands. He took just the little food offered, just so many yards of cotton cloth, no more. He could never be induced to take any other gift. With all these marvellous ideas, he was strict, because that made him free. The monk in India is the friend of the prince today, dines with him; and tomorrow he is with the beggar, sleeps under a tree.[45]

He used to love me intensely, which made many quite jealous of me. He knew one's character by sight, and never changed his opinion. He could perceive, as it were, supersensual things, while we try to know one's character by reason, with the result that our judgments are often fallacious. He called some persons his Antarangas or "belonging to the inner circle," and he used to teach them the secrets of his own nature and those of Yoga. To the outsiders or Bahirangas he taught those parables now known as "Sayings." He used to prepare those young men (the former class) for his work, and though many complained to him about them, he paid no heed. I may have perhaps a better opinion of a Bahiranga than an Antaranga through his actions, but I have a superstitious regard for the latter. "Love me, love my dog," as they say. I love that Brahmin priest intensely, and therefore, love whatever he used to love, whatever he used to regard! He was afraid about me that I might create a sect, if left to myself.

He used to say to some, "You will not attain spirituality in this life." He sensed everything, and this will explain his apparent partiality to some. He, as a scientist, used to see that different people required different treatment. None except those of the "inner circle" were allowed to sleep in his room. It is not true that those who have not seen him will not attain salvation; neither is it true that a man who has seen him thrice will attain Mukti.[46]

It has become a trite saying that idolatry is wrong, and every man swallows it at the present time without questioning. I once thought so, and to pay the penalty of that I had to learn my lesson sitting at the feet of a man who realised everything through idols; I allude to Ramakrishna Paramahamsa. If such Ramakrishna Paramahamsas are produced by idol-worship, what will you have—the reformer's creed or any number of idols?... Take a thousand idols more if you can produce Ramakrishna Paramahamsas through idol-worship, and may God speed you![47]

Despite the many iniquities that have found entrance into the practices of image-worship as it is in vogue now, I do not condemn it. Ay, where would I have been if I had not been blessed with the dust of the holy feet of that orthodox, image-worshipping Brahmin![48]

When my Master, Sri Ramakrishna, fell ill, a Brahmin suggested to him that he apply his tremendous mental power to cure himself. He said that if my Master would only concentrate his mind on the diseased part of the body, it would heal. Sri Ramakrishna answered, "What! Bring down the mind that I've given to God to this little body!" He refused to think of body and illness. His mind was continually conscious of God; it was dedicated to Him utterly. He would not use it for any other purpose.[49]

Am I able to sit quiet?... Two or three days before Sri Ramakrishna's passing away, She whom he used to call "Kali" entered this body. It is She who takes me here and there and makes me work, without letting me remain quiet or allowing me to look to my personal comforts. [*Question: Are you speaking metaphorically?*] Oh, no; two or three days before his leaving the body, he called me to his side one day, and asking me to sit before him, looked steadfastly at me and fell into Samadhi. Then I really felt that a subtle force like an electric shock was entering my body! In a little while, I also lost outward consciousness and sat motionless. How long I stayed in that condition I do not remember; when consciousness returned I found Sri Ramakrishna shedding tears. On questioning him, he answered me affectionately, "Today, giving you my all, I have become a beggar. With this power you are to do many works for the world's good before you will return." I feel that power is constantly directing me to this or that work. This body has not been made for remaining idle.[50]

[*Question: Did Sri Ramakrishna, out of his own lips, ever say that he was God, the all-perfect Brahman?*] Yes, he did so many times.

And he said this to all of us. One day while he was staying at the Cossipore garden, his body in imminent danger of falling off for ever, by the side of his bed I was saying in my mind, "Well, now if you can declare that you are God, then only will I believe you are really God Himself." It was only two days before he passed away. Immediately, he looked up towards me all on a sudden and said, "He who was Rama, He who was Krishna, verily is He now Ramakrishna in this body. And that not merely from the standpoint of your Vedanta!" At this I was struck dumb. Even we haven't had yet the perfect faith, after hearing it again and again from the holy lips of our Lord himself—our minds still get disturbed now and then with doubt and despair—and so, what shall we speak of others being slow to believe? It is indeed a very difficult matter to be able to declare and believe a man with a body like ours to be God Himself. We may just go to the length of declaring him to be a "perfected one," or a "knower of Brahman." Well, it matters nothing, whatever you may call him or think of him, a saint, or a knower of Brahman, or anything. But take it from me, never did come to this earth such an all-perfect man as Sri Ramakrishna. In the utter darkness of the world, this great man is like the shining pillar of illumination in this age. And by his light alone will man now cross the ocean of Samsara.[51]

Never during his life did [Sri Ramakrishna] refuse a single prayer of mine; millions of offences has he forgiven me; such great love even my parents never had for me. There is no poetry, no exaggeration in all this. It is the bare truth and every disciple of his knows it. In times of great danger, great temptation, I wept in extreme agony with the prayer, "O God, do save me," but no response came from anybody; but this wonderful saint, or Avatara, or anything else he may be, came to know of all my affliction through his powers of insight into human hearts and lifted it off—in spite of my desire to the contrary—after getting me brought to his presence.... Him alone I have found in this world to be like an ocean of unconditioned mercy.[52]

Time and again have I received in this life marks of his grace. He stands behind and gets all this work done by me. When lying helpless under a tree in an agony of hunger, when I had not even a scrap of cloth for Kaupina, when I was resolved on travelling penniless round the world, even then help came in all ways by the grace of Sri Ramakrishna. And again when crowds jostled with one another in the streets of Chicago to have a sight of this Vivekananda, then also, just because I had his grace, I could digest without difficulty all that honour—a hundredth part of which would have been enough to turn mad any ordinary man; and by his will, victory followed everywhere.[53]

[Sri Ramakrishna] was all Bhakti without; but within he was all Jnana. I am all Jnana without; but in my heart all is Bhakti.[54]

You have touched another chord in my heart, the deepest of all, and that is the mention of my teacher, my master, my hero, my ideal, my God in life—Sri Ramakrishna Paramahamsa. If there has been anything achieved by me, by thoughts, or words, or deeds, if from my lips has ever fallen one word that has helped any one in the world, I lay no claim to it, it was his. But if there have been curses falling from my lips, if there has been hatred coming out of me, it is all mine and not his. All that has been weak has been mine, and all that has been life-giving, strengthening, pure, and holy, has been his inspiration, his words, and he himself.[55]

He himself is his own parallel. Has he any exemplar?... What shall I say about myself? You see, I must be one of his demons. In his presence even, I would sometimes speak ill of him, hearing which he would laugh.[56]

Truly, I tell you, I have understood him very little. He appears to me to have been so great, that whenever I have to speak anything of him, I am afraid lest I ignore or explain away the truth, lest my little power does not suffice, lest in trying to extol him I present his picture by painting him according to my lights and belittle him thereby.[57]

His was a different case. What comparison can there be between him and ordinary men? He practised in his life all the different ideals of religion to show that each of them leads but to the One Truth. Shall you or I ever be able to do all that he has done? None of us has understood him fully. So, I do not venture to speak about him anywhere and everywhere. He only knows what he himself really was; his frame was a human one only, but everything else about him was entirely different from others.[58]

The fact is that Sri Ramakrishna is not exactly what the ordinary followers have comprehended him to be. He had infinite moods and phases. Even if you might form an idea of the limits of Brahmajnana, the knowledge of the Absolute, you could not have any idea of the unfathomable depths of his mind. Thousands of Vivekanandas may spring forth through one gracious glance of his eyes! But instead of doing that, he has chosen to get things done this time through me as his single instrument, and what can I do in this matter?[59]

Travelling this world over I find that save and except his circle alone, everywhere else thought and act are at variance. For those that belong to him, I have the utmost love, the utmost confidence. I have no alternative in the matter. Call me one-sided if you will, but there you have my bona fide avowal.

If but a thorn pricks the foot of one who has surrendered himself to Sri Ramakrishna, it makes my bones ache. All others I love; you will find very few men so unsectarian as I am; but you must excuse me, I have that bit of bigotry. If I do not appeal to his name, whose else shall I? It will be time enough to seek for a big Guru in our next birth; but in this, it is that unlearned Brahmin who has bought this body of mine for ever.[60]

CHAPTER THREE

SRI RAMAKRISHNA, MY MASTER

OVER THE COURSE of time . . . the descendants of the Aryans deviated from proper conduct; they lost their spirit of renunciation and their sharp intelligence and became deeply attached to popular customs. They even failed to understand the import of the Puranas, thinking them contradictory to one another because each one taught by emphasizing only a particular aspect of the spiritual ideal and because each taught people of ordinary intelligence the abstruse truths of Vedanta by using concrete imagery and elaborate language. They divided the whole of the Sanatana Dharma—the sum total of all religious ideals—into many sects. They enkindled the fire of sectarian jealousy and anger and tried to throw each other into it. When the degraded Aryans had almost turned India, the land of religion, into a hell, Bhagavan Sri Ramakrishna incarnated himself to demonstrate the true religion of the Aryan race. He made visible the unity among the innumerable sects and denominations of the Hindu religion that had cropped up throughout the country over a vast period of time. At that time the Hindu religion had been devastated by continuous sectarian fights, and was seemingly divided into many sects. Its various sects were overrun by hideous customs, and Hinduism had become confusing to Indians and an object of contempt to foreigners. Over time, this eternal religion had been debased, but Sri Ramakrishna incorporated its universal and eternal aspects in his own life to become a living example of the eternal religion, which he lived before all for the good of humanity....

Before the effulgence of this new awakening, the glory of all past revivals of Aryan society will pale like stars before the rising sun....

So at the dawn of this momentous epoch, the message of the harmony of religions has been proclaimed. This boundless and all-embracing idea, which has been hidden in the Vedic scriptures and religion, has been rediscovered and declared to humanity with a clarion call.

This new religion of the age will benefit the whole world, but most especially India. Bhagavan Sri Ramakrishna, the founder of this new religion, is the reconstructed manifestation of the earlier founders of religions. O human beings, have faith in this and realize it.[1]

Every new religious wave requires a new centre. The old religion can only be revivified by a new centre. Hang your dogmas or doctrines, they never pay. It is a character, a life, a centre, a God-man that must lead the way, that must be the centre round which all other elements will gather themselves and then fall like a tidal wave upon the society, carrying all before it, washing away all impurities.

Again, a piece of wood can only easily be cut along the grain. So the old Hinduism can only be reformed through Hinduism, and not through the new-fangled reform movements. At the same time the reformers must be able to unite in themselves the culture of both the East and the West. Now do you not think that you have already seen the nucleus of such a great movement, that you have heard the low rumblings of the coming tidal wave? That centre, that God-man to lead was born in India. He was the great Ramakrishna Paramahamsa.[2]

[Shankara] had a great head, [Ramanuja] a large heart, and the time was ripe for one to be born, the embodiment of both this head and heart; the time was ripe for one to be born who in one body would have the brilliant intellect of Shankara and the wonderfully expansive, infinite heart of Chaitanya; one who would see in every sect the same spirit working, the same God; one who would see God in every being, one whose heart would weep for the poor, for the weak, for the outcast, for the downtrodden, for every one in this world, inside India or outside India; and at the same time whose grand brilliant intellect would conceive of such noble thoughts as would harmonise all conflicting sects, not only in India but outside of India, and bring a marvellous harmony, the universal religion of head and heart, into existence. Such a man was born, and I had the good fortune to sit at his feet for years.[3]

It was while reforms of various kinds were being inaugurated in India that a child was born of poor Brahmin parents on the eighteenth of February, 1836, in one of the remote villages of Bengal. The father and mother were very orthodox people....

Very poor they were and yet many a time the mother would starve herself a whole day to help a poor man. Of them this child was born; and he was a peculiar child from very boyhood. He remembered his past from his birth, and was conscious for what purpose he came into the world, and every power was devoted to the fulfilment of that purpose.

While he was quite young his father died; and the boy was sent to school.... [Seeing the Pandits arguing at a gathering], he gathered this moral out of it: "This is the outcome of all their knowledge. Why are they fighting so hard? It is simply for money; the man who can show the highest learning here will get the best pair of cloth[s], and that is all these people are struggling for. I will not go to school any more." And he did not; that was the end of his going to school. But this boy had an elder brother, a learned professor, who took him to Calcutta ... to study with him. After a short time the boy became convinced that the aim of all secular learning was mere material advancement, and he resolved to give up study and devote himself to the pursuit of spiritual knowledge. The father being dead, the family was very poor, and this boy had to make his own living. He went to a place near Calcutta and became a temple priest....

In the temple was an image of the "Blissful Mother." This boy had to conduct the worship morning and evening, and by degrees this one idea filled his mind: "Is there anything behind this image? Is it true that there is a Mother of Bliss in the universe? Is it true that She lives and guides this universe, or is it all a dream? Is there any reality in religion?"...

This idea took possession of the boy, and his whole life became concentrated upon that. Day after day he would weep and say, "Mother, is it true that Thou existest, or is it all poetry? Is the Blissful Mother an imagination of poets and misguided people, or is there such a reality?" We have seen that of books, of education in our sense of the word, he had none, and so much the more natural, so much the more healthy, was his mind, so much the purer his thoughts, undiluted by drinking in the thoughts of others.... However, this thought—whether God can be seen—which was uppermost in his mind, gained in strength every day until he could think of nothing else. He could no more conduct the worship properly, could no more attend to the various details in all their minuteness. Often he would forget to place the food offering before the image, sometimes he would forget to wave the light; at other times he would wave it for hours, and forget everything else.

And that one idea was in his mind every day: "Is it true

that Thou existest, O Mother? Why dost Thou not speak? Art Thou dead?"... At last it became impossible for him to serve in the temple. He left it and entered into a little wood that was near and lived there. About this part of his life he has told me many times that he could not tell when the sun rose or set, nor how he lived. He lost all thought of himself and forgot to eat. During this period he was lovingly watched over by a relative who put into his mouth food which he mechanically swallowed.

Days and nights thus passed with the boy. When a whole day would pass, towards the evening, when the peal of bells in the temples, and the voices singing, would reach the wood, it would make the boy very sad, and he would cry, "Another day is gone in vain, Mother, and Thou dost not come. Another day of this short life has gone and I have not known the Truth." In the agony of his soul, sometimes he would rub his face against the ground and weep, and this one prayer burst forth: "Do Thou manifest Thyself in me, Thou Mother of the universe! See that I need Thee and nothing else!" Verily, he wanted to be true to his own ideal.

He had heard that the Mother never came until everything had been given up for Her. He had heard that the Mother wanted to come to everyone, but they would not have Her, that people wanted all sorts of foolish little idols to pray to, that they wanted their own enjoyments, and not the Mother, and that the moment they really wanted Her with their whole soul, and nothing else, that moment She would come. So he began to break himself into that idea; he wanted to be exact, even on the plane of matter. He threw away all the little property he had, and took a vow that he would never touch money, and this one idea, "I will not touch money," became a part of him. It may appear to be something occult, but even in after-life when he was sleeping, if I touched him with a piece of money his hand would become bent, and his whole body would become, as it were, paralysed. The other idea that came into his mind was that lust was the other enemy. Man is a soul, and soul is sexless, neither man nor woman. The idea of sex and the idea of money were the two things, he thought, that prevented him from seeing the Mother. This whole universe is the manifestation of the Mother, and She lives in every woman's body. "Every woman represents the Mother; how can I think of woman in mere sex relation?" That was the idea: Every woman was his Mother, he must bring himself to the state when he would see nothing but Mother in every woman. And he carried it out in his life.[4]

We have seen in Sri Ramakrishna how he had this idea of divine motherhood in every woman, of whatever caste she might be, or whatever might be her worth.[5]

[This] illiterate boy, possessed of renunciation, turned the heads of your great old Pandits. Once at the Dakshineswar Temple the Brahmana who was in charge of the worship of Vishnu broke a leg of the image. Pandits were brought together at a meeting to give their opinions, and they, after consulting old books and manuscripts, declared that the worship of this broken image could not be sanctioned according to the Shastras and a new image would have to be consecrated. There was, consequently, a great stir. Sri Ramakrishna was called at last. He heard and asked, "Does a wife forsake her husband in case he becomes lame?" What followed? The Pandits were struck dumb, all their Shastric commentaries and erudition could not withstand the force of this simple statement.... Why should Sri Ramakrishna come down to this earth, and why should he discourage mere book-learning so much? That new life-force which he brought with him has to be instilled into learning and education.[6]

Later on, this very man said to me: "My child, suppose there is a bag of gold in one room, and a robber in the next room, do you think that the robber can sleep? He cannot. His mind will be always thinking how to get into that room and obtain possession of that gold. Do you think then that a man firmly persuaded that there is a Reality behind all these appearances, that there is a God, that there is One who never dies, One who is infinite bliss, a bliss compared with which these pleasures of the senses are simply playthings, can rest contented without struggling to attain It? Can he cease his efforts for a moment? No. He will become mad with longing." This divine madness seized the boy. At that time he had no teacher, nobody to tell him anything, and everyone thought that he was out of his mind....

So days, weeks, months passed in continuous struggle of the soul to arrive at Truth. The boy began to see visions, to see wonderful things; the secrets of his nature were beginning to open to him. Veil after veil was, as it were, being taken off. Mother Herself became the teacher, and initiated the boy into the truths he sought. At this time there came to this place a woman of beautiful appearance, learned beyond compare. Later on this saint used to say about her that she was not learned, but was the embodiment of learning; she was learning itself, in human form....

She was a Sannyasini; for women also give up the world, throw away their property, do not marry, and devote themselves to the worship of the Lord. She came; and when she heard of this boy in the grove she offered to go and see him; and hers was the first help he received. At once she recognised what his trouble was, and she said to him, "My son, blessed is the man upon whom such madness comes.... [People may] call you mad; but yours is the right kind of madness. Blessed is the man who is mad after God. Such men are very few."

This woman remained near the boy for years, taught him the forms of the religions of India, initiated him in the different practices of Yoga, and, as it were, guided and brought into harmony this tremendous river of spirituality.

Later there came to the same grove a Sannyasin, one of the begging friars of India, a learned man, a philosopher. He was a peculiar man, he was an idealist. He did not believe that this world existed in reality, and to demonstrate that he would never go under a roof; he would always live out of doors, in storm and sunshine alike. This man began to teach the boy the philosophy of the Vedas, and he found very soon, to his astonishment, that the pupil was in some respects wiser than the master. He spent several months there with the boy, after which he initiated him into the order of Sannyasins, and took his departure.

When as a temple priest his extraordinary worship made people think him deranged in his head, his relatives took him home and married him to a little girl, thinking that that would turn his thoughts and restore the balance of his mind. But he came back and ... merged deeper in his madness.... The husband had entirely forgotten he had a wife.

In her far-off home the girl had heard that her husband had become a religious enthusiast and that he was even considered insane by many. She resolved to learn the truth for herself, so she set out and walked to the place where her husband was. When at last she stood in her husband's presence, he at once admitted her right to his life, although in India any person, man or woman, who embraces a religious life is thereby freed from all other obligations. The young man fell at the feet of his wife and said, "As for me, the Mother has shown me that She resides in every woman, and so I have learnt to look upon every woman as Mother. That is the one idea I can have about you; but if you wish to drag me into the world, as I have been married to you, I am at your service."

The maiden was a pure and noble soul, and was able to understand her husband's aspirations and sympathise with them. She quickly told him that she had no wish to drag him down to a life of worldliness; but that all she desired was to remain near him, to serve him, and to learn of him. She became one of his most devoted disciples, always revering him as a divine being. Thus through his wife's consent the last barrier was removed, and he was free to lead the life he had chosen.[7]

That was the woman. The husband went on and became a monk in his own way; and from a distance the wife went on helping as much as she could. And later, when the man had become a great spiritual giant, she came—really, she was the first disciple—and she spent the rest of her life taking care of the body of this man. He never knew whether he was living or dying, or anything. Sometimes, when talking, he would get so excited that if he sat on live charcoals, he did not know it. Live charcoals! Forgetting all about his body, all the time.[8]

The next desire that seized upon the soul of this man was to know the truth about the various religions. Up to that time he had not known any religion but his own. He wanted to understand what other religions were like. So he sought teachers of other religions. By teachers you must always remember what we mean in India, not a book-worm, but a man of realisation, one who knows truth at first hand and not through an intermediary. He found a Mohammedan saint and placed himself under him; he underwent the disciplines prescribed by him, and to his astonishment found that when faithfully carried out, these devotional methods led him to the same goal he had already attained. He gathered similar experience from following the true religion of Jesus the Christ.

He went to all the sects he could find, and whatever he took up he went into with his whole heart. He did exactly as he was told, and in every instance he arrived at the same result. Thus from actual experience he came to know that the goal of every religion is the same, that each is trying to teach the same thing, the difference being largely in method, and still more in language....

That is what my Master found, and he then set about to learn humility, because he had found that the one idea in all religions is, "Not me, but Thou," and he who says, "Not me," the Lord fills his heart.... He now set himself to accomplish this. As I have told you, whenever he wanted to do anything he never confined himself to fine theories, but would enter into the practice immediately. We see many persons talking the most wonderfully fine things about charity and about equality and the rights of other people and all that, but it is only in theory. I was so fortunate as to find one who was able to carry theory into practice. He had the most wonderful faculty of carrying everything into practice which he thought was right.

Now, there was a family of Pariahs living near the place.... My Master would go to a Pariah and ask to be allowed to clean his house. The business of the Pariah is to clean the streets of the cities and to keep houses clean.... By birth the Brahmin stands for holiness, and the Pariah for the very reverse. And this Brahmin asked to be allowed to do the menial services in the house of the Pariah. The Pariah of course could not allow that, for they all think that if they allow a Brahmin to do such menial work it will be an awful sin, and they will become extinct. The Pariah would not permit it; so in the dead of night, when all were sleeping, Ramakrishna would enter the house. He had long hair, and with his hair he would wipe the place, saying, "Oh, my Mother, make me the servant of the Pariah, make me feel that I am even lower than the Pariah"....

For years he thus educated himself. One of the Sadhanas was to root out the sex idea. Soul has no sex, it is neither male nor female. It is only in the body that sex exists, and the man who desires to reach the spirit cannot at the same time hold to sex distinctions. Having been born in a masculine body, this man wanted to bring the feminine idea into everything. He began to think that he was a woman; he dressed like a woman, spoke like a woman, gave up the occupations of men, and lived in the household among the women of a good family, until, after years of this discipline, his mind became changed, and he entirely forgot the idea of sex; thus the whole view of life became changed to him.

We hear in the West about worshipping woman, but this is usually for her youth and beauty. This man meant by worshipping woman, that to him every woman's face was that of the Blissful Mother, and nothing but that. I myself have seen this man standing before those women whom society would not touch, and falling at their feet bathed in tears, saying, "Mother, in one form Thou art in the street, and in another form Thou art the universe. I salute Thee, Mother, I salute Thee."

Think of the blessedness of that life from which all carnality has vanished, which can look upon every woman with that love and reverence—when every woman's face becomes transfigured, and only the face of the Divine Mother, the Blissful One, the Protectress of the human race shines upon it!... Such purity is absolutely necessary if real spirituality is to be attained.

This rigorous, unsullied purity came into the life of that man. All the struggles which we have in our lives were past for him. His hard-earned jewels of spirituality, for which he had given three-quarters of his life, were now ready to be given to humanity, and then began his mission. His teaching and preaching were peculiar. In our country a teacher is a most highly venerated person, he is regarded as God Himself. We have not even the same respect for our father and mother. Father and mother give us our body, but the teacher shows us the way to salvation. We are his children, we are born in the spiritual line of the teacher. All Hindus come to pay respect to an extraordinary teacher, they crowd around him. And here was such a teacher, but the teacher had no thought whether he was to be respected or not, he had not the least idea that he was a great teacher, he thought that it was Mother who was doing everything and not he. He always said, "If any good comes from my lips, it is the Mother who speaks; what have I to do with it?" That was his one idea about his work, and to the day of his death he never gave it up. This man sought no one. His principle was, first form character, first earn spirituality, and results will come of themselves. His favourite illustration was, "When the lotus opens, the bees come of their own accord to seek the honey; so let the lotus of your character be full-blown and the results will follow." This is a great lesson to learn. My Master taught me this lesson hundreds of times, yet I often forget it.[9]

[Sri Ramakrishna], too, practised the Tantra, but not in [the old] way. Where there is the injunction of drinking wine, he would simply touch his forehead with a drop of it. The Tantrika form of worship is a very slippery ground.[10]

Sri Ramakrishna wept and prayed to the Divine Mother to send him such a one to talk with as would not have in him the slightest tinge of Kama-kanchana [lust and greed]; for he would say, "My lips burn when I talk with the worldy-minded." He also used to say that he could not even bear the touch of the worldly-minded and the impure.[11]

[*Question: Where did this habit of seeing every people from their strongest aspect come from?*] It must have been the training under Ramakrishna Paramahamsa. We all went by his path to some extent. Of course it was not so difficult for us as he made it for himself. He would eat and dress like the people he wanted to understand, take their initiation, and use their language. "One must learn," he said, "to put oneself into another man's very soul." And this method was his own! No one ever before in India became Christian and Mohammedan and Vaishnava, by turn![12]

I know one whom the world used to call mad, and this was his answer: "My friends, the whole world is a lunatic asylum. Some are mad after worldly love, some after name, some after fame, some after money, some after salvation and going to heaven. In this big lunatic asylum I am also mad, I am mad after God. If you are mad after money, I am mad after God. You are mad; so am I. I think my madness is after all the best."[13]

Sometimes the mind is concentrated on a set of ideas—this is called meditation with Vikalpa or oscillation. But when the mind becomes almost free from all activities, it melts in the inner Self, which is the essence of infinite Knowledge, One, and Itself Its own support. This is what is called Nirvikalpa Samadhi, free from all activities. In Sri Ramakrishna we have again and again noticed both these forms of Samadhi. He had not to struggle to get these states. They came to him spontaneously, then and there. It was a wonderful phenomenon. It was by seeing him that we could rightly understand these things.[14]

It is not a very difficult matter to bring under control the material powers and to flaunt a miracle; but I do not find a more marvellous miracle than the way this "mad Brahmin" used to handle human minds like lumps of clay, breaking, moulding, and remoulding them at ease, and filling them with new ideas by a mere touch.[15]

Sri Ramakrishna never spoke a harsh word against anyone. So beautifully tolerant was he that every sect thought that he belonged to them. He loved everyone. To him all religions were true. He found a place for each one. He was free, but free in love, not in "thunder." The mild type creates, the thundering type spreads....

Ramakrishna came to teach the religion of today, constructive, not destructive. He had to go afresh to Nature to ask for facts, and he got scientific religion, which never says "believe," but "see"; "I see, and you too can see." Use the same means and you will reach the same vision. God will come to everyone, harmony is within the reach of all. Sri Ramakrishna's teachings are "the gist of Hinduism"; they were not peculiar to him. Nor did he claim that they were; he cared naught for name or fame.

He began to preach when he was about forty; but he never went out to do it. He waited for those who wanted his teachings to come to him....

Sri Ramakrishna is worshipped in India as one of the great Incarnations, and his birthday is celebrated there as a religious festival.[16]

The other idea of his life was intense love for others. The first part of my Master's life was spent in acquiring spirituality, and the remaining years in distributing it.... Men came in crowds to hear him, and he would talk twenty hours in the twenty-four, and that not for one day, but for months and months, until at last the body broke down under the pressure of this tremendous strain. His intense love for mankind would not let him refuse to help even the humblest of the thousands who sought his aid. Gradually there developed a vital throat disorder, and yet he could not be persuaded to refrain from these exertions. As soon as he heard that people were asking to see him, he would insist upon having them admitted and would answer all their questions. When expostulated with, he replied, "I do not care. I will give up twenty thousand such bodies to help one man. It is glorious to help even one man." There was no rest for him. Once a great man asked him, "Sir, you are a great Yogi, why do you not put your mind a little on your body and cure your disease?" At first he did not answer, but when the question had been repeated he gently said, "My friend, I thought you were a sage, but you talk like other men of the world. This mind has been given to the Lord. Do you mean to say that I should take it back and put it upon the body which is but a mere cage of the soul?"

So he went on preaching to the people, and the news spread that his body was about to pass away, and the people began to flock to him in greater crowds than ever ... and my Master went on teaching them without the least regard for his health. We could not prevent this. Many of the people came from long distances, and he would not rest until he had answered their questions. "While I can speak I must teach them," he would say, and he was as good as his word. One day he told us that he would lay down the body that day, and repeating the most sacred word of the Vedas he entered into Samadhi and passed away.[17]

I could not believe my own ears when I heard Western people talking so much of consciousness! Consciousness? What does consciousness matter! Why, it is nothing compared with the unfathomable depths of the subconscious and the heights of the superconscious! In this I could never be misled, for had

I not seen Ramakrishna Paramahamsa gather in ten minutes, from a man's subconscious mind, the whole of his past, and determine from that his future and his powers?[18]

Sri Ramakrishna was quite unable to take food in [an] indiscriminate way from the hands of any and all. It happened many a time that he would not accept food touched by a certain person or persons, and on rigorous investigation it would turn out that these had some particular stain to hide.[19]

Sri Ramakrishna used to deprecate lukewarmness in spiritual attainments, as for instance, saying that religion would come gradually, and that there was no hurry for it.[20]

We have seen how Sri Ramakrishna would encourage even those whom we considered as worthless, and change the very course of their lives thereby. His very method of teaching was a unique phenomenon....

He never destroyed a single man's special inclinations. He gave words of hope and encouragement even to the most degraded of persons and lifted them up.[21]

The history of the past has gone to develop the inner life of India, and the activity [i.e. the outer life] of the West. Hitherto these have been divergent. The time has now come for them to unite. Ramakrishna Paramahamsa was alive to the depths of his being, yet on the outer plane who was more active? This is the secret. Let your life be as deep as the ocean, but let it also be as wide as the sky.[22]

The artistic faculty was highly developed in our Lord, Sri Ramakrishna, and he used to say that without this faculty none can be truly spiritual.[23]

There are many things to learn, we must struggle for new and higher things till we die—struggle is the end of human life.

Sri Ramakrishna used to say, "As long as I live, so long do I learn." That man or that society which has nothing to learn is already in the jaws of death.[24]

A certain young man of little understanding used always to blame the Hindu Shastras before Sri Ramakrishna. One day he praised the *Bhagavad Gita*, on which Sri Ramakrishna said, "Methinks, some European Pandit has praised the Gita, and so he has also followed suit."[25]

It was no new truth that Ramakrishna Paramahamsa came to preach, though his advent brought the old truths to light. In other words, he was the embodiment of all the past religious thoughts of India. His life alone made me understand what the Shastras really meant, and the whole plan and scope of the old Shastras.[26]

And the most wonderful part of it was that his life's work was just near a city which was full of Western thought, a city which had run mad after these occidental ideas, a city which had become more Europeanised than any other city in India. There he lived, without any book-learning whatsoever; this great intellect never learnt even to write his own name, but the most brilliant graduates of our university found in him an intellectual giant. He was a strange man, this Sri Ramakrishna Paramahamsa ... the fulfilment of the Indian sages, the sage for the time, one whose teaching is just now, in the present time, most beneficial. And mark the divine power working behind the man. The son of a poor priest, born in an out-of-the-way village, unknown and unthought of, today is worshipped literally by thousands in Europe and America, and tomorrow will be worshipped by thousands more. Who knows the plans of the Lord! ... Let me say now that if I have told you one word of truth, it was his and his alone, and if I have told you many things which were not true, which were not correct, which were not beneficial to the human race, they were all mine, and on me is the responsibility.[27]

It requires striving through many births to reach perfection or the ultimate stage with regard to a single one of [the] devotional attitudes. But Sri Ramakrishna, the king of the realm of spiritual sentiment, perfected himself in no less than eighteen different forms of devotion! He also used to say that his body would not have endured, had he not held himself on to this play of spiritual sentiment.[28]

To remove all this corruption in religion, the Lord has incarnated Himself on earth in the present age in the person of Sri Ramakrishna. The universal teachings that he offered, if spread all over the world, will do good to humanity and the world. Not for many a century past has India produced so great, so wonderful, a teacher of religious synthesis.[29]

Ramakrishna Paramahamsa came for the good of the world. Call him a man, or God, or an Incarnation, just as you please. Accept him each in your own light.

He who will bow before him will be converted to purest gold that very moment.[30]

From the day Sri Ramakrishna was born dates the growth of modern India and of the Golden Age.[31]

It is my opinion that Sri Ramakrishna was born to vivify all branches of art and culture in this country.[32]

In the Ramakrishna Incarnation there is knowledge, devotion, and love—infinite knowledge, infinite love, infinite work, infinite compassion for all beings. You have not yet been able to understand him.... What the whole Hindu race has thought in ages, he lived in one life. His life is the living commentary to the Vedas of all nations. People will come to know him by degrees.[33]

The future, you say, will call Ramakrishna Paramahamsa an Incarnation of Kali? Yes, I think there's no doubt that She worked up the body of Ramakrishna for Her own ends.[34]

He was contented simply to live that great life and to leave it to others to find the explanation.[35]

Everybody who has gone to Sri Ramakrishna has advanced in spirituality, is advancing, and will advance. Sri Ramakrishna used to say that the perfected Rishis of a previous Kalpa [cycle] take human bodies and come on earth with the Avataras. They are the associates of the Lord. God works through them and propagates His religion. Know this for a truth that they alone are the associates of the Avatara who have renounced all self for the sake of others, who, giving up all sense-enjoyments with repugnance, spend their lives for the good of the world, for the welfare of Jivas....

One [drop] from the full ocean of his spirituality, if realised, will make gods of men. Such a synthesis of universal ideas you will not find in the history of the world again. Understand from this who was born in the person of Sri Ramakrishna. When he used to instruct his Sannyasin disciples, he would rise from his seat and look about to see if any householder was coming that way or not. If he found none, then in glowing words he would depict the glory of renunciation and austerity. As a result of the rousing power of that fiery dispassion, we have renounced the world and become averse to worldliness.[36]

When the Avatara comes, then with him are born liberated persons as helpers in his world-play. Only Avataras have the power to dispel the darkness of a million souls and give them salvation in one life. This is known as grace....

The way ... is to call on him. Calling on him, many are blessed with his vision—can see him in human form just like ours and obtain his grace....

Those who have seen Sri Ramakrishna are really blessed. Their family and birth have become purified by it.... Nobody has been able to understand who came on earth as Sri Ramakrishna. Even his own nearest devotees have got no real clue to it. Only some have got a little inkling of it. All will understand it afterwards.[37]

In the highest reality of the Parabrahman, there is no distinction of sex. We notice this only in the relative plane. And the more the mind becomes introspective, the more that idea of difference vanishes. Ultimately, when the mind is wholly merged in the homogeneous and undifferentiated Brahman, such ideas as this is a man or that a woman do not remain at all. We have actually seen this in the life of Sri Ramakrishna.[38]

You will find that no one of the great teachers of the world went into these various explanations of texts; on their part there is no attempt at "text-torturing," no saying, "This word means this, and this is the philological connection between this and that word." You study all the great teachers the world has produced, and you will see that no one of them goes that way. Yet they taught.[39]

If anyone accepts Paramahamsa Deva as [an] Avatara, it is all right; if he doesn't do so, it is just the same. The truth about it is that in point of character, Paramahamsa Deva beats all previous records; and as regards teaching, he was more liberal, more original, and more progressive than all his predecessors. In other words, the older Teachers were rather one-sided, while the teaching of this new Incarnation or Teacher is that the best points of Yoga, devotion, knowledge, and work must be combined now so as to form a new society.... The older ones were no doubt good, but this is the new religion of this age—the synthesis of Yoga, knowledge, devotion, and work—the propagation of knowledge and devotion to all, down to the very lowest, without distinction of age or sex. The previous Incarnations were all right, but they have been synthesised in the person of Ramakrishna.[40]

That Ramakrishna Paramahamsa was God incarnate, I have not the least doubt; but then you must let people find out for themselves what he used to teach—you cannot thrust these things upon them....

Without studying Ramakrishna Paramahamsa first, one can never understand the real import of the Vedas, the Vedanta, of the Bhagavata and the other Puranas. His life is a searchlight of infinite power thrown upon the whole mass of Indian religious thought. He was the living commentary to the Vedas and to their aim. He had lived in one life the whole cycle of the national religious existence in India....

Ramakrishna Paramahamsa is the latest and the most perfect [Avatara]—the concentrated embodiment of knowledge, love, renunciation, catholicity, and the desire to serve mankind. So where is anyone to compare with him? He must have been born in vain who cannot appreciate him! My supreme good fortune is that I am his servant through life after life. A single word of his is to me far weightier than the Vedas and the Vedanta. *Tasya dāsadāsadāso'ham*—Oh, I am the servant of the servants of his servants.... Certain fishermen and illiterate people called Jesus Christ a God, but the literate people killed him. Buddha was honoured in his lifetime by a number of merchants and cowherds. But Ramakrishna has been worshipped in his lifetime—towards the end of this nineteenth century—by the demons and giants of the university as God incarnate.... Here is a man in whose company we have been day and night and yet consider him to be a far greater personality than any of [the earlier Avataras].[41]

[Our] ideal is, of course, the abstract Brahman. But as ... all cannot be inspired by an abstract ideal, [we] must have a personal ideal. [We] have got that in the person of Sri Ramakrishna.... In order that Vedanta may come to everyone, there must be a person who is in sympathy with the present generation. This is fulfilled in Sri Ramakrishna. So now you should place him before everyone. Whether one accepts him as a Sadhu or an Avatara does not matter.

He said he would come once more with us. Then, I think, he will embrace Videha-Mukti [liberation on the fall of the body].[42]

The minds of those who have truly received his grace cannot be attached to worldliness. The test of his grace is—unattachment to lust or wealth. If that has not come in anyone's life, then he has not truly received his grace.[43]

We have heard the great Minister of the Brahmo Samaj, the late revered Acharya Sri Keshab Chandra Sen, speaking in his charming way that Sri Ramakrishna's simple, sweet, colloquial language breathed a superhuman purity; though in his speech could be noticed some such words as we term obscene, the use of those words, on account of his uncommon childlike innocence and of their being perfectly devoid of the least breath of sensualism, instead of being something reproachable, served rather the purpose of embellishment.[44]

Know truth for yourself, and there will be many to whom you can teach it afterwards; they will all come. This was the attitude of my Master. He criticised no one. For years I lived with that man, but never did I hear those lips utter one word of condemnation for any sect. He had the same sympathy for all sects; he had found the harmony between them. A man may be intellectual, or devotional, or mystic, or active; the various religions represent one or the other of these types. Yet it is possible to combine all the four in one man, and this is what future humanity is going to do. That was his idea. He condemned no one, but saw the good in all.[45]

It was given to me to live with a man who was as ardent a dualist, as ardent an Advaitist, as ardent a Bhakta, as a Jnani. And living with this man first put it into my head to understand the Upanishads and the texts of the scriptures from an independent and better basis than by blindly following the commentators; and in my opinion and in my researches, I came to the conclusion that these texts are not at all contradictory.[46]

The life of Sri Ramakrishna was an extraordinary searchlight under whose illumination one is able to really understand the whole scope of Hindu religion. He was the object-lesson of all the theoretical knowledge given in the Shastras. He showed by his life what the Rishis and Avataras really wanted to teach. The books were theories, he was the realisation. This man had in fifty-one years lived the five thousand years of national spiritual life and so raised himself to be an object-lesson for future generations. The Vedas can only be explained and the Shastras reconciled by his theory of Avasthā or stages—that we must not only tolerate others, but positively embrace them, and that truth is the basis of all religions....

He had a whole world of knowledge to teach.[47]

[*Question: Did he found a sect?*] No, his whole life was spent in breaking down the barriers of sectarianism and dogma. He formed no sect. Quite the reverse. He advocated and strove to establish absolute freedom of thought. He was a great Yogi.[48]

Others, who have nothing to teach, will take a word and write a three-volume book on its origin and use. As my Master used to say, what would you think of men who went into a mango orchard and busied themselves in counting leaves, the size of twigs, the number of branches, and so forth, while only one of them had the sense to begin to eat the mangoes?[49]

There is another set of teachers, the Christs of the world. These Teachers of all teachers represent God Himself in the form of man. They are much higher; they can transmit spirituality with a touch, with a wish, which makes even the lowest and most degraded characters saints in one second.... They are the Teachers of all teachers, the greatest manifestations of God to man; we cannot see God except through them. We cannot help worshipping them, and they are the only beings we are bound to worship.[50]

The Guru has to bear the disciple's burden of sin; and that is the reason why diseases and other ailments appear even in the bodies of powerful Acharyas....

It is easier to become a Jivanmukta [free in this very life] than to be an Acharya. For the former knows the world as a dream and has no concern with it; but an Acharya knows it as a dream and yet has to remain in it and work. It is not possible for everyone to be an Acharya. He is an Acharya through whom the divine power acts.

The body in which one becomes an Acharya is very different from that of any other man. There is a science for keeping that body in a perfect state. His is the most delicate organism, very susceptible, capable of feeling intense joy and intense suffering....

Sri Ramakrishna is a force. You should not think that his doctrine is this or that. But he is a power, living even now in his disciples and working in the world. I saw him growing in his ideas. He is still growing. Sri Ramakrishna was both a Jivanmukta and an Acharya.[51]

The highest ideal of Ishvara which the human mind can grasp is the Avatara. Beyond this there is no relative knowledge. Such knowers of Brahman are rarely born in the world. And very few people can understand them. They alone are the proof of the truths of the scriptures—the towers of light in the ocean of the world. By the company of such Avataras and by their grace, the darkness of the mind disappears in a trice and realisation flashes immediately in the heart. Why or by what process it comes cannot be ascertained. But it does come. I have seen it happen like that.[52]

The work which the Jnani does only conduces to the well-being of the world. Whatever a man of realisation says or does contributes to the welfare of all. We have observed Sri Ramakrishna; he was, as it were, *"Dehastho'pi na dehasthaḥ*—in the body, but not of it." About the motive of the actions of such personages only this can be said: "*Lokavattu līlākaivalyam*—everything they do like men, simply by way of sport."[53] *

Whoever could have thought that the life and teachings of a boy born of poor Brahmin parents in a wayside Bengal village would, in a few years, reach such distant lands as our ancestors never even dreamed of? I refer to Bhagavan Ramakrishna.[54]

From the very date that he was born, has sprung the Satya-Yuga (Golden Age). Henceforth there is an end to all sorts of distinctions, and everyone down to the Chandala will be

---

* *Brahma-Sutras*, 2.1.33

a sharer in the Divine Love. The distinction between man and woman, between the rich and the poor, the literate and illiterate, Brahmins and Chandalas—he lived to root out all. And he was the harbinger of Peace—the separation between Hindus and Mohammedans, between Hindus and Christians, all are now things of the past. That fight about distinctions that there was, belonged to another era. In this Satya-Yuga the tidal wave of Sri Ramakrishna's Love has unified all.... Whoever—man or woman—will worship Sri Ramakrishna, be he or she ever so low, will be then and there converted into the very highest....

He was the saviour of women, saviour of the masses, saviour of all, high and low.[55]

In the presence of my Master I found out that man could be perfect, even in this body. Those lips never cursed anyone, never even criticised anyone. Those eyes were beyond the possibility of seeing evil, that mind had lost the power of thinking evil. He saw nothing but good. That tremendous purity, that tremendous renunciation is the one secret of spirituality. "Neither through wealth, nor through progeny, but through renunciation alone, is immortality to be reached," say the Vedas. "Sell all that thou hast and give to the poor, and follow me," says the Christ. So all great saints and prophets have expressed it, and have carried it out in their lives. How can great spirituality come without that renunciation? Renunciation is the background of all religious thought wherever it be, and you will always find that as this idea of renunciation lessens, the more will the senses creep into the field of religion, and spirituality will decrease in the same ratio.

That man was the embodiment of renunciation. In our country it is necessary for a man who becomes a Sannyasin to give up all worldly wealth and position, and this my Master carried out literally. There were many who would have felt themselves blessed if he would only have accepted a present from their hands, who would gladly have given him thousands of rupees if he would have taken them, but these were the only men from whom he would turn away. He was a triumphant example, a living realisation of the complete conquest of lust and of desire for money. He was beyond all ideas of either, and such men are necessary for this century. Such renunciation is necessary in these days when men have begun to think that they cannot live a month without what they call their "necessities," and which they are increasing out of all proportion. It is necessary in a time like this that a man shall arise to demonstrate to the sceptics of the world that there yet breathes a man who does not care a straw for all the gold or all the fame that is in the universe.[56]

Such a man, then, was necessary; and such renunciation is what this age requires....

Lay down your lives. Make yourselves servants of humanity. Be living sermons. This, and not talk, is renunciation. Stand up and strike! The very sight of you will fill the worldly mind, the wealth-seeking mind, with terror....

Stand you up, and realise God! If you can renounce all wealth and all sex, it will not be necessary for you to speak. Your lotus will have blossomed, and the spirit will spread. Whoever approaches you will be warmed, as it were, by the fire of your spirituality.

This is the message of Sri Ramakrishna to the modern world. Care not for doctrines or for dogmas, for sects or for churches. All these count for but little, compared with that essence of existence, which is in each one, and called spirituality. The more this is developed in a man, the more powerful is he for good. He who has most of it can do most good to his fellow-men. First, then, acquire that.... Only those who have seen it will understand this; but such spirituality can be given to others, even though they be unconscious of the gift. Only those who have attained to this power are amongst the great teachers of mankind. They are the powers of light.

Then be you this! The more of such men any country produces, the higher is that country raised. That land where no such men exist, is doomed. Nothing can save it. Therefore my Master's message to the world is, "Be ye all spiritual! Get ye first realisation!" And to the young and strong of every country he would cry that the time is come for renunciation. Renounce for the sake of humanity! You have talked of the love of man till the thing is in danger of becoming words alone. The time is come to act. The call now is, Do! Leap into the breach and save the world.[57]

While I am on earth, Sri Ramakrishna is working through me.[58]

Others love me personally. But they little dream that what they love me for is Ramakrishna; leaving Him, I am only a mass of foolish selfish emotions.[59]

Sri Sarada Devi, 1898

Mother has been born to revive that wonderful Shakti in India . . . To me, Mother's grace is a hundred thousand times more valuable than Father's. Mother's grace, Mother's blessings are all paramount to me. . . . fie on him who has no devotion for the Mother.

At the Parliament of Religions, Chicago, September 1893

I bowed down to Devi Sarasvati and stepped up, and Dr. Barrows introduced me. I made a short speech. I addressed the assembly as "Sisters and Brothers of America," a deafening applause of two minutes followed.... The next day all the papers announced that my speech was the hit of the day, and I became known to the whole of America.

Madras, 1897

India I loved before I came away. Now the very dust of India has become holy to me, the very air is now to me holy; it is now the holy land, the place of pilgrimage, the Tirtha.

Belur Math

When I installed Sri Ramakrishna on the Math grounds, I felt as if his ideas shot forth from this place and flooded the whole universe.

Swami Vivekananda Temple, Belur Math

CHAPTER FOUR

THE BARANAGORE MATH AND DAYS OF WANDERING

The Master's Passing Away

THEN CAME THE SAD DAY when our old teacher died. We nursed him the best we could. We had no friends. Who would listen to a few boys, with their crank notions? Nobody. At least, in India, boys are nobodies. Just think of it—a dozen boys, telling people vast, big ideas, saying they are determined to work these ideas out in life. Why, everybody laughed. From laughter it became serious; it became persecution. Why, the parents of the boys came to feel like spanking every one of us. And the more we were derided, the more determined we became.[1]

Sri Ramakrishna used to say, "In the morning and evening the mind remains highly imbued with Sattva ideas; those are the times when one should meditate with earnestness."

After the passing away of Sri Ramakrishna we underwent a lot of religious practice at the Baranagore Math. We used to get up at 3 AM, and after washing our face etc.—some after bath, and others without it—we would sit in the worship-room and become absorbed in Japa and meditation. What a strong spirit of dispassion we had in those days! We had no thought even as to whether the world existed or not. Ramakrishnananda busied himself day and night with the duties pertaining to Sri Ramakrishna's worship and service, and occupied the same position in the Math as the mistress of the house does in a family. It was he who would procure, mostly by begging, the requisite articles for Sri Ramakrishna's worship and our subsistence. There have been days when the Japa and meditation continued from morning till four or five in the afternoon. Ramakrishnananda waited and waited with our meals ready, till at last he would come and snatch us from our meditation by sheer force. Oh, what a wonderful constancy of devotion we have noticed in him!...

We were Sadhus, and what would come by begging and other means, would be utilised for defraying the Math expenses. Today both Suresh Babu [Surendra Nath Mitra] and Balaram Babu [Balaram Bose] are no more; had they been alive they would have been exceedingly glad to see this Math [at Belur]. You have doubtless heard Suresh Babu's name. It was he who used to bear all the expenses of the Baranagore Math. It was this Suresh Mitra who used to think most for us in those days. His devotion and faith have no parallel!...

Owing to want of funds I would sometimes fight for abolishing the Math altogether. But I could never induce Ramakrishnananda to accede to the proposal. Know Ramakrishnananda to be the central figure of the Math. There have been days when the Math was without a grain of food. If some rice was collected by begging, there was no salt to take it with! On some days there would be only rice and salt, but nobody cared for it in the least. We were then being carried away by a tidal wave of spiritual practice. Boiled *bimba* leaves, rice, and salt—this was the menu for a month at a stretch. Oh, those wonderful days! The austerities of that period were enough to dismay supernatural beings, not to speak of men. But it is a tremendous truth that if there be real worth in you, the more are circumstances against you, the more will that inner power manifest itself. But the reason why I have provided for beds and a tolerable living in this Math is that the Sannyasins that are enrolling themselves nowadays will not be able to bear so much strain as we did. There was the life of Sri Ramakrishna before us, and that was why we did not care much for privations and hardships. Boys of this generation will not be able to undergo so much hardship. Hence it is that I have provided for some sort of habitation and a bare subsistence for them. If they get just enough food and clothing, the boys will devote themselves to religious practice and will learn to sacrifice their lives for the good of humanity....

[*Question: Outside people say a good deal against this sort of bedding and furniture.*] Let them say. Even in jest they will at least once think of this Math. And they say, it is easier to attain liberation through cherishing a hostile spirit.[2]

After Sri Ramakrishna's passing away, all forsook us as so many worthless, ragged boys. Only people like Balaram, Suresh, Master [Mahendranath Gupta or "M"], and Chuni Babu [Chunilal Basu] were our friends at that hour of need. And we shall never be able to repay our debts to them.[3]

Then came a terrible time—for me personally and for all the other boys as well. But to me came such misfortune! On the one side was my mother, my brothers. My father died at that time, and we were left poor. Oh, very poor, almost starving all the time! I was the only hope of the family, the only one who could do anything to help them. I had to stand between my two worlds. On the one hand, I would have to see my mother and brothers starve unto death; on the other, I had believed that [Sri Ramakrishna's] ideas were for the good of India and the world, and had to be preached and worked out. And so the fight went on in my mind for days and months. Sometimes I would pray for five or six days and nights together without stopping. Oh, the agony of those days! I was living in hell!

The natural affections of my boy's heart drawing me to my family—I could not bear to see those who were the nearest and dearest to me suffering. On the other hand, nobody to sympathise with me. Who would sympathise with the imaginations of a boy—imaginations that caused so much suffering to others? Who would sympathise with me? None—except one [Sri Sarada Devi]. That one's sympathy brought blessing and hope....

Well, that lady, [Sri Ramakrishna's] wife, was the only one who sympathised with the idea of those boys. But she was powerless. She was poorer than we were. Never mind! We plunged into the breach. I believed, as I was living, that these ideas were going to rationalise India and bring better days to many lands and foreign races. With that belief, came the realisation that it is better that a few persons suffer than that such ideas should die out of the world. What if a mother or two brothers die? It is a sacrifice. Let it be done. No great thing can be done without sacrifice. The heart must be plucked out and the bleeding heart placed upon the altar. Then great things are done. Is there any other way? None have found it. I appeal to each one of you, to those who have accomplished any great thing. Oh, how much it has cost! What agony! What torture! What terrible suffering is behind every deed of success in every life! You know that, all of you.

And thus we went on, that band of boys. The only thing we got from those around us was a kick and a curse—that was all. Of course, we had to beg from door to door for our food: got hips and haws—the refuse of everything—a piece of bread here and there. We got hold of a broken-down old house, with hissing cobras living underneath; and because that was the cheapest, we went into that house and lived there.

Thus we went on for some years, in the meanwhile making excursions all over India, trying to bring about the idea gradually. Ten years were spent without a ray of light! Ten more years! A thousand times despondency came; but there was one thing always to keep us hopeful—the tremendous faithfulness to each other, the tremendous love between us. I have got a hundred men and women around me; if I become the devil himself tomorrow, they will say, "Here we are still! We will never give you up!" That is a great blessing. In happiness, in misery, in famine, in pain, in the grave, in heaven, or in hell, who never gives me up is my friend. Is such friendship a joke? A man may have salvation through such friendship. That brings salvation if we can love like that. If we have that faithfulness, why, there is the essence of all concentration. You need not worship any gods in the world if you have that faith, that strength, that love. And that was there with us all throughout that hard time. That was there. That made us go from the Himalayas to Cape Comorin, from the Indus to the Brahmaputra.

This band of boys began to travel about. Gradually we began to draw attention: ninety percent was antagonism, very little of it was helpful. For we had one fault: we were boys—in poverty and with all the roughness of boys. He who has to make his own way in life is a bit rough, he has not much time to be smooth and suave and polite—"my lady and my gentleman," and all that. You have seen that in life, always. He is a rough diamond, he has not much polish, he is a jewel in an indifferent casket.

And there we were. "No compromise!" was the watchword. "This is the ideal, and this has got to be carried out. If we meet the king, though we die, we must give him a bit of our minds; if the peasant, the same." Naturally, we met with antagonism.

But, mind you, this is life's experience; if you really want the good of others, the whole universe may stand against you and cannot hurt you. It must crumble before your power of the Lord Himself in you if you are sincere and really unselfish. And those boys were that. They came as children, pure and fresh from the hands of nature. Said our Master: I want to offer at the altar of the Lord only those flowers that have not even been smelled, fruits that have not been touched with the fingers. The words of the great man sustained us all. For he saw through the future life of those boys that he collected from the streets of Calcutta, so to say. People used to laugh at him when he said, "You will see—this boy, that boy, what he becomes." His faith was unalterable: "Mother showed it to me. I may be weak, but when She says this is so—She can never make mistakes—it must be so."

So things went on and on for ten years without any light, but with my health breaking all the time. It tells on the body in the long run: sometimes one meal at nine in the evening, another time a meal at eight in the morning, another after two days, another after three days—and always the poorest and roughest thing. Who is going to give to the beggar the good things he has? And then, they have not much in India. And most of the time walking, climbing snow peaks, sometimes ten miles of hard mountain climbing, just to get a meal. They eat unleavened bread in India, and sometimes they have it stored away for twenty or thirty days, until it is harder than bricks; and then they will give a square of that. I would have to go from house to house to collect sufficient for one meal. And then the bread was so hard, it made my mouth bleed to eat it. Literally, you can break your teeth on that bread. Then I would put it in a pot and pour over it water from the river. For months and months I existed that way—of course it was telling on the health.[4]

He who has a dogged determination like that shall have everything. Only some may have it sooner, and others a little later, that is all. But one is bound to reach the goal. It is because we had such a determination that we have attained the little that we have. Otherwise, what dire days of privation we have had to pass through! One day, for want of food I fainted in the outer platform of a house on the roadside and quite a shower of rain had passed over my head before I recovered my senses! Another day, I had to do odd jobs in Calcutta for the whole day without food, and had my meal on my return to the Math at ten or eleven in the night. And these were not solitary instances.[5]

Sri Ramakrishna was a wonderful gardener. Therefore he has made a bouquet of different flowers and formed his Order. All different types and ideas have come into it, and many more will come. Sri Ramakrishna used to say, "Whoever has prayed to God sincerely for one day, must come here." Know each of those who are here [the Sannyasin disciples of Sri Ramakrishna], to be of great spiritual power.... When they will go out, they will be the cause of the awakening of spirituality in people. Know them to be part of the spiritual body of Sri Ramakrishna, who was the embodiment of infinite religious ideas. I look upon them with that eye. See, for instance, Brahmananda, who is here—even I have not the spirituality which he has. Sri Ramakrishna looked upon him as his mind-born son; and he lived and walked, ate and slept with him. He is the ornament of our Math—our king. Similarly Premananda, Turiyananda, Trigunatitananda, Akhandananda, Saradananda, Ramakrishnananda, Subodhananda, and others; you may go round the world, but it is doubtful if you will find men of such spirituality and faith in God like them. They are each a centre of religious power, and in time that power will manifest.[6]

To create a band of men who are tied and bound together with a most undying love in spite of difference—is it not wonderful?[7]

The disciples of Jesus were all Sannyasins. The direct recipients of the grace of Shankara, Ramanuja, Sri Chaitanya and Buddha were the all-renouncing Sannyasins. It is men of this stamp who have been through succession of disciples spreading the Brahma-vidya [knowledge of Brahman] in the world. Where and when have you heard that a man being the slave of lust and wealth has been able to liberate another or to show the path of God to him? Without himself being free, how can he make others free? In Veda, Vedanta, Itihasa [history], Purana [ancient tradition], you will find everywhere that the Sannyasins have been the teachers of religion in all ages and climes. History repeats itself. It will also be likewise now. The capable Sannyasin children of Sri Ramakrishna, the teacher of the great synthesis of religions, will be honoured everywhere as the teachers of men.[8]

The ways, movements, and ideas of our Master were all cast in a new mould, so we are also of a new type. Sometimes dressed like gentlemen, we are engaged in lecturing; at other times, throwing all aside, with "Hara, Hara, Vyom Vyom" on the lips, ash-clad, we are immersed in meditation and austerities in mountains and forests.[9]

Let me tell you a little personal experience. When my Master left the body, we were a dozen penniless and unknown young men. Against us were a hundred powerful organisations, struggling hard to nip us in the bud. But Ramakrishna had given us one great gift, the desire, and the lifelong struggle not to talk alone, but to *live the life*. And today all India knows and reverences the Master, and the truths he taught are spreading like wild fire. Ten years ago I could not get a hundred persons together to celebrate his birthday anniversary. Last year there were fifty thousand.[10]

His thoughts and his message were known to very few who were capable of giving them out. Among others, he left a few young boys who had renounced the world, and were ready to carry on his work. Attempts were made to crush them. But they stood firm, having the inspiration of that great life before them. Having had the contact of that blessed life for years, they stood their ground. These young men, living as Sannyasins, begged through the streets of the city where they were born, although some of them came from high families. At first they met with great antagonism, but they persevered and went on from day to day spreading all over India the message of that great man, until the whole country was filled with the ideas he had preached.[11]

I am not taking pride in this. But, mark you, I have told the story of that group of boys. Today there is not a village, not a man, not a woman in India that does not know their work and bless them. There is not a famine in the land where these boys do not plunge in and try to work and rescue as many as they can.[12]

I believed and still believe that without my giving up the world, the great mission which Ramakrishna Paramahamsa, my great Master, came to preach would not see the light, and where would those young men be who have stood as bulwarks against the surging waves of materialism and luxury of the day? These have done a great amount of good to India, especially to Bengal, and this is only the beginning. With the Lord's help they will do things for which the whole world will bless them for ages. So on the one hand, my vision of the future of Indian religion and that of the whole world, my love for the millions of beings sinking down and down for ages with nobody to help them, nay, nobody with even a thought for them; on the other hand, making those who are nearest and dearest to me miserable; I choose the former. "Lord will do the rest." He is with me, I am sure of that if of anything. So long as I am sincere, nothing can resist me, because He will be my help. Many and many in India could not understand me; and how could they, poor men? Their thoughts never strayed beyond the everyday routine business of eating and drinking.... But appreciation or no appreciation, I am born to organise these young men; nay, hundreds more in every city are ready to join me; and I want to send them rolling like irresistible waves over India, bringing comfort, morality, religion, education to the doors of the meanest and the most downtrodden. And this I will do or die.[13]

We are a unique company. Nobody amongst us has a right to force his faith upon the others. Many of us do not believe in any form of idolatry.... What harm is there in some people worshipping their Guru when that Guru was a hundred times more holy than even your historical prophets all taken together? If there is no harm in worshipping Christ, Krishna, or Buddha, why should there be any in worshipping this man who never did or thought anything unholy, whose intellect only through intuition stands head and shoulders above all the other prophets, because they were all one-sided?[14]

Glimpses from Letters and Conversations

Baranagore, 25 March 1887 · I have attained my present state of mind as a result of much suffering and pain.... I now realize that without trials and tribulations one cannot resign oneself to God and depend on Him absolutely.[15]

Baranagore, 9 April 1887 · Whatever spiritual disciplines we are practising here are in obedience to the Master's command. But it is strange that Ram Babu criticizes us for our spiritual practices. He says: "We have seen [Sri Ramakrishna]. What need have we of any such practice?"... But the Master asked us to practise Sadhana....

Now and then I feel great scepticism. At Baburam's house it seemed to me that nothing existed—as if there were no such thing as God.[16]

Calcutta, 7 May 1887 · I don't care for anything.... I shall fast to death for the realization of God....

It seems there is no God. I pray so much, but there is no reply—none whatsoever.

How many visions I have seen! How many mantras shining in letters of gold! How many visions of the Goddess Kali! How many other divine forms! But still I have no peace.[17]

I saw many great men in Hrishikesh. One case that I remember was that of a man who seemed to be mad. He was coming nude down the street, with boys pursuing and throwing stones at him. The whole man was bubbling over with laughter while blood was streaming down his face and neck. I took him and bathed the wound, putting ashes on it to stop the bleeding. And all the time with peals of laughter he told me of the fun the boys and he had been having, throwing the stones. "So the Father plays," he said.

Many of these men hide, in order to guard themselves against intrusion. People are a trouble to them. One had human bones strewn about his cave and gave it out that he lived on corpses. Another threw stones. And so on....

Sometimes the thing comes upon them in a flash. There was a boy, for instance, who used to come to read the Upanishads with Abhedananda. One day he turned and said, "Sir, is all this really true?"

"Oh yes!" said Abhedananda, "It may be difficult to realize, but it is certainly true." And next day, that boy was a silent Sannyasin, nude, on his way to Kedarnath![18]

Baranagore, 19 November 1888 · A good deal of study, in fact, is given to Sanskrit scriptures in this Math. The Vedas may well be said to have fallen quite out of vogue in Bengal. Many here in this Math are conversant with Sanskrit, and they have a mind to master the Samhita portions of the Vedas. They are of opinion that what has to be done must be done to a finish. So, believing that a full measure of proficiency in the Vedic language is impossible without first mastering Panini's grammar, which is the best available for the purpose, a copy of the latter was felt to be a necessity.... This Math is not wanting in men of perseverance, talent, and penetrative intellect. I may hope that by the grace of our Master, they will acquire in a short time Panini's system and then succeed in restoring the Vedas to Bengal.[19]

Baranagore, 4 February 1889 · Your letter of invitation to the heavenly city of Varanasi reached me. I accept it as the call of Vishveshvara.... He must be made of stone whose mind does not melt at the sight of Kashi and its Lord!... I am coming as soon as I can. It all depends ultimately on Vishveshvara's will.[20]

Antpur, 7 February 1889 · My heart leaps with joy—and it is a wonder that I do not go mad when I find anybody thoroughly launched into the midst of the doctrine which is to shower peace on earth hereafter.[21]

Baghbazar, 21 March 1889 · I am very ill at present; there is fever now and then, but there is no disorder in the spleen or other organs. I am under homeopathic treatment. Now I have had to give up completely the intention of going to Varanasi. Whatever God dispenses will happen later on, according to the state of the body.[22]

Calcutta, 4 July 1889 · By the will of God, the last six or seven years of my life have been full of constant struggles with hindrances and obstacles of all sorts. I have been vouchsafed the ideal Shastra; I have seen the ideal man; and yet fail myself to get on with anything to the end—this is my profound misery.

And particularly, I see no chance of success while remaining near Calcutta. In Calcutta live my mother and two brothers. I am the eldest; the second is preparing for the First Arts Examination, and the third is young. They were quite well off before, but since my father's death, it is going very hard with them—they even have to go fasting at times! To crown all, some relatives, taking advantage of their helplessness, drove them away from the ancestral residence. Though a part of it is recovered through suing at the High Court, destitution is now upon them—a matter of course in litigation.

Living near Calcutta I have to witness their adversity, and the quality of Rajas prevailing, my egotism sometimes develops into the form of a desire that rises to plunge me into action; in such moments, a fierce fighting ensues in my mind, and so I wrote that the state of my mind was terrible. Now their lawsuit has come to an end.[23]

Baranagore, 17 August 1889 · I have no partiality for any party in this caste question, because I know it is a social law and is based on diversity of Guna and Karma. It also means grave harm if one bent on going beyond Guna and Karma cherishes in mind any caste distinctions. In these matters, I have got some settled ideas through the grace of my Guru ... [24]

Baghbazar, 2 September 1889 · Your advice to me to give up arguing and disputing is very true indeed, and that is really the goal of life for the individual—"Sundered are the knots of the heart, torn off are all his doubts, and the seeds of his Karma wear off, when the sight of the Transcendent One is gained." But then, as my Master used to say, when a pitcher is being filled [by immersing it in a pond], it gurgles, but when full, it is noiseless; know my condition to be the same.[25]

Vaidyanath, 24 December 1889 · I have been putting up here for some days with a gentleman of Calcutta, but my mind is much longing for Varanasi. My idea is to remain there for some time, and to watch how Vishvanatha and Annapurna deal it out to my lot. And my resolve is something like *śarīraṁ vā pātayāmi mantraṁ vā sādhayāmi*—either to lay down my life or realise my ideal—so help me the Lord of Kashi.[26]

Allahabad, 30 December 1889 · I was to go to Varanasi in a day or two, but who can nullify the decree of Providence? News reached me that a brother-disciple, Yogen by name [Swami Yogananda], had been attacked with smallpox after arriving here from a pilgrimage to Chitrakuta, Omkarnath, etc., and so I came to this place to nurse him. He has now completely recovered. Some Bengali gentlemen here are of a greatly pious and loving disposition. They are very lovingly taking care of me....

I am going to try my best to slip away ... and betake myself to the holy realm of the Lord of Varanasi.... Let me see how the Lord of Kashi disposes.[27]

Ghazipur, 30 January 1890 · I am now stopping with Satish Babu at Ghazipur. Of the few places I have recently visited, this is the healthiest. The water of Vaidyanath is very bad—it leads to indigestion. Allahabad is very congested. The few days I passed at Varanasi, I suffered from fever day and night—the place is so malarious! Ghazipur has a very salubrious climate—specially the quarter I am living in. I have visited Pavhari Baba's house—there are high walls all round, and it is fashioned like an English bungalow. There is a garden inside and big rooms and chimneys, etc. He allows nobody to enter. If he is so inclined, he comes up to the door and speaks from inside—that is all. One day I went and waited and waited in the cold and had to return. I shall go to Varanasi on Sunday next. If the meeting with the Babaji takes place in the meantime, all right, otherwise I bid him good-bye.[28]

Ghazipur, 4 February 1890 · Through supreme good fortune, I have obtained an interview with Babaji [Pavhari Baba]. A great sage indeed!—it is all very wonderful, and in this atheistic age, a towering representation of marvellous power born of Bhakti and Yoga! I have sought refuge in his grace; and he has given me hope—a thing very few may be fortunate enough to obtain. It is Babaji's wish that I stay on for some days here, and he would do me some good. So following this saint's bidding I shall remain here for some time.... Unless one is face to face with the life of such men, faith in the scriptures does not grow in all its real integrity.[29]

Ghazipur, 7 February 1890 · Apparently in his features, the Babaji is a Vaishnava, the embodiment, so to speak, of Yoga, Bhakti, and humility. His dwelling has walls on all sides with a few doors in them. Inside these walls, there is one long underground burrow wherein he lays himself up in Samadhi. He talks to others only when he comes out of the hole. Nobody knows what he eats, and so they call him Pavhari Baba. Once he did not come out of the hole for five years, and people thought he had given up the body. But now again he is out. But this time he does not show himself to people and talks from behind the door. Such sweetness in speech I have never come across! He does not give a direct reply to questions but says, "What does this servant know?" But then fire comes out as the talking goes on. On my pressing him very much he said, "Favour me highly by staying here some days." But he never speaks in this way; so from this I understood he meant to reassure me; and whenever I am importunate, he asks me to stay on. So I wait in hope. He is a learned man no doubt but nothing in the line betrays itself. He performs scriptural ceremonials, for from the full-moon day to the last day of the month, sacrificial oblations go on. So it is sure, he is not retiring into the hole during this period.[30]

After [Sri Ramakrishna's] leaving the body, I associated for some time with Pavhari Baba of Ghazipur. There was a garden not far distant from his ashrama where I lived. People used to say it was a haunted garden, but as you know, I am a sort of demon myself and have not much fear of ghosts. In the garden there were many lemon trees which bore numerous fruits. At that time I was suffering from diarrhoea, and there no food could be had except bread. So, to increase the digestive powers, I used to take plenty of lemons. Mixing with Pavhari Baba, I liked him very much, and he also came to love me deeply. One day I thought that I did not learn any art for making this weak body strong, even though I lived with Sri Ramakrishna for so many years. I had heard that Pavhari Baba knew the science of Hatha-Yoga. So I thought I would learn the practices of Hatha-Yoga from him, and through them strengthen the body.

You know, I have a dogged resolution, and whatever I set my heart on, I always carry out. On the eve of the day on which I was to take initiation, I was lying on a cot thinking; and just then I saw the form of Sri Ramakrishna standing on my right side, looking steadfastly at me, as if very much grieved. I had dedicated myself to him, and at the thought that I was taking another Guru I was much ashamed and kept looking at him. Thus perhaps two or three hours passed, but no words escaped from my mouth. Then he disappeared all on a sudden. My mind became upset seeing Sri Ramakrishna that night, so I postponed the idea of initiation from Pavhari Baba for the day. After a day or two again the idea of initiation from Pavhari Baba arose in the mind—and again in the night there was the appearance of Sri Ramakrishna as on the previous occasion. Thus when for several nights in succession I had the vision of Sri Ramakrishna, I gave up the idea of initiation altogether, thinking that as every time I resolved on it, I was getting such a vision, then no good but harm would come from it.[31]

I once knew a Yogi, a very old man, who lived in a hole in the ground all by himself. All he had was a pan or two to cook his meals in. He ate very little, and wore scarcely anything, and spent most of his time meditating.

With him all people were alike. He had attained to non-injuring. What he saw in everything, in every person, in every animal, was the Soul, the Lord of the Universe. With him, every person and every animal was "My Lord." He never addressed any person or animal in any other way. Well, one day a thief came his way and stole one of his pans. He saw him and ran after him. The chase was a long one. At last the thief from exhaustion had to stop, and the Yogi, running up to him, fell on his knees before him and said, "My Lord, you do me a great honour to come my way. Do me the honour to accept the other pan. It is also yours." This old man is dead now. He was full of love for everything in the world. He would have died for an ant. Wild animals instinctively knew this old man to be their friend. Snakes and ferocious animals would go into his hole and sleep with him. They all loved him and never fought in his presence.[32]

One of the greatest lessons I have learnt in my life is to pay as much attention to the means of work as to its end. He was a great man from whom I learnt it, and his own life was a practical demonstration of this great principle. I have been always learning great lessons from that one principle, and it appears to be that all the secret of success is there; to pay as much attention to the means as to the end.[33]

One of [Pavhari Baba's] great peculiarities was his entire absorption at the time in the task in hand, however trivial. The same amount of care and attention was bestowed in cleaning a copper pot as in the worship of Sri Raghunathji, he himself being the best example of the secret he once told us of work: "The means should be loved and cared for as if it were the end itself."

Neither was his humility kindred to that which means pain and anguish or self-abasement. It sprang naturally from the realisation of that which he once so beautifully explained to us, "O King, the Lord is the wealth of those who have nothing—yes, of those," he continued, "who have thrown away all desires of possession, even that of one's own soul." He would never directly teach, as that would be assuming the role of a teacher and placing himself in a higher position than another. But once the spring was touched, the fountain welled up with infinite wisdom; yet always the replies were indirect....

The present writer owes a deep debt of gratitude to the departed saint, and dedicates these lines, however unworthy, to the memory of one of the greatest Masters he has loved and served.[34]

Ghazipur, 14 February 1890 · If Mother [Sri Sarada Devi] has come, please convey to her my countless salutations, and ask her to bless me that I may have unflinching perseverance. Or, if that be impossible in this body, may it fall off soon![35]

Ghazipur, 19 February 1890 · Well, you may smile ... to see me weaving all this web of Maya—and that is no doubt the fact. But then there is the chain of iron, and there is the chain of gold. Much good comes of the latter; and it drops off by itself when all the good is reaped. The sons of my Master are indeed the great objects of my service, and here alone I feel I have some duty left for me.[36]

Ghazipur, March 1890 · My motto is to learn whatever good things I may come across anywhere. This leads many friends to think that it will take away from my devotion to the Guru. These ideas I count as those of lunatics and bigots. For all gurus are one and are fragments and radiations of God, the Universal Guru.[37]

Ghazipur, 3 March 1890 · I am a very soft-natured man in spite of the stern Vedantic views I hold. And this proves to be my undoing. At the slightest touch I give myself away; for howsoever I may try to think only of my own good, I slip off in spite of myself to think of other peoples' interests. This time it was with a very stern resolve that I set out to pursue my own good, but I had to run off at the news of the illness of a brother at Allahabad! And now comes this news from Hrishikesh, and my mind has run off with me there....

The lumbago obstinately refuses to leave me, and the pain is very great. For the last few days I haven't been able to go to see Pavhariji, but out of his kindness he sends every day for my report. But now I see the whole matter is inverted in its bearings! While I myself have come, a beggar, at his door, he turns round and wants to learn of me! This saint perhaps is not yet perfected—too much of rites, vows, observances, and too much of self-concealment....

By my stay here I have been cured of all other symptoms of malaria, only the pain in the loins makes me frantic; day and night it is aching and chafes me very much.... I find wonderful endurance in Babaji, and that's why I am begging something of him; but no inkling of the mood to give, only receiving and receiving! So I also fly off....

To no big person am I going any longer—"Remain, O mind, within yourself"... says the poet Kamalakanta.

So now the great conclusion is that Ramakrishna has no peer; nowhere else in this world exists that unprecedented perfection, that wonderful kindness for all that does not stop to justify itself, that intense sympathy for man in bondage. Either he must be the Avatara as he himself used to say, or else the ever-perfected divine man, whom the Vedanta speaks of as the free one who assumes a body for the good of humanity. This is my conviction sure and certain; and the worship of such a divine man has been referred to by Patanjali in the aphorism: "Or the goal may be attained by meditating on a saint."[38]

Ghazipur, 15 March 1890 · I am leaving this place tomorrow. Let me see which way destiny leads![39]

Ghazipur, 31 March 1890 · I haven't been here for the last few days and am again going away today. I have asked brother Gangadhar [Swami Akhandananda] to come here; and if he comes, we go over to [Varanasi] together. For some special reasons, I shall continue to stay in secret in a village some distance from this place.... The news of his arrival has not yet been received, and, his health being bad, I am rather anxious for his sake. I have behaved very cruelly towards him—that is, I have harassed him much to make him leave my company.

There's no help, you see; I am so very weak-hearted, so much overmastered by the distractions of love!... What shall I say to you about the condition of my mind! Oh, it is as if the hell-fire is burning there day and night! Nothing, nothing could I do yet! And this life seems muddled away in vain; I feel quite helpless as to what to do! The Babaji throws out honeyed words and keeps me from leaving. Ah, what shall I say? I am committing hundreds of offenses against you—please excuse them as so many misdoings of a man driven mad with mental agonies.... My Gurubhais must be thinking me very cruel and selfish. Oh, what can I do? Who will see deep down into my mind? Who will know how much I am suffering day and night?...

My lumbago is as before.[40]

Baghbazar, 26 May 1890 · I am Ramakrishna's slave; having laid my body at his feet "with Til and Tulasi leaves," I cannot disregard his behest. If it is in failure that that great sage laid down his life after having attained to superhuman heights of Jnana, Bhakti, love, and powers, and after having practised for forty years stern renunciation, non-attachment, holiness, and great austerities, then where is there anything for us to count on? So I am obliged to trust his words as the words of one identified with truth.

Now his behest to me was that I should devote myself to the service of the order of all-renouncing devotees founded by him, and in this I have to persevere, come what may, being ready to take heaven, hell, salvation, or anything that may happen to me.

His command was that his all-renouncing devotees should group themselves together, and I am entrusted with seeing to this. Of course, it matters not if any one of us goes out on visits to this place or that, but these shall be but visits, while his own opinion was that absolute homeless wandering suited him alone who was perfected to the highest point. Before that state, it is proper to settle somewhere to dive down into practice. When all the ideas of body and the like are dissolved of themselves, a person may then pursue whatever state comes to him. Otherwise, it is baneful for a practising aspirant to be always wandering.

So in pursuance of this his commandment, his group of Sannyasins are now assembled in a dilapidated house at Baranagore, and two of his lay disciples, Babu Suresh Chandra Mitra and Babu Balaram Bose, so long provided for their food and house-rent.

For various reasons, the body of Bhagavan Ramakrishna had to be consigned to fire. There is no doubt that this act was very blameable. The remains of his ashes are now preserved, and if they be now properly enshrined somewhere on the banks of the Ganga, I presume we shall be able in some measure to expiate the sin lying on our head. These sacred remains, his seat, and his picture are every day worshipped in our Math in proper form ... a brother-disciple of mine, of Brahmin parentage, is occupied day and night with the task. The expenses of the worship used also to be borne by the two great souls mentioned above.

What greater regret can there be than this, that no memorial could yet be raised in this land of Bengal in the very neighbourhood of the place where he lived his life of Sadhana—he by whose birth the race of Bengalis has been sanctified, the land of Bengal has become hallowed, he who came on earth to save the Indians from the spell of the worldly glamour of Western culture and who therefore chose most of his all-renouncing disciples from university men?

The two gentlemen mentioned above had a strong desire to have some land purchased on the banks of the Ganga and see the sacred remains enshrined on it, with the disciples living there together; and Suresh Babu had offered a sum of Rs. 1,000 for the purpose, promising to give more, but for some inscrutable purpose of God he left this world yesternight! And the news of Balaram Babu's death is already known ...

Now there is no knowing as to where his disciples will stand with his sacred remains and his seat ... The disciples are Sannyasins and are ready forthwith to depart anywhere their way may lie. But I, their servant, am in an agony of sufferings, and my heart is breaking to think that a small piece of land could not be had in which to install the remains of Bhagavan Ramakrishna....

I have not the slightest qualm to beg from door to door for this noble cause, for the sake of my Lord and his children.... To my mind, if all these sincere, educated, youthful Sannyasins of good birth fail to live up to the ideals of Sri Ramakrishna owing to want of an abode and help, then alas for our country!

If [asked], "You are a Sannyasin, so why do you trouble over these desires?"—I would then reply, I am Ramakrishna's servant, and I am willing even to steal and rob, if by doing so I can perpetuate his name in the land of his birth and Sadhana and help even a little his disciples to practise his great ideals....

I returned to Calcutta for this reason.[41]

Baghbazar, 6 July 1890 · I had no wish to leave Ghazipur this time, and certainly not to come to Calcutta, but Kali's [Swami Abhedananda's] illness made me go to Varanasi, and Balaram's sudden death brought me to Calcutta.... I intend shortly, as soon as I can get my fare, to go up to Almora and thence to some place in Gharwal on the Ganga where I can settle down for a long meditation. Gangadhar is accompanying me. Indeed it was with this desire and intention that I brought him down from Kashmir....

You have not yet attempted the one thing you should do, that is, be resolved to sit down and meditate. I don't think Jnana is a thing like rousing a maiden suddenly from sleep by saying, "Get up, dear girl, your marriage ceremony is waiting for you!" as we say. I am strongly of opinion that very few persons in any Yuga attain Jnana, and therefore we should go on striving and striving even unto death. That's my old-fashioned way, you know. About the humbug of modern Sannyasins' Jnana I know too well....

I am in fine health now, and the good I gained by my stay in Ghazipur will last, I am sure, for some time. I am longing for a flight to the Himalayas. This time I shall not go to Pavhari Baba or any other saint—they divert one from his highest purpose. Straight up![42]

Travels in India as an Unknown Sannyasin

I was once travelling in the Himalayas, and the long road stretched before us. We poor monks cannot get anyone to carry us, so we had to make all the way on foot. There was an old man with us. The way goes up and down for hundreds of miles, and when that old monk saw what was before him, he said, "Oh sir, how to cross it; I cannot walk any more; my chest will break." I said to him, "Look down at your feet." He did so, and I said, "The road that is under your feet is the road that you have passed over and is the same road that you see before you; it will soon be under your feet." The highest things are under your feet, because you are Divine Stars; all these things are under your feet. You can swallow the stars by the handful if you want; such is your real nature. Be strong, get beyond all superstitions, and be free.[43]

Many times I have been in the jaws of death, starving, foot-sore, and weary; for days and days I had had no food, and often could walk no farther; I would sink down under a tree, and life would seem [to be] ebbing away. I could not speak, I could scarcely think, but at last the mind reverted to the idea: "I have no fear nor death; I never hunger nor thirst. I am It! I am It! The whole of nature cannot crush me; it is my servant. Assert thy strength, thou Lord of lords and God of gods! Regain thy lost empire! Arise and walk and stop not!" And I would rise up, reinvigorated, and here am I, living, to-day. Thus, whenever darkness comes, assert the reality, and everything adverse must vanish.[44]

Once when I was in Varanasi, I was passing through a place where there was a large tank of water on one side and a high wall on the other. It was in the grounds where there were many monkeys. The monkeys of Varanasi are huge brutes and are sometimes surly. They now took it into their heads not to allow me to pass through their street, so they howled and shrieked and clutched at my feet as I passed. As they pressed closer, I began to run, but the faster I ran, the faster came the monkeys and they began to bite at me. It seemed impossible to escape, but just then I met a stranger who called out to me, "Face the brutes!" I turned and faced the monkeys, and they fell back and finally fled. That is a lesson for all life—face the terrible, face it boldly. Like the monkeys, the hardships of life fall back when we cease to flee before them.[45]

Once in Western India I was travelling in the desert country on the coast of the Indian Ocean. For days and days I used to travel on foot through the desert, but it was to my surprise that I saw every day beautiful lakes, with trees all around them, and the shadows of the trees upside down and vibrating there. "How wonderful it looks and they call this a desert country!" I said to myself. Nearly a month I travelled, seeing these wonderful lakes and trees and plants. One day I was very thirsty and wanted to have a drink of water, so I started to go to one of these clear, beautiful lakes, and as I approached, it vanished. And with a flash it came to my brain, "This is the mirage about which I have read all my life," and with that came also the idea that throughout the whole of this month, every day, I had been seeing the mirage and did not know it. The next morning I began my march. There was again the lake, but with it came also the idea that it was the mirage and not a true lake.

So is it with this universe. We are all travelling in this mirage of the world day after day, month after month, year after year, not knowing that it is a mirage. One day it will break up, but it will come back again; the body has to remain under the power of past Karma, and so the mirage will come back. This world will come back upon us so long as we are bound by Karma: men, women, animals, plants, our attachments and duties, all will come back to us, but not with the same power. Under the influence of the new knowledge the strength of Karma will be broken, its poison will be lost. It becomes transformed, for along with it there comes the idea that we know it now, that the sharp distinction between the reality and the mirage has been known."[46]

Real monasticism is not easy to attain. There is no order of life so rigorous as this. If you stumble ever so little, you are hurled down a precipice—and are smashed to pieces. One day I was travelling on foot from Agra to Vrindavan. There was not a farthing with me. I was about a couple of miles from Vrindavan when I found a man smoking on the roadside, and I was seized with a desire to smoke. I said to the man, "Hallo, will you let me have a puff at your Chillum?" He seemed to be hesitating greatly and said, "Sire, I am a sweeper." Well, there was the influence of old Samskaras, and I immediately stepped back and resumed my journey without smoking. I had gone a short distance when the thought occurred to me that I was a Sannyasin, who had renounced caste, family, prestige, and everything—and still I drew back as soon as the man gave himself out as a sweeper, and could not smoke at the Chillum touched by him! The thought made me restless at heart; then I had walked on half a mile. Again I retraced my steps and came to the sweeper whom I found still sitting there. I hastened to tell him, "Do prepare a Chillum of tobacco for me, my dear friend." I paid no heed to his objections and insisted on having it. So the man was compelled to prepare a Chillum for me. Then I gladly had a puff at it and proceeded to Vrindavan. When one has embraced the monastic life, one has to test whether one has gone beyond the prestige of caste and birth, etc. It is so difficult to observe the monastic vow in right earnest! There must not be the slightest divergence between one's words and actions.[47]

You find that in every religion mortifications and asceticisms have been practised. In these religious conceptions the Hindus always go to the extremes. You will find men with their hands up all their lives, until their hands wither and die.... I once saw a man who had kept his hands raised in this way, and I asked him how it felt when he did it first. He said it was awful torture. It was such torture that he had to go to a river and put himself in water, and that allayed the pain for a little while. After a month he did not suffer much. Through such practices powers can be attained.[48]

When I was in Jaipur, I met a great grammarian and felt a desire to study Sanskrit grammar with him. Although he was a great scholar in that branch, he had not much aptitude for teaching. He explained to me the commentary on the first aphorism for three days continuously; still I could not grasp a bit of it. On the fourth day the teacher got annoyed and said, "Swamiji, I could not make you understand the meaning of the first aphorism even in three days; I fear, you will not be much benefited by my teaching." Hearing these words, a great self-reproach came over me. Putting food and sleep aside, I set myself to study the commentary on the first aphorism independently. Within three hours the sense of the commentary stood explained before me as clearly as anything; then going to my teacher I gave him the sense of the whole commentary. My teacher, hearing me, said, "How could you gather the sense so excellently within three hours, which I failed to explain to you in three days?" After that, every day I began to read chapter after chapter, with the greatest ease. Through concentration of mind everything can be accomplished—even mountains can be crushed to atoms.[49]

In Malabar ... the women lead in everything. Exceptional cleanliness is apparent everywhere and there is the greatest impetus to learning. When I myself was in that country, I met many women who spoke good Sanskrit, while in the rest of India not one woman in a million can speak it.[50]

Once when travelling in the Himalayas I had to take up my abode for a night in a village of the hill-people. Hearing the beating of drums in the village some time after nightfall, I came to know upon inquiring of my host that one of the villagers had been possessed by a Devata or good spirit. To meet his importunate wishes and to satisfy my own curiosity, we went out to see what the matter really was. Reaching the spot, I found a great concourse of people. A tall man with long, bushy hair was pointed out to me, and I was told that person had got the devata on him. I noticed an axe being heated in fire close by the man; and after a while, I found the red-hot thing being seized and applied to parts of his body and also to his hair! But wonder of wonders, no part of his body or hair thus branded with the red-hot axe was found to be burnt, and there was no expression of any pain in his face. I stood mute with surprise. The headman of the village, meanwhile, came up to me and said, "Maharaj, please exorcise this man out of your mercy." I felt myself in a nice fix, but moved to do something, I had to go near the possessed man. Once there, I felt a strong impulse to examine the axe rather closely, but the instant I touched it, I burnt my fingers, although the thing had been cooled down to blackness. The smarting made me restless and all my theories about the axe phenomenon were spirited away from my mind! However, smarting with the burn, I placed my hand on the head of the man and repeated [Japa] for a short while.... It was a matter of surprise to find that the man came round in ten or twelve minutes. Then oh, the gushing reverence the villagers showed to me! I was taken to be some wonderful man! But, all the same, I couldn't make any head or tail of the whole business. So without a word one way or the other, I returned with my host to his hut. It was about midnight, and I went to bed. But what with the smarting burn in the hand and the impenetrable puzzle of the whole affair, I couldn't have any sleep that night. Thinking of the burning axe failing to harm living human flesh, it occurred again and again to my mind, "There are more things in heaven and earth, Horatio, than are dreamt of in your philosophy"....

But Sri Ramakrishna used to disparage these supernatural powers; his teaching was that one cannot attain to the supreme truth if the mind is diverted to the manifestation of these powers. The human mind, however, is so weak that, not to speak of householders, even ninety per cent of the Sadhus happen to be votaries of these powers. In the West, men are lost in wonderment if they come across such miracles. It is only because Sri Ramakrishna has mercifully made us understand the evil of these powers as being hindrances to real spirituality that we are able to take them at their proper value.[51]

Once while I was putting up at Manmatha Babu's place, I dreamt one night that my mother had died. My mind became much distracted. Not to speak of corresponding with anybody at home, I used to send no letters in those days even to our Math. The dream being disclosed to Manmatha, he sent a wire to Calcutta to ascertain facts about the matter. For the dream had made my mind uneasy on the one hand, and on the other, our Madras friends, with all arrangements ready, were insisting on my departing for America immediately, and I felt rather unwilling to leave before getting any news of my mother. So Manmatha, who discerned this state of my mind, suggested our repairing to a man living some way off from town, who having acquired mystic powers over spirits could tell fortunes and read the past and the future of a man's life. So at Manmatha's request and to get rid of my mental suspense, I agreed to go to this man. Covering the distance partly by railway and partly on foot, we four of us—Manmatha, Alasinga, myself, and another—managed to reach the place, and what met our eyes there was a man with a ghoulish, haggard, soot-black appearance, sitting close to a cremation ground. His attendants used some jargon of South Indian dialect to explain to us that this was the man with perfect power over the ghosts. At first the man took absolutely no notice of us; and then, when we were about to retire from the place, he made a request for us to wait.

Our Alasinga was acting as the interpreter, and he explained the requests to us. Next, the man commenced drawing some figures with a pencil, and presently I found him getting perfectly still in mental concentration. Then he began to give out my name, my genealogy, the history of my long line of forefathers, and said that Sri Ramakrishna was keeping close to me all through my wanderings, intimating also to me good news about my mother. He also foretold that I would have to go very soon to far-off lands for preaching religion. Getting good news thus about my mother, we all travelled back to town, and after arrival received by wire from Calcutta the assurance of my mother's doing well.... Everything that the man had foretold came to be fulfilled to the letter, call it some fortuitous concurrence or anything you will....

Well, I am not a fool to believe anything and everything without direct proof. And coming into this realm of Mahamaya, oh, the many magic mysteries I have come across alongside this bigger magic conjuration of a universe! Maya, it is all Maya![52]

I once heard of a man who, if any one went to him with questions in his mind, would answer them immediately; and I was also informed that he foretold events. I was curious and went to see him with a few friends. We each had something in our minds to ask, and, to avoid mistakes, we wrote down our questions and put them in our pockets. As soon as the man saw one of us, he repeated our questions and gave the answers to them. Then he wrote something on paper, which he folded up, asked me to sign on the back, and said, "Don't look at it; put it in your pocket and keep it there till I ask for it again." And so on to each one of us. He next told us about some events that would happen to us in the future. Then he said, "Now, think of a word or a sentence, from any language you like." I thought of a long sentence from Sanskrit, a language of which he was entirely ignorant. "Now, take out the paper from your pocket," he said. The Sanskrit sentence was written there! He had written it an hour before with the remark, "In confirmation of what I have written, this man will think of this sentence." It was correct. Another of us who had been given a similar paper which he had signed and placed in his pocket, was also asked to think of a sentence. He thought of a sentence in Arabic, which it was still less possible for the man to know; it was some passage from the Koran. And my friend found this written down on the paper. Another of us was a physician. He thought of a sentence from a German medical book. It was written on his paper. Several days later I went to this man again, thinking possibly I had been deluded somehow before. I took other friends, and on this occasion also he came out wonderfully triumphant.[53]

Another time I was in the city of Hyderabad in India, and I was told of a Brahmin there who could produce numbers of things from where, nobody knew. This man was in business there; he was a respectable gentleman. And I asked him to show me his tricks. It so happened that this man had a fever, and in India there is a general belief that if a holy man puts his hand on a sick man he would be well. This Brahmin came to me and said, "Sir, put your hand on my head, so that my fever may be cured." I said, "Very good; but you show me your tricks." He promised. I put my hand on his head as desired, and later he came to fulfil his promise. He had only a strip of cloth about his loins, we took off everything else from him. I had a blanket which I gave him to wrap round himself, because it was cold, and made him sit in a corner. Twenty-five pairs of eyes were looking at him. And he said, "Now, look, write down anything you want." We all wrote down names of fruits that never grew in that country, bunches of grapes, oranges, and so on. And we gave him those bits of paper. And there came from under his blanket, bushels of grapes, oranges, and so forth, so much that if all that fruit was weighed, it would have been twice as heavy as the man. He asked us to eat the fruit. Some of us objected, thinking it was hypnotism; but the man began eating himself—so we all ate. It was all right.

He ended by producing a mass of roses. Each flower was perfect, with dew-drops on the petals, not one crushed, not one injured. And masses of them! When I asked the man for an explanation, he said, "It is all sleight of hand."

Whatever it was, it seemed to be impossible that it could be sleight of hand merely. From whence could he have got such large quantities of things?

Well, I saw many things like that....

All these extraordinary powers are in the mind of man.[54]

I know very little of this science [of mind], but [for] the little that I gained I worked for thirty years of my life, and for six years I have been telling people the little that I know. It took me thirty years to learn it; thirty years of hard struggle. Sometimes I worked at it twenty hours during the twenty-four; sometimes I slept only one hour in the night; sometimes I worked whole nights; sometimes I lived in places where there was hardly a sound, hardly a breath; sometimes I had to live in caves. Think of that. And yet I know little or nothing; I have barely touched the hem of the garment of this science. But I can understand that it is true and vast and wonderful.[55]

First, the practice of meditation has to proceed with some one object before the mind. Once I used to concentrate my mind on some black point. Ultimately, during those days, I could not see the point any more, nor notice that the point was before me at all—the mind used to be no more—no wave of functioning would rise, as if it were all an ocean without any breath of air. In that state I used to experience glimpses of supersensuous truth. So I think, the practice of meditation even with some trifling external object leads to mental concentration. But it is true that the mind very easily attains calmness when one practises meditation with anything on which one's mind is most apt to settle down. This is the reason why we have in this country so much worship of the images of gods and goddesses.[56]

I have met some who told me they did remember their previous life. They had reached a point where they could remember their former incarnations.[57]

[*Question: Do you know your previous births?*] Yes, I do.... I can know them—I do know them—but I prefer not to say anything in detail.[58]

In the course of my wanderings I was in a certain place where people came to me in crowds and asked for instruction. Though it seems almost unbelievable, people came and made me talk for three days and nights without giving me a moment's rest. They did not even ask me whether I had eaten. On the third night, when all the visitors had left, a low-caste poor man came up to me and said, "Swamiji, I am much pained to see that you have not had any food these three days. You must be very tired and hungry. Indeed, I have noticed that you have not even taken a glass of water." I thought that the Lord Himself had come in the form of this low-caste man to test me. I asked him, "Can you give me something to eat?" The man said, "Swamiji, my heart is yearning to give you food, but how can you eat Chapatis baked with my hands! If you allow me I shall be most glad to bring flour, lentils and other things, and you may cook them yourself."

At that time, according to the monastic rules, I did not touch fire; so I said to him, "You had better give me the Chapatis cooked by you. I shall gladly take them." Hearing this, the man shrank in fear; he was a subject of the Maharaja of Khetri and was afraid that if the latter came to hear that he, a cobbler, had given Chapatis to a Sannyasin, he would be severely dealt with and possibly banished from the state. I told him, however, that he need not fear, that the Maharaja would not punish him. He did not believe me; but out of the kindness of his heart, even though he feared the consequences, he brought me the cooked food. I doubted just then whether it would have been more palatable even if Indra himself, King of the Devas, had held a cup of nectar in a golden basin before me. I shed tears of love and gratitude, and thought, "Thousands of such large-hearted men live in lowly huts, and we despise them as low-castes and untouchables!"

When I became well acquainted with the Maharaja, I told him of the noble act of this man. Accordingly, within a few days the latter was called to the presence of the Prince. Frightened beyond words, the man came shaking all over, thinking that some dire punishment was to be inflicted upon him. But the Maharaja praised him and put him beyond all want.[59]

Don't be afraid for me. It is true I often sleep under a banyan tree with a bowl of rice given me by a kindly peasant, but it is equally true that I also am sometimes the guest in the palace of a great Maharaja, and a slave girl is appointed to wave a peacock feather fan over me all night long! I am used to temptation, and you need not fear for me![60]

Oh, the days of suffering I passed through! Once, after eating nothing for three days, I fell down senseless on the road. I do not know how long I was in that state. When I regained consciousness I found my clothing wet through from a shower of rain. Drenched, I felt somewhat refreshed. I arose, and after trudging along some distance, I reached a monastery. My life was saved by the food that I received there.[61]

I used to beg my food from door to door in the Himalayas. Most of the time I spent in spiritual practices which were rigorous; and the food that was available was very coarse, and often that too was insufficient to appease the hunger. One day I thought that my life was useless. These hill people are very poor themselves. They cannot feed their own children and family properly. Yet they try to save a little for me. Then what is the use of such a life? I stopped going out for food. Two days thus passed without any food. Whenever I was thirsty I drank the water of the streams using my palms as a cup. Then I entered a deep jungle. There I meditated sitting on a piece of stone. My eyes were open, and suddenly I was aware of the presence of a striped tiger of a large size. It looked at me with its shining eyes. I thought, "At long last I shall find peace and this animal its food. It is enough that this body will be of some service to this creature." I shut my eyes and waited for it, but a few seconds passed and I was not attacked. So, I opened my eyes and saw it receding in the forest. I was sorry for it and then smiled, for I knew it was the Master who was saving me till his work be done.[62]

Kakrighat, near Almora, August 1890 [after a profound meditation] · I have just passed through one of the greatest moments of my life. Here under this peepul tree one of the greatest problems of my life has been solved: I have found the oneness of the macrocosm with the microcosm. In this microcosm of the body everything that is there [in the macrocosm] exists. I have seen the whole universe within an atom.[63]

BARANAGORE MATH & DAYS OF WANDERING

Preparations for the Journey West

Hyderabad, 11 February 1893 · So all my plans have been dashed to the ground. That is why I wanted to hurry off from Madras early. In that case I would have months left in my hands to seek out for somebody amongst our northern princes to send me over to America. But alas, it is now too late. First, I cannot wander about in this heat—I would die. Secondly, my fast friends in Rajputana would keep me bound down to their sides if they get hold of me and would not let me go over to Europe. So my plan was to get hold of some new person without my friends' knowledge. But this delay at Madras has dashed all my hopes to the ground, and with a deep sigh I give it up, and the Lord's will be done!... However, man learns as he lives, and experience is the greatest teacher in the world.

"Thy will be done on earth as it is in heaven, for Thine is the glory and the kingdom for ever and ever."[64]

Khetri, May 1893 · I had from before a desire to go to Chicago. When [I was] at Madras, the people there, of their own accord, in conjunction with H. H. of Mysore and Ramnad made every arrangement to send me up.... Between H. H. of Khetri and myself there are the closest ties of love. Well, I, as a matter of course, wrote to him that I was going to America. Now the Raja of Khetri thought in his love that I was bound to see him once before I departed, especially as the Lord has given him an heir to the throne and great rejoicings were going on here; and to make sure of my coming he sent his private secretary all the way to Madras to fetch me ...[65]

Bombay, 22 May 1893 · Reached Bombay a few days ago and would start off in a few days....

The private secretary of H. H. of Khetri and I are now

residing together. I cannot express my gratitude to him for his love and kindness to me. He is what they call a Tazimi Sardar in Rajputana, i.e., one of those whom the Rajas receive by rising from their seats. Still he is so simple, and sometimes his service for me makes me almost ashamed.

... Often and often, we see that the very best of men even are troubled and visited with tribulations in this world; it may be inexplicable; but it is also the experience of my life that the heart and core of everything here is good, that whatever may be the surface waves, deep down and underlying everything, there is an infinite basis of goodness and love; and so long as we do not reach that basis, we are troubled; but having once reached that zone of calmness, let winds howl and tempests rage. The house which is built on a rock of ages cannot shake.[66]

Bombay, 24 May 1893 · Arrangements are all ready for my starting for America on the 31st next.[67]

CHAPTER FIVE

THE DIVINE CALL AND THE PARLIAMENT OF RELIGIONS

I AM NOW LEAVING Kashi, and shall not return until I have burst on society like a bomb-shell; and it will follow me like a dog.[1]

I go forth, to preach a religion of which Buddhism is nothing but a rebel child, and Christianity, with all her pretensions, only a distant echo.[2]

I am called by the Lord for this. I have been dragged through a whole life full of crosses and tortures, I have seen the nearest and dearest die, almost of starvation; I have been ridiculed, distrusted, and have suffered for my sympathy for the very men who scoff and scorn. Well, my boy, this is the school of misery, which is also the school for great souls and prophets for the cultivation of sympathy, of patience, and, above all, of an indomitable iron will which quakes not even if the universe be pulverised at our feet.[3]

I do not care for liberation, or for devotion; I would rather go to a hundred thousand hells, "*vasantavallokahitaṁ carantaḥ*—doing good to others (silently) like the spring"—this is my religion.[4]

I do not take into any consideration whether people accept [Sri Ramakrishna's] name or not, but I am ready to lay down my life to help his teachings, his life, and his message spread all over the world.[5]

Yes, my own life is guided by the enthusiasm of a certain great personality, but what of that? Inspiration was never filtered out to the world through one man!

It is true I believe Ramakrishna Paramahamsa to have been inspired. But then I am myself inspired also. And you are inspired. And your disciples will be; and theirs after them; and so on, to the end of time![6]

I stand at nobody's dictation. I know my mission in life, and no chauvinism about me; I belong as much to India as to the world ... What country has any special claim on me? Am I any nation's slave?[7]

I see a greater Power than man, or God, or devil at my back.[8]

I hate cowardice; I will have nothing to do with cowards or political nonsense. I do not believe in any politics. God and truth are the only politics in the world, everything else is trash.[9]

Truth is my God, the universe my country.[10]

Before proceeding to America I wrote to Mother [Sri Sarada Devi] to bless me. Her blessings came, and at one bound I cleared the ocean.[11]

The Parliament of Religions is being organized for this [*pointing to himself*]. My mind tells me so. You will see it verified at no distant date.[12]

I want to give them dry, hard reason, softened in the sweetest syrup of love and made spicy with intense work, and cooked in the kitchen of Yoga, so that even a baby can easily digest it.[13]

To put the Hindu ideas into English and then make out of dry philosophy and intricate mythology and queer startling psychology, a religion which shall be easy, simple, popular, and at the same time meet the requirements of the highest minds—is a task only those can understand who have attempted it. The dry, abstract Advaita must become living—poetic—in everyday life; out of hopelessly intricate mythology must come concrete moral forms; and out of bewildering Yogi-ism must come the most scientific and practical psychology—and all this must be put in a form so that a child may grasp it. That is my life's work.[14]

I thought, I have tried India: it is time for me to try another country. At that time [the] Parliament of Religions was to be held, and someone was to be sent from India. I was just a vagabond, but I said, "If you send me, I am going. I have not much to lose, and I do not care if I lose that." It was very difficult to find the money, but after a long struggle they got together just enough to pay for my passage—and I came. Came one or two months earlier, so that I found myself drifting about in the streets here, without knowing anybody.[15]

That I went to America was not my doing or your doing; but the God of India who is guiding her destiny sent me, and will send hundreds of such to all the nations of the world. No power on earth can resist it.[16]

To America

Yokohama, Japan, 10 July 1893 · Excuse my not keeping you constantly informed of my movements. One is so busy every day, and especially myself who am quite new to the life of possessing things and taking care of them. That consumes so much of my energy. It is really an awful botheration.

From Bombay we reached Colombo. Our steamer remained in port for nearly the whole day, and we took the opportunity of getting off to have a look at the town. We drove through the streets, and the only thing I remember was a temple in which was a very gigantic Murti [image] of the Lord Buddha in a reclining posture, entering Nirvana....

The next station was Penang, which is only a strip of land along the sea in the body of the Malay Peninsula.... On our way from Penang to Singapore, we had glimpses of Sumatra with its high mountains, and the Captain pointed out to me several places as the favourite haunts of pirates in days gone by.

Singapore ... has a fine botanical garden with the most splendid collection of palms. The beautiful fan-like palm, called the traveller's palm, grows here in abundance, and the bread-fruit tree everywhere. The celebrated mangosteen is as plentiful here as mangoes in Madras, but mango is nonpareil....

Hong Kong next. You feel that you have reached China, the Chinese element predominates so much. All labour, all trade seems to be in their hands. And Hong Kong is real China. As soon as the steamer casts anchor, you are besieged with hundreds of Chinese boats to carry you to the land....

We remained three days at Hong Kong and went to see Canton, which is eighty miles up a river.... What a scene of bustle and life! What an immense number of boats almost covering the waters! And not only those that are carrying on the trade, but hundreds of others which serve as houses to live in. And quite a lot of them so nice and big! In fact, they are big houses two or three storeys high, with verandahs running round and streets between, and all floating!

We landed on a strip of ground given by the Chinese Government to foreigners to live in. Around us on both sides of the river for miles and miles is the big city—a wilderness of human beings, pushing, struggling, surging, roaring. But with all its population, all its activity, it is the dirtiest town I saw, not in the sense in which a town is called dirty in India, for as to that not a speck of filth is allowed by the Chinese to go waste; but because of the Chinaman, who has, it seems, taken a vow never to bathe!...

I went to see several Chinese temples. The biggest in Canton is dedicated to the memory of the first Buddhistic Emperor and the five hundred first disciples of Buddhism. The central figure is of course Buddha, and next beneath Him is seated the Emperor, and ranging on both sides are the statues of the disciples, all beautifully carved out of wood.

From Canton I returned back to Hong Kong, and from thence to Japan. The first port we touched was Nagasaki. We landed for a few hours and drove through the town. What a contrast! The Japanese are one of the cleanliest peoples on earth. Everything is neat and tidy. Their streets are nearly all broad, straight, and regularly paved. Their little houses are cage-like, and their pine-covered evergreen little hills form the background of almost every town and village.... Japan is the land of the picturesque! Almost every house has a garden at the back, very nicely laid out according to Japanese fashion with small shrubs, grass-plots, small artificial waters, and small stone bridges.

From Nagasaki to Kobe. Here I gave up the steamer and took the land-route to Yokohama, with a view to see the interior of Japan....

I saw quite a lot of temples. In every temple there are some Sanskrit Mantras written in Old Bengali characters.[17]

Metcalf, Massachusetts, 20 August 1893 · From Japan I reached Vancouver. The way was by the Northern Pacific. It was very cold and I suffered much for want of warm clothing. However, I reached Vancouver anyhow, and thence went through Canada to Chicago. I remained about twelve days in Chicago. And almost every day I used to go to the Fair. It is a tremendous affair. One must take at least ten days to go through it....

The expense I am bound to run into here is awful.... On an average it costs me £1 every day; a cigar costs eight annas of our money. The Americans are so rich that they spend money like water, and by forced legislation keep up the price of everything so high that no other nation on earth can approach it. Every common coolie earns nine or ten rupees a day and spends as much. All those rosy ideas we had before starting have melted, and I have now to fight against impossibilities. A hundred times I had a mind to go out of the country and go back to India. But I am determined, and I have a call from Above; I see no way, but His eyes see. And I must stick to my guns, life or death....

Just now I am living as the guest of an old lady in a village near Boston. I accidentally made her acquaintance in the railway train, and she invited me to come over and live with her. I have an advantage in living with her, in saving for some time my expenditure of £1 per day, and she has the advantage of inviting her friends over here and showing them a curio from India! And all this must be borne. Starvation, cold, hooting in the streets on account of my quaint dress, these are what I have to fight against. But, my dear boy, no great things were ever done without great labour....

This is the land of Christians, and any other influence than that is almost zero. Nor do I care a bit for the enmity of any ——ists in the world. I am here amongst the children of the Son of Mary, and the Lord Jesus will help me. They like much the broad views of Hinduism and my love for the Prophet of Nazareth. I tell them that I preach nothing against the Great One of Galilee. I only ask the Christians to take in the Great Ones of India along with the Lord Jesus, and they appreciate it.

Winter is approaching and I shall have to get all sorts of warm clothing, and we require more warm clothing than the natives....

In Chicago, the other day, a funny thing happened. The Raja of Kapurthala was here, and he was being lionised by some portion of Chicago society. I once met the Raja in the Fair grounds, but he was too big to speak with a poor Fakir. There was an eccentric Mahratta Brahmin selling nail-made pictures in the Fair, dressed in a dhoti. This fellow told the reporters all sorts of things against the Raja—that he was a man of low caste, that those Rajas were nothing but slaves, and that they generally led immoral lives, etc., etc. And these truthful editors, for which America is famous, wanted to give to the boy's stories some weight; and so the next day they wrote huge columns in their papers about the description of a man of wisdom from India, meaning me—extolling me to the skies, and putting all sorts of words in my mouth, which I never even dreamt of, and ascribing to me all those remarks made by the Mahratta Brahmin about the Raja of Kapurthala. And it was such a good brushing that Chicago society gave up the Raja in hot haste.... These newspaper editors made capital out of me to give my countryman a brushing. That shows, however, that in this country intellect carries more weight than all the pomp of money and title.

Yesterday Mrs. Johnson, the lady superintendent of the women's prison, was here. They don't call it prison but reformatory here. It is the grandest thing I have seen in America. How the inmates are benevolently treated, how they are reformed and sent back as useful members of society; how grand, how beautiful, you must see to believe! And, oh, how my heart ached to think of what we think of the poor, the low, in India. They have no chance, no escape, no way to climb up. The poor, the low, the sinner in India have no friends, no help—they cannot rise, try however they may. They sink lower and lower every day, they feel the blows showered upon them by a cruel society, and they do not know whence the blow comes. They have forgotten that they too are men. And the result is slavery. Thoughtful people within the last few years have seen it, but unfortunately laid it at the door of the Hindu religion, and to them, the only way of bettering is by crushing this grandest religion of the world. Hear me, my friend, I have discovered the secret through the grace of the Lord. Religion is not in fault. On the other hand, your religion teaches you that every being is only your own self multiplied. But it was the want of practical application, the want of sympathy—the want of heart. The Lord once more came to you as Buddha and taught you how to feel, how to sympathise with the poor, the miserable, the sinner, but you heard Him not....

Balaji and G. G. may remember one evening at Pondicherry—we were discussing the matter of sea-voyage with a Pandit, and I shall always remember his brutal gestures and his *Kadāpi na!* [never!] They do not know that India is a very small part of the world ... This state of things must be removed, not by destroying religion but by following the great teachings of the Hindu faith, and joining with it the wonderful sympathy of that logical development of Hinduism—Buddhism....

I have travelled twelve years with this load in my heart and this idea in my head. I have gone from door to door of the so-called rich and great. With a bleeding heart I have crossed half the world to this strange land, seeking for help. The Lord is great. I know He will help me. I may perish of cold or hunger in this land, but I bequeath to you, young men, this sympathy, this struggle for the poor, the ignorant, the oppressed....

It is not the work of a day, and the path is full of the most deadly thorns.... But we are the sons of Light and children of God. Glory unto the Lord, we will succeed. Hundreds will fall in the struggle, hundreds will be ready to take it up. I may die here unsuccessful, another will take up the task.... Faith, sympathy—fiery faith and fiery sympathy! Life is nothing, death is nothing, hunger nothing, cold nothing. Glory unto the Lord—march on, the Lord is our General. Do not look back to see who falls—forward—onward! Thus and thus we shall go on, brethren. One falls, and another takes up the work.

I must first go and buy some clothing in Boston. If I am to live longer here, my quaint dress will not do. People gather by hundreds in the streets to see me. So what I want is to dress myself in a long black coat, and keep a red robe and turban to wear when I lecture....

In America, there are no classes in the railway except in Canada. So I have to travel first-class, as that is the only class; but I do not venture in the Pullmans. They are very comfortable—you sleep, eat, drink, even bathe in them, just as if you were in a hotel—but they are too expensive.

It is very hard work getting into society and making yourself heard. Now nobody is in the towns, they are all away in summer places. They will all come back in winter. Therefore I must wait. After such a struggle, I am not going to give up easily. Only try your best to help me as much as you can; and even if you cannot, I must try to the end. And even if I die of cold or disease or hunger here, you take up the task. Holiness, sincerity, and faith. I have left instructions with Cooks to forward any letter or money to me wherever I am. Rome was not built in a day. If you can keep me here for six months at least, I hope everything will come right. In the meantime

I am trying my best to find any plank I can float upon. And if I find out any means to support myself, I shall wire to you immediately.

First I will try in America; and if I fail, try in England; if I fail, go back to India and wait for further commands from [on] High.[18]

I am the first monk to come over to these Western countries—it is the first time in the history of the world that a Hindu monk has crossed the ocean.[19]

When I, a poor, unknown, friendless Sannyasin was going to America, going beyond the waters to America without any introductions or friends there, I called on the leader of the Theosophical Society. Naturally I thought he, being an American and a lover of India, perhaps would give me a letter of introduction to somebody there. He asked me, "Will you join my Society?" "No," I replied, "how can I? For I do not believe in most of your doctrines." "Then, I am sorry, I cannot do anything for you," he answered. That was not paving the way for me. I reached America, as you know, through the help of a few friends in Madras.... I arrived in America several months before the Parliament of Religions began. The money I had with me was little, and it was soon spent. Winter approached, and I had only thin summer clothes. I did not know what to do in that cold, dreary climate, for if I went to beg in the streets, the result would have been that I would have been sent to jail. There I was with the last few dollars in my pocket.

I sent a wire to my friends in Madras. This came to be known to the Theosophists, and one of them wrote, "Now the devil is going to die; God bless us all." Was that paving the way for me? I would not have mentioned this now; but, as my countrymen wanted to know, it must come out. For three years I have not opened my lips about these things; silence has been my motto; but today the thing has come out. That was not all. I saw some Theosophists in the Parliament of Religions, and I wanted to talk and mix with them. I remember the looks of scorn which were on their faces, as much as to say, "What business has the worm to be here in the midst of the gods?"[20]

It must be particularly remembered that the same ideals and activities do not prevail in all societies and countries; our ignorance of this is the main cause of much of the hatred of one nation towards another. An American thinks that whatever an American does in accordance with the custom of his country is the best thing to do, and that whoever does not follow his custom must be a very wicked man. A Hindu thinks that his customs are the only right ones and are the best in the world, and that whosoever does not obey them must be the most wicked man living. This is quite a natural mistake which all of us are apt to make. But it is very harmful; it is the cause of half the uncharitableness found in the world. When I came to this country and was going through the Chicago Fair, a man from behind pulled at my turban. I looked back and saw that he was a very gentlemanly-looking man, neatly dressed. I spoke to him; and when he found that I knew English, he became very much abashed. On another occasion in the same Fair another man gave me a push. When I asked him the reason, he also was ashamed and stammered out an apology saying, "Why do you dress that way?" The sympathies of these men were limited within the range of their own language and their own fashion of dress. Much of the oppression of powerful nations on weaker ones is caused by this prejudice. It dries up their fellow-feeling for fellow men. That very man who asked me why I did not dress as he did and wanted to ill-treat me because of my dress may have been a very good man, a good father, and a good citizen; but the kindliness of his nature died out as soon as he saw a man in a different dress.

Strangers are exploited in all countries, because they do not know how to defend themselves; thus they carry home false impressions of the peoples they have seen. Sailors, soldiers, and traders behave in foreign lands in very queer ways, although they would not dream of doing so in their own country; perhaps this is why the Chinese call Europeans and Americans "foreign devils." They could not have done this if they had met the good, the kindly sides of Western life.[21]

I landed [in Boston] once, a stranger in a strange land. My coat was like this red one and I wore my turban. I was proceeding up a street in the busy part of the town when I became aware that I was followed by a great number of men and boys. I hastened my pace and they did too. Then something struck my shoulder and I began to run, dashing around a corner, and up a dark passage, just before the mob in full pursuit swept past—and I was safe![22]

Before I knew the customs of this country, I received such a shock when the son, in a very refined family, got up and called the mother by name! However, I got used to that. That is the custom of the country. But with us, we never pronounce the name of our parents when they are present.[23]

I belong to an Order very much like what you have in the Mendicant Friars of the Catholic Church; that is to say, we have to go about without very much in the way of dress and beg from door to door, live thereby, preach to people when they want it, sleep where we can get a place—that way we have to follow. And the rule is that the members of this Order have to call every woman "mother"; to every woman and little girl we have to say "mother"; that is the custom. Coming to the West, that old habit remained and I would say to ladies, "Yes, mother," and they are horrified. I could not understand why they should be horrified. Later on, I discovered the reason: because that would mean that they are old.[24]

Chicago, 2 October 1893 · I dropped in on the Congress in the eleventh hour, and quite unprepared; and that kept me very very busy for some time.... I was speaking almost every day in the Congress ... The Congress is now over....

I was so so afraid to stand before that great assembly of fine speakers and thinkers from all over the world and speak; but the Lord gave me strength, and I almost every day heroically faced the platform and the audience. If I have done well, He gave me the strength for it; if I have miserably failed—I knew that beforehand—for I am hopelessly ignorant.

... Prof. Bradley was very kind to me and he always cheered me on. And oh! everybody is so kind here to me who am nothing—that it is beyond my power of expression. Glory unto Him in the highest in whose sight the poor ignorant monk from India is the same as the learned divines of this mighty land. And how the Lord is helping me every day of my life, brother—I sometimes wish for a life of [a] million million ages to serve Him through the work, dressed in rags and fed by charity....

I am now going to be reconciled to my life here. All my life I have been taking every circumstance as coming from Him and calmly adapting myself to it. At first in America I was almost out of my water. I was afraid I would have to give up the accustomed way of being guided by the Lord and *cater* for myself—and what a horrid piece of mischief and ingratitude was that. I now clearly see that He who was guiding me on the snow tops of the Himalayas and the burning plains of India is here to help me and guide me. *Glory unto Him* in the highest. So I have calmly fallen into my old ways. Somebody or other gives me a shelter and food, somebody or other comes to ask me to speak about Him, and I know He sends them and mine is to obey. And then He is supplying my necessities, and His *will be done*!

"He who rests [in] Me and gives up all other self-assertion and struggles I carry to him whatever he needs" (Gita).

So it is in Asia. So in Europe. So in America. So in the deserts of India. So in the rush of business in America. For is He not here also? And if He does not, I only would take for granted that He wants that I should lay aside this three minutes' body of clay—and hope to lay it down gladly.

"He who gets hold of the One in this world of many—the one constant existence in a world of flitting shadows—the one life in a world of death—he alone crosses this sea of misery and struggle. None else, none else" (Vedas).

"He who is the Brahman of the Vedantins, Ishvara of the Naiyayikas, Purusha of the Sankhyas, *cause* of the Mimamsakas, *law* of the Buddhists, *absolute zero* of the Atheists, and love infinite unto those that love, may [He] take us all under His merciful protection": Udayanacharya—a great philosopher of the Nyaya or dualistic school.[25]

Chicago, 10 October 1893 · Just now I am lecturing about Chicago—and am doing as I think very well; it is ranging from 30 to 80 dollars a lecture, and just now I have been so well advertised in Chicago gratis by the Parliament of Religions that it is not advisable to give up this field now.... Yesterday I returned from Streator where I got 87 dollars for a lecture. I have engagements every day this week.[26]

Chicago, 26 October 1893 · I am doing well here, and ... almost everybody has been very kind to me, except of course the very orthodox. Many of the men brought together here from far-off lands have got projects and ideas and missions to carry out, and America is the only place where there is a chance of success for everything. But I thought better and have given up speaking about my project entirely—because I am sure now—the heathen draws more than his project. So I want to go to work earnestly for my own project only keeping the project in the background and working like any other lecturer.

He who has brought me hither and has not left me yet will not leave me ever I am here. You will be glad to know that I am doing well and expect to do very well in the way of getting money. Of course I am too green in the business but would soon learn my trade. I am very popular in Chicago. So I want to stay here a little more and get *money*.

Tomorrow I am going to lecture on Buddhism at the ladies' fortnightly club—which is the most influential in this city.... Now I think the success of my project probable.[27]

Chicago, 2 November 1893 · The Lord sent me friends. At a village near Boston I made the acquaintance of Dr. Wright, Professor of Greek in the Harvard University. He sympathised with me very much and urged upon me the necessity of going to the Parliament of Religions, which he thought would give me an introduction to the nation. As I was not acquainted with anybody, the Professor undertook to arrange everything for me, and eventually I came back to Chicago. Here I, together with the oriental and occidental delegates to the Parliament of Religions, were all lodged in the house of a gentleman.

On the morning of the opening of the Parliament, we all assembled in a building called the Art Palace, where one huge and other smaller temporary halls were erected for the sittings of the Parliament. Men from all nations were there. From India were Mazoomdar of the Brahmo Samaj, and Nagarkar of Bombay, Mr. Gandhi representing the Jains, and Mr. Chakravarti representing Theosophy with Mrs. Annie Besant. Of these, Mazoomdar and I were, of course, old friends, and Chakravarti knew me by name. There was a grand procession, and we were all marshalled on to the platform. Imagine a hall below and a huge gallery above, packed with six or seven thousand men and women representing the best culture of the country, and on the platform learned men of all the nations of the earth. And I, who never spoke in public in my life, to address this august assemblage!! It was opened in great form with music and ceremony and speeches; then the delegates were introduced one by one, and they stepped up and spoke. Of course my heart was fluttering, and my tongue nearly dried up; I was so nervous and could not venture to speak in the morning. Mazoomdar made a nice speech, Chakravarti a nicer one, and they were much applauded. They were all prepared and came with ready-made speeches. I was a fool and had none, but bowed down to Devi Sarasvati and stepped up, and Dr. Barrows introduced me. I made a short speech. I addressed the assembly as "Sisters and Brothers of America," a deafening applause of two minutes followed, and then I proceeded; and when it was finished, I sat down, almost exhausted with emotion. The next day all the papers announced that my speech was the hit of the day, and I became known to the whole of America. Truly has it been said by the great commentator Sridhara—"*Mūkaṁ karoti vācālam*—who maketh the dumb a fluent speaker." His name be praised! From that day I became a celebrity, and the day I read my paper of Hinduism, the hall was packed as it had never been before. I quote to you from one of the papers: "Ladies, ladies, ladies packing every place—filling every corner, they patiently waited and waited while the papers that separated them from Vivekananda were read," etc. You would be astonished if I sent over to you the newspaper cuttings, but you already know that I am a hater of celebrity. Suffice it to say, that whenever I went on the platform, a deafening applause would be raised for me. Nearly all the papers paid high tributes to me, and even the most bigoted had to admit that "This man with his handsome face and magnetic presence and wonderful oratory is the most prominent figure in the Parliament," etc., etc. Sufficient for you to know that never before did an Oriental make such an impression on American society.

And how to speak of their kindness? I have no more wants now, I am well off, and all the money that I require to visit Europe I shall get from here....

I am now out of want. Many of the handsomest houses in this city are open to me. All the time I am living as a guest of somebody or other....

Day by day I am feeling that the Lord is with me, and I am trying to follow His direction. His will be done.... We will do great things for the world, and that for the sake of doing good and not for name and fame....

It is a great art to press the largest amount of thought into the smallest number of words. Even Manilal Dvivedi's paper had to be cut very short. More than a thousand papers were read, and there was no time to give to such wild perorations. I had a good long time given to me over the ordinary half hour ... because the most popular speakers were always put down last, to hold the audience. And Lord bless them, what sympathy they have, and what patience! They would sit from ten o'clock in the morning to ten o'clock at night—only a recess of half an hour for a meal, and paper after paper read, most of them very trivial, but they would wait and wait to hear their favourites.

Dharmapala of Ceylon was one of the favourites. But unfortunately he was not a good speaker. He had only quotations from Max Müller and Rhys Davids to give them. He is a very sweet man, and we became very intimate during the Parliament....

Lecturing is a very profitable occupation in this country and sometimes pays well. Mr. Ingersoll gets five to six hundred dollars a lecture. He is the most celebrated lecturer in this country.[28]

At the Parliament

Sisters and Brothers of America,

It fills my heart with joy unspeakable to rise in response to the warm and cordial welcome which you have given us. I thank you in the name of the most ancient order of monks in the world; I thank you in the name of the mother of religions; and I thank you in the name of millions and millions of Hindu people of all classes and sects.

My thanks, also, to some of the speakers on this platform who, referring to the delegates from the Orient, have told you that these men from far-off nations may well claim the honour of bearing to different lands the idea of toleration. I am proud to belong to a religion which has taught the world both tolerance and universal acceptance. We believe not only in universal toleration, but we accept all religions as true. I am proud to belong to a nation which has sheltered the persecuted and the refugees of all religions and all nations of the earth. I am proud to tell you that we have gathered in our bosom the purest remnant of the Israelites, who came to Southern India and took refuge with us in the very year in which their holy temple was shattered to pieces by Roman tyranny. I am proud to belong to the religion which has sheltered and is still fostering the remnant of the grand Zoroastrian nation. I will quote to you, brethren, a few lines from a hymn which I remember to have repeated from my earliest boyhood, which is every day repeated by millions of human beings: *"As the different streams having their sources in different places all mingle their water in the sea, so, O Lord, the different paths which men take through different tendencies, various though they appear, crooked or straight, all lead to Thee."* ...

I fervently hope that the bell that tolled this morning in honour of this convention may be the death-knell of all fanaticism, of all persecutions with the sword or with the pen, and of all uncharitable feelings between persons wending their way to the same goal.[29]

I came here [to America] to seek aid for my impoverished people, and I fully realised how difficult it was to get help for heathens from Christians in a Christian land.[30]

I remember, as a boy, hearing a Christian missionary preach to a crowd in India. Among other sweet things he was telling them was that if he gave a blow to their idol with his stick, what could it do? One of his hearers sharply answered, "If I abuse your God, what can He do?" "You would be punished," said the preacher, "when you die." "So my idol will punish you when you die," retorted the Hindu.

The tree is known by its fruits. When I have seen amongst them that are called idolaters, men, the like of whom in morality and spirituality and love I have never seen anywhere, I stop and ask myself, "Can sin beget holiness?"[31]

I am one of those monks who have been described as beggarly. That is the pride of my life. I am proud in that sense to be Christ-like. I eat what I have today and think not of tomorrow. "Behold the lilies of the field; they toil not, neither do they spin." The Hindu carries that out literally. Many gentlemen present in Chicago sitting on this platform can testify that for the last twelve years I never knew whence my next meal was coming. I am proud to be a beggar for the sake of the Lord.[32]

In my first speech in this country, in Chicago, I addressed that audience as "Sisters and Brothers of America," and you know that they all rose to their feet. You may wonder what made them do this, you may wonder if I had some strange power. Let me tell you that I did have a power and this is it—never once in my life did I allow myself to have even one sexual thought. I trained my mind, my thinking, and the powers that man usually uses along that line I put into a higher channel, and it developed a force so strong that nothing could resist it.[33]

I spoke at the Parliament of Religions, and with what effect I may quote to you from a few newspapers and magazines ready at hand. I need not be self-conceited, but to you in confidence I am bound to say, because of your love, that no Hindu made such an impression in America, and if my coming has done nothing, it has done this that the Americans have come to know that India even today produces men at whose feet even the most civilised nations may learn lessons of religion and morality. Don't you think that is enough to say for the Hindu nation sending over here their Sannyasin?...

These I quote from the journals: "But eloquent as were many of the brief speeches, no one expressed as well the spirit of the Parliament (of religions) and its limitations as the Hindu monk. I copy his address in full, but I can only suggest its effect upon the audience; for he is an orator by Divine right, and his strong intelligent face in its picturesque setting of yellow and orange was hardly less interesting than these earnest words and the rich rhythmical utterance he gave them." (Here the speech is quoted *in extenso*.) *New York Critique*.

"He has preached in clubs and churches until his faith has become familiar to us.... His culture, his eloquence, and his fascinating personality have given us *a new idea of Hindu civilisation*.... His fine, intelligent face and his deep musical voice, prepossessing one at once in his favour.... He speaks without notes, presenting his facts and his conclusions with the greatest art and the most convincing sincerity, and rising often to rich inspiring eloquence." (*ibid*.)

"Vivekananda is undoubtedly the greatest figure in the Parliament of Religions. After hearing him we feel how foolish it is to send missionaries to this learned nation." *Herald* (the greatest paper here).

I cease from quoting more lest you think me conceited ...

I am the same here as in India, only here in this highly cultural land there is an appreciation, a sympathy which our ignorant fools never dream of. There our people grudge us monks a crumb of bread, here they are ready to pay one thousand rupees a lecture and remain grateful for the instructions for ever.

I am appreciated by these strangers more than I was ever in India. I can, if I will, live here all my life in the greatest luxury; but I am a Sannyasin, and "India, with all thy faults I love thee still." So I am coming back after some months, and go on sowing the seeds of religion and progress from city to city as I was doing so long, although amongst a people who know not what appreciation and gratefulness are....

Now after these quotations, do you think it was worthwhile to send a Sannyasin to America?

Please do not publish [them]. I hate notoriety in the same manner as I did in India.

I am doing the Lord's work, and wherever He leads I follow.

Mūkaṁ karoti vācālam etc.—he who makes the dumb eloquent and the lame cross a mountain, He will help me. I do not care for human help. He is ready to help me in India, in America, on the North Pole, if He thinks fit. If He does not, none else can help me. Glory unto the Lord for ever and ever.[34]

The Parliament of Religions was organised with the intention of proving the superiority of the Christian religion over other forms of faith, but the philosophic religion of Hinduism was able to maintain its position notwithstanding.[35]

The Parliament of Religions, as it seems to me, was intended for a "heathen show" before the world: but it turned out that the heathens had the upper hand and made it a Christian show all around. So the Parliament of Religions was a failure from the Christian standpoint, seeing that the Roman Catholics, who were the organisers of that Parliament, are, when there is talk of another Parliament at Paris, now steadily opposing it. But the Chicago Parliament was a tremendous success for India and Indian thought. It helped on the tide of Vedanta, which is flooding the world. The American people—of course, *minus* the fanatical priests and Church-women—are very glad of the results of the Parliament.[36]

What a wonderful achievement was that World's Fair at Chicago! And that wonderful Parliament of Religions where voices from every corner of the earth expressed their religious ideas! I was also allowed to present my own ideas through the kindness of Dr. Barrows and Mr. Bonney. Mr. Bonney is such a wonderful man! Think of that mind that planned and carried out with great success that gigantic undertaking, and he, no clergyman, a lawyer, presiding over the dignitaries of all the churches—the sweet, learned, patient Mr. Bonney with all his soul speaking through his bright eyes.[37]

CHAPTER SIX

MARCH OF EVENTS

My mission in America was not to the Parliament of Religions. That was only something by the way, it was only an opening, an opportunity, and for that we are very thankful to the members of the Parliament; but really, our thanks are due to the great people of the United States, the American nation, the warm-hearted, hospitable, great nation of America, where more than anywhere else the feeling of brotherhood has been developed. An American meets you for five minutes on board a train, and you are his friend, and the next moment he invites you as a guest to his home and opens the secret of his whole living there. That is the character of the American race, and we highly appreciate it. Their kindness to me is past all narration, it would take me years yet to tell you how I have been treated by them most kindly and most wonderfully.[1]

I have heard many stories about the American home: of liberty running into licence, of unwomanly women smashing under their feet all the peace and happiness of home-life in their mad liberty-dance, and much nonsense of that type. And now after a year's experience of American homes, of American women, how utterly false and erroneous that sort of judgment appears! American women! A hundred lives would not be sufficient to pay my deep debt of gratitude to you! I have not words enough to express my gratitude to you. "The Oriental hyperbole" alone expresses the depth of Oriental gratitude—"If the Indian Ocean were an inkstand, the highest mountain of the Himalaya the pen, the earth the scroll and time itself the writer," still it will not express my gratitude to you!

Last year I came to this country in summer, a wandering preacher of a far distant country, without name, fame, wealth, or learning to recommend me—friendless, helpless, almost in a state of destitution—and American women befriended me, gave me shelter and food, took me to their homes and treated me as their own son, their own brother. They stood my friends even when their own priests were trying to persuade them to give up the "dangerous heathen"—even when day after day their best friends had told them not to stand by this "unknown foreigner, may be, of dangerous character." But they are better judges of character and soul—for it is the pure mirror that catches the reflection.

And how many beautiful homes I have seen, how many mothers whose purity of character, whose unselfish love for their children are beyond expression, how many daughters and pure maidens, "pure as the icicle on Diana's temple," and withal with much culture, education, and spirituality in the highest sense! Is America then full of only wingless angels in the shape of women? There is good and bad everywhere, true—but a nation is not to be judged by its weaklings called the wicked, as they are only the weeds which lag behind, but by the good, the noble, and the pure who indicate the national life-current to be flowing clear and vigorous....

And then the modern American women—I admire their broad and liberal minds. I have seen many liberal and broad-minded men too in this country, some even in the narrowest churches, but here is the difference—there is danger with the men to become broad at the cost of religion, at the cost of spirituality—women broaden out in sympathy to everything that is good everywhere, without losing a bit of their own religion.[2]

Nowhere in the world are women like those of this country. How pure, independent, self-relying, and kind-hearted! It is the women who are the life and soul of this country. All learning and culture are centred in them ....

There are thousands of women here whose minds are as pure and white as the snow of this country.[3]

When I came into this country I was surprised to meet so many liberal men and women. But after the Parliament of Religions a great Presbyterian paper came out and gave me the benefit of a seething article. This the editor called enthusiasm.[4]

Just think, with all your claims to civilisation in this country, on one occasion I was refused a chair to sit on, because I was a Hindu.[5]

It struck me more than once that I should have to leave my bones on foreign shores owing to the prevalence of religious intolerance.[6]

"Fifty years ago," said Ingersoll to me, "you would have been hanged in this country if you had come to preach. You would have been burnt alive or you would have been stoned out of the villages."[7]

I pity the Hindu who does not see the beauty in Jesus Christ's character. I pity the Christian who does not reverence the Hindu Christ.[8]

Had I lived in Palestine, in the days of Jesus of Nazareth, I would have washed his feet, not with my tears, but with my heart's blood![9]

Letters Reveal the Struggle

Chicago, 15 November 1893 · I have seen many strange sights and grand things.... America is a grand country. It is a paradise of the poor and women. There is almost no poor in the country, and nowhere else in the world women are so free, so educated, so cultured. They are everything in society.

This is a great lesson. The Sannyasin has not lost a bit of his Sannyasinship, even his mode of living. And in this most hospitable country, every home is open to me. The Lord who guides me in India, would He not guide me here? And He has.

You may not understand why a Sannyasin should be in America, but it was necessary. Because the only claim you have to be recognised by the world is your religion, and good specimens of our religious men are required to be sent abroad to give other nations an idea that India is not dead....

And a Sannyasin who has no idea of doing good to his fellows is a brute, not a Sannyasin.

I am neither a sightseer nor an idle traveller; but you will see, if you live to see, and bless me all your life.[10]

Chicago, November 1894 · Here were ...; they were all trying to lecture and get money thereby. They did something, but I succeeded better than they—why, I did not put myself as a bar to their success. It was the will of the Lord. But all these ... have fabricated and circulated the most horrible lies about me in this country, and behind my back....

I do not care what they say. I love my God, my religion, my country, and above all, myself, a poor beggar. I love the poor, the ignorant, the downtrodden, I feel for them—the Lord knows how much. He will show me the way. I do not care a fig for human approbation or criticism. I think of most of them as ignorant, noisy children—they have not penetrated into the inner nature of sympathy, into the spirit which is all love.

I have that insight through the blessing of Ramakrishna. I am trying to work with my little band, all of these poor beggars like me, you have seen them. But the Lord's works have been always done by the lowly, by the poor.... The only way is love and sympathy. The only worship is love.[11]

Minneapolis, Minnesota, 24 November 1893 · The day I came here they had their first snow, and it snowed all through the day and night, and I had great use for the arctics [a waterproof overshoe]. I went to see the frozen Minnehaha Falls. They are very beautiful. The temperature today is 21° below zero, but I had been out sleighing and enjoyed it immensely. I am not the least afraid of losing the tips of my ears or nose.

The snow scenery here has pleased me more than any other sight in this country.

I saw people skating on a frozen lake yesterday.[12]

Detroit, 20 February 1894 · My lectures here are over. I have made some very good friends here, amongst them Mr. Palmer, President of the late World's Fair. I am thoroughly disgusted with this Slayton [an unscrupulous lecture agent] business and am trying hard to break loose. I have lost at least $5,000 by joining this man....

It is rather wearisome, these constant receptions and dinners; and their horrible dinners—a hundred dinners concentrated into one—and when in a man's club, why, smoking on between the courses and then beginning afresh. I thought the Chinese alone make a dinner run through half a day with intervals of smoking! However, they are very gentlemanly men and, strange to say, an Episcopal clergyman and a Jewish rabbi take great interest in me and eulogize me. Now the man who got up the lectures here got at least a thousand dollars. So in every place. And this is Slayton's duty to do for me. Instead, he, the liar, had told me often that he has agents everywhere and would advertise and do all that for me. And this is what he is doing. His will be done. I am going home. Seeing the liking the American people have for me, I could have, by this time, got a pretty large sum. But Jimmy Mills and Slayton were sent by the Lord to stand in the way. His ways are inscrutable.

However, this is a secret. President Palmer has gone to Chicago to try to get me loose from this liar of a Slayton. Pray that he may succeed. Several judges here have seen my contract, and they say it is a shameful fraud and can be broken any moment; but I am a monk—no self defence. Therefore, I had better throw up the whole thing and go to India.[13]

Detroit, 12 March 1894 · I am now living with Mr. Palmer. He is a very nice gentleman.... I spoke at an opera house for two hours and a half. People were very much pleased.... To tell you the truth, the more I am getting popularity and facility in speaking, the more I am getting fed up. My last address was the best I ever delivered. Mr. Palmer was in ecstasies and the audience remained almost spellbound, so much so that it was after the lecture that I found I had spoken so long. A speaker always feels the uneasiness or inattention of the audience. Lord save me from such nonsense, I am fed up.[14]

Detroit, 15 March 1894 · I am pulling on well with old Palmer. He is a very jolly, good old man....

The funniest thing said about me here was in one of the papers which said, "The cyclonic Hindu has come and is a guest with Mr. Palmer. Mr. Palmer has become a Hindu and is going to India; only he insists that two reforms should be carried out: firstly that the Car of Jagannath should be drawn by Percherons raised in Mr. Palmer's Loghouse Farm, and secondly that the Jersey cow be admitted into the pantheon of Hindu sacred cows." Mr. Palmer is passionately fond of both Percheron horse and Jersey cow and has a great stock of both in his Loghouse Farm.

The first lecture was not properly managed, the cost of the hall being 150 dollars. I have given up Holden [a lecture agent in Detroit]. Here is another fellow cropped up; let me see if he does better. Mr. Palmer makes me laugh the whole day. Tomorrow there is going to be another dinner party. So far all is well; but I do not know—I have become very sad in my heart since I am here—do not know why.

I am wearied of lecturing and all that nonsense. This mixing with hundreds of varieties of the human animal has disturbed me. I will tell you what is to my taste; I cannot write, and I cannot speak, but I can think deeply, and when I am heated, can speak fire. It should be, however, to a select, a very select few. Let them, if they will, carry and scatter my ideas broadcast—not I. This is only a just division of labour. The same man never succeeded both in thinking and in scattering his thoughts. A man should be free to think, especially spiritual thoughts.

Just because this assertion of independence, this proving that man is *not a machine*, is the essence of all religious thought, it is impossible to think it in the routine mechanical way. It is this tendency to bring everything down to the level of a machine that has given the West its wonderful prosperity. And it is this which has driven away all religion from its doors. Even the little that is left, the West has reduced to a systematic drill.

I am really not "cyclonic" at all. Far from it. What I want is not here, nor can I longer bear this "cyclonic" atmosphere. This is the way to perfection, to strive to be perfect, and to strive to make perfect a few men and women. My idea of doing good is this: to evolve out a few giants, and not to strew pearls before swine, and so lose time, health, and energy.

Just now I got a letter from Flagg. He cannot help me in lecturing. He says, "First go to Boston." Well, I do not care for lecturing any more. It is too disgusting, this attempt to bring me to suit anybody's or any audience's fads ... [15]

Detroit, 16 March 1894 · I am in no way very anxious. I am taking life very easy in my natural way. I have no particular wish to go anywhere, Boston or no Boston. I am just in a nice come-what-may mood. Something should turn up, bad or good. I have enough now to pay my passage back and a little sight-seeing to boot. As to my plans of *work*, I am fully convinced that at the rate it is progressing I will have to come back four or five times to put it in any shape.

As to informing others and doing good that way, I have failed to persuade myself that I have really anything to convey to the world. So I am very happy just now and quite at my ease. With almost nobody in this vast house and a cigar between my lips, I am dreaming just now and philosophising upon that *work* fever which was upon me. It is all nonsense. I am nothing, the world is nothing, the Lord alone is the only *worker*. We are simply tools in His hands ... [16]

Detroit, 17 March 1894 · I have returned today to Mrs. Bagley's as she was sorry that I would remain so long with Mr. Palmer. Of course in Palmer's house there was real "good time." He is a real jovial heartwhole fellow, and likes "good time" a little too much and his "hot scotch." But he is right along innocent and childlike in his simplicity. He was very sorry that I came away, but I could not help.[17]

Detroit, 18 March 1894 · My heartfelt thanks for your kindly sending me the letter from Calcutta. It was from my brethren at Calcutta, and it is written on the occasion of a private invitation to celebrate the birthday of my Master about whom you have heard so much from me—so I send it over to you. The letter says that Mazoomdar has gone back to Calcutta and is preaching that Vivekananda is committing every sin under the sun in America—especially 'unchastity' of the most degraded type!!! Lord bless his soul. You need not be sorry—I am too well known in my native land as to my character, and my brethren, my life-long companions, know me too well to believe such trash. They only laugh at Mazoomdar's attempts as very clumsy. This is your America's *wonderful spiritual man*! It is not their fault; until one is really spiritual, that is, until one has got a real insight into the nature of one's own soul and has got a glimpse of the world of the soul, one cannot distinguish chaff from seed, tall talk from depth, and so on. I am sorry for poor Mazoomdar that he should stoop so low! ... Lord bless the old boy ...

The address inside the letter is in English and is my old, old name as written by a companion of my childhood who has also taken orders. It is a very poetic name. That written in the letter is an abbreviation, the full name being Narendra meaning the "Chief of men" ("nara" means "man," and "indra" stands for "ruler," "chief")—very ludicrous, isn't it? But such are the names in our country; we cannot help, but I am glad I have given that up.[18]

Chicago, 19 March 1894 · I have no wants in this country, but mendicancy has no vogue here, and I have to labour, that is, lecture in places. It is as cold here as it is hot. The summer is not a bit less hot than in Calcutta. And how to describe the cold in winter! The whole country is covered with snow, three or four feet deep, nay, six or seven feet at places! In the southern parts there is no snow. Snow, however, is a thing of little consideration here. For it snows when the mercury stands at 32° F [0° C]. In Calcutta it scarcely comes down to 60° [15° C] and it rarely approaches zero in England. But here, your mercury sinks to *minus* 4° or 5° [-20° C]. In Canada, in the north, mercury becomes condensed, when they have to use the alcohol thermometer. When it is too cold, that is, when the mercury stands even below 20° F, it does not snow. I used to think that it must be an exceedingly cold day on which the snow falls. But it is not so, it snows on comparatively warm days. Extreme cold produces a sort of intoxication. No carriages would run; only the sledge, which is without wheels, slides on the ground! Everything is frozen stiff—even an elephant can walk on rivers and canals and lakes. The massive falls of Niagara, of such tremendous velocity, are frozen to marble!! But I am doing nicely. I was a little afraid at first, but necessity makes me travel by rail to the borders of Canada one day, and the next day finds me lecturing in south U.S.A! The carriages are kept quite warm, like your own room, by means of steam pipes, and all around are masses of snow, spotlessly white. Oh, the beauty of it!

I was mortally afraid that my nose and ears would fall off, but to this day they are all right. I have to go out, however, dressed in a heap of warm clothing surmounted by a fur-coat, with boots encased in a woollen jacket, and so on. No sooner do you breathe out than the breath freezes among the beard and moustache! Notwithstanding all this, the fun of it is that they won't drink water indoors without putting a lump of ice into it. This is because it is warm indoors. Every room and the staircase are kept warm by steam pipes. They are first and foremost in art and appliances, foremost in enjoyment and luxury, foremost in making money, and foremost in spending it. The daily wages of a coolie are six rupees, as also are those of a servant; you cannot hire a cab for less than three rupees, nor get a cigar for less than four annas. A decent pair of shoes costs twenty-four rupees, and a suit, five hundred rupees. As they earn, so they spend. A lecture fetches from two hundred up to three thousand rupees. I have got up to five hundred. Of course now I am in the very heyday of fortune. They like me, and thousands of people come to hear me speak.

As it pleased the Lord, I met here Mr. Mazoomdar. He was very cordial at first, but when the whole Chicago population began to flock to me in overwhelming numbers, then grew the canker in his mind!... I was astounded to see and hear these things.... Mazoomdar slandered me to the missionaries in the Parliament of Religions, saying that I was a nobody, a thug and a cheat, and he accused me of coming here and pretending to be a monk. Thus he greatly succeeded in prejudicing their minds against me. He so prejudiced President Barrows that he didn't even speak to me decently. In their books and pamphlets they tried their best to snub me, but the Guru is my help. What could Mazoomdar say? And the whole American nation loves and respects me, pays my expenses, and reveres me as a Guru.... It was not in the power of your priests to do anything against me. Moreover, they are a nation of scholars.... What they want is philosophy, learning; and empty talk will no more do....

Brother, I have been brought to my senses.... "*Ye nighnanti nirarthakaṁ parahitaṁ te ke na jānīmahe*—We do not know what sort of people they are who for nothing hinder the welfare of others." [Bhartrihari.] Brother, we can get rid of everything, but not of that cursed jealousy.... That is a national sin with us, speaking ill of others, and burning at heart at the greatness of others. Mine alone is the greatness, none else should rise to it!!...

A country where millions of people live on flowers of the Mohua plant, and a million or two of Sadhus and a hundred million or so of Brahmins suck the blood out of these poor people, without even the least effort for their amelioration—is that a country or hell? Is that a religion, or the devil's dance? My brother, here is one thing for you to understand fully—I have travelled all over India, and seen this country too—can there be an effect without cause? Can there be punishment without sin?

Sarvaśāstrapurāṇeṣu vyāsasya vacanaṁ dhruvam |
Paropakāraḥ puṇyāya pāpāya parapīḍanam ||

"Amidst all the scriptures and Puranas, know this statement of Vyāsa to be true, that doing good to others conduces to merit, and doing harm to them leads to sin"....

In view of all this, specially of the poverty and ignorance [in India], I had no sleep. At Cape Comorin sitting in Mother Kumari's temple, sitting on the last bit of Indian rock—I hit upon a plan: We are so many Sannyasins wandering about, and teaching the people metaphysics—it is all madness.

Did not our Gurudeva use to say, "An empty stomach is no good for religion"? That those poor people are leading the life of brutes is simply due to ignorance. We have for all ages been sucking their blood and trampling them underfoot.

...Suppose some disinterested Sannyasins, bent on doing good to others, go from village to village, disseminating education and seeking in various ways to better the condition of all down to the Chandala, through oral teaching, and by means of maps, cameras, globes, and such other accessories—can't that bring forth good in time?... The long and the short of it is—if the mountain does not come to Mohammed, Mohammed must go to the mountain. The poor are too poor to come to schools and Pāthashālās... We, as a nation, have lost our individuality, and that is the cause of all mischief in India. We have to give back to the nation its lost individuality and *raise the masses*....

To effect this, the first thing we need is men, and the next is funds. Through the grace of our Guru I was sure to get from ten to fifteen men in every town. I next travelled in search of funds, but do you think the people of India were going to spend money!... Selfishness personified—are they to spend anything? Therefore I have come to America, to earn money myself, and then return to my country and devote the rest of my days to the realisation of this one aim of my life.

As our country is poor in social virtues, so this country [America] is lacking in spirituality. I give them spirituality, and they give me money. I do not know how long I shall take to realise my end.... These people are not hypocrites, and jealousy is altogether absent in them. I depend on no one in Hindusthan. I shall try to earn the wherewithal myself to the best of my might and carry out my plans, or die in the attempt. "*Sannimitte varaṁ tyāgo vināśe niyate sati*—When death is certain, it is best to sacrifice oneself for a good cause."

You may perhaps think what Utopian nonsense all this is! You little know what is in me. If any of you help me in my plans, all right, or Gurudeva will show me the way out.[19]

U.S.A., Summer 1894 · This is a very funny country. It is now summer; this morning it was as hot as April in Bengal, but now it is as cold as February at Allahabad! So much fluctuation within four hours! The hotels of this country beggar description. For instance, there is a hotel in New York where a room can be hired for up to Rs. 5,000 a day, excluding boarding charges. Not even in Europe is there a country like this in point of luxury. It is indeed the richest country in the world, where money is drained off like water. I seldom live in hotels, but am mostly the guest of big people here. To them I am a widely known man. The whole country knows me now; so wherever I go they receive me with open arms into their homes. Mr. Hale's home is my centre in Chicago. I call his wife mother, and his daughters call me brother. I scarcely find a family so highly pure and kind. Or why should God shower His blessings on them in such abundance, my brother? Oh, how wonderfully kind they are! If they chance to learn that a poor man is in a strait at such and such a place, there they will go, ladies and gentlemen, to give him food and clothing, and find him some job!...

By the bye, nowadays we have plenty of Hilsa fish here. Eat your fill, but everything digests. There are many kinds of fruits; plantain, lemon, guava, apple, almond, raisin, and grape are in abundance; besides many other fruits come from California. There are plenty of pineapples but there are no mangoes or lichis, or things of that sort. There is a kind of spinach, which, when cooked, tastes just like our *note* of Bengal, and another class, which they call asparagus, tastes exactly like the tender *dengo* herb, but you can't have our *charchari* made of it here. There is no *kalai* or any other pulse; they do not even know of them. There is rice, and bread, and numerous varieties of fish and meat, of all descriptions. Their menu is like that of the French. There is your milk, rarely curd, but plenty of whey. Cream is an article of everyday use. In tea and coffee and everything there is that cream—not the hardened crust of boiled milk, mind you—and there is your butter, too, and ice-water—no matter whether it is summer or winter, day or night, whether you have got a bad cold or fever—you have ice-water in abundance. These are scientific people and laugh when they are told that ice-water aggravates cold. The more you take, the better. And there is plenty of ice-cream, of all sorts of shapes. I have seen the Niagara Falls seven or eight times, the Lord be praised! Very grand no doubt, but not quite as you have heard them spoken of. One day, in winter, we had the aurora borealis....

As for lectures and so forth, I don't prepare them beforehand. Only one I wrote out, which you have printed. The rest I deliver off-hand, whatever comes to my lips—Gurudeva backs me up. I have nothing to do with pen and paper. Once at Detroit I held forth for three hours at a stretch. Sometimes I myself wonder at my own achievement—to think that there was such stuff in this pate![20]

Power comes to him who observes unbroken Brahmacharya for a period of twelve years, with the sole object of realising God. I have practised that kind of Brahmacharya myself, and so a screen has been removed, as it were, from my brain. For that reason, I need not any more think over or prepare myself for any lectures on such a subtle subject as philosophy. Suppose I have to lecture tomorrow; all that I shall speak about will pass tonight before my eyes like so many pictures; and the next day I put into words during my lecture all those things that I saw.[21]

Those that are very emotional no doubt have their Kundalini rushing quickly upwards, but it is as quick to come down as to go up. And when it does come down, it leaves the devotee in a state of utter ruin.... [If] through a momentary impulse, that power is made to course upwards ... it is never enduring. On the contrary when it traces back its course, it rouses violent lust in the individual. Listening to my lectures in America, through temporary excitement many among the audience used to get into an ecstatic state, and some would even become motionless like statues. But on inquiry I afterwards found that many of them had an excess of the carnal instinct immediately after that state. But this happens simply owing to a lack of steady practice in meditation and concentration.[22]

A friend criticised the use of European terms of philosophy and religion in my addresses. I would have been very glad to use Sanskrit terms; it would have been much more easy, as being the only perfect vehicle of religious thought. But the friend forgot that I was addressing an audience of Western people; and although a certain Indian missionary declared that the Hindus had forgotten the meaning of their Sanskrit books, and that it was the missionaries who unearthed the meaning, I could not find one in that large concourse of missionaries who could understand a line in Sanskrit—and yet some of them read learned papers criticising the Vedas, and all the sacred sources of the Hindu religion![23]

Detroit, 30 March 1894 · Next summer, if I do not go away, which Mrs. Bagley insists I should not, I may go to Annisquam where Mrs. Bagley has engaged a nice house. Mrs. Bagley is a very spiritual lady, and Mr. Palmer a spirituous gentleman but very good.... I am all right in nice health of body and mind.... By the by, Mrs. Sherman has presented me with a lot of things amongst which is a nail set and letter holder and a little satchel etc., etc. Although I objected, especially to the nail set, as very dudish with mother-of-pearl handles, she insisted and I had to take them, although I do not know what to do with that brushing instrument. Lord bless them all. She gave me one advice—never to wear this Afrikee dress in society. Now I am a society man! Lord! What comes next? Long life brings queer experiences![24]

New York, 9 April 1894 · I have lectured in many of the big towns of America, and have got enough to pay my passage back after paying the awful expenses here. I have made a good many friends here, some of them very influential. Of course, the orthodox clergymen are against me; and seeing that it is not easy to grapple with me, they try to hinder, abuse, and vilify me in every way; and Mazoomdar has come to their help. He must have gone mad with jealousy. He has told them that

I was a big fraud, and a rogue! And again in Calcutta he is telling them that I am leading a most sinful life in America, specially unchaste! Lord bless him! My brother, no good thing can be done without obstruction. It is only those who persevere to the end that succeed.... I believe that the Satya Yuga [Golden Age] will come when there will be one caste, one Veda, and peace and harmony. This idea of Satya Yuga is what would revivify India. Believe it.[25]

Chicago, Spring, 1894 · I am very sorry to hear of Mazoomdar's doings. One always behaves thus in trying to push oneself before all others. I am not much to blame. Mazoomdar came here ten years ago, and got much reputation and honour; now I am in flying colours. Such is the will of the Guru, what shall I do? It is childishness on Mazoomdar's part to be annoyed at this. Never mind ... great men like you should pay no heed to what he says. Shall we, children of Sri Ramakrishna, nourished with his heart's blood, be afraid of worm-bites? "The wicked criticise the conduct of the magnanimous, which is extraordinary and whose motives are difficult to fathom"—remember all this and forgive this fool. It is the will of the Lord that people of this land have their power of introspection roused, and does it lie in anybody to check His progress? I want no name—I want to be a voice without a form. I do not require anybody to defend me ... who am I to check or to help the course of His march?[26]

New York, 10 April 1894 · As for lecturing, I have given up raising money. I cannot degenerate myself any more. When a certain purpose was in view, I could work; with that gone I cannot earn for myself. I have sufficient for going back. I have not tried to earn a penny here, and have refused some presents which friends here wanted to make to me.... I had in Detroit tried to refund the money back to the donors, and told them that, there being almost no chance of my succeeding in my enterprise, I had no right to keep their money; but they refused and told me to throw that into the waters if I liked. But I cannot take any more conscientiously. I am very well off, Mother. Everywhere the Lord sends me kind persons and homes; so there is no use of my going into beastly worldliness at all.

The New York people, though not so intellectual as the Bostonians, are, I think, more sincere. The Bostonians know well how to take advantage of everybody. And I am afraid even water cannot slip through their closed fingers!!! Lord bless them!!! I have promised to go and I must go; but, Lord, make me live with the sincere, ignorant and the poor, and not cross the shadow of the hypocrites and tall talkers who, as my Master used to say, are like vultures who soar high and high in their talks, but the heart is really on a piece of carrion on the ground....

Went to see Barnum's circus the other day. It is no doubt a grand thing. I have not been as yet downtown. This street is very nice and quiet.

I heard a beautiful piece of music the other day at Barnum's—they call it a Spanish Serenada. Whatever it be, I liked it so much.[27]

[Western Music] is very good; there is in it a perfection of harmony, which we [Indians] have not attained. Only, to our untrained ears, it does not sound well, hence we do not like it, and think that the singers howl like jackals. I also had the same sort of impression, but when I began to listen to the music with attention and study it minutely, I came more and more to understand it, and I was lost in admiration.[28]

New York, 26 April 1894 · The mail you sent yesterday from India was really ... a good news after a long interval.... There was a little pamphlet published in Calcutta about me—revealing that once at least in my life the prophet has been honoured in his own country. There are extracts from American and Indian papers and magazines about me. The extracts printed from Calcutta papers were especially gratifying, although the strain is so fulsome that I refuse to send the pamphlet over to you. They call me illustrious, wonderful, and all sorts of nonsense, but they forward me the gratitude of the whole nation. Now I do not care what they even of my own people say about me—except for one thing. I have an old mother. She has suffered much all her life and in the midst of all she could bear to give me up for the service of God and man; but to have given up the most beloved of her children—her hope—to live a beastly immoral life in a far distant country, as Mazoomdar was telling in Calcutta, would have simply killed her. But the Lord is great, none can injure His children.

The cat is out of the bag—without my seeking at all. And who do you think is the editor of one of our leading papers which praise me so much and thank God that I came to America to represent Hinduism? Mazoomdar's cousin!!—poor Mazoomdar—he has injured his cause by telling lies through jealousy. Lord knows I never attempted any defence.[29]

New York, 1 May 1894 · I could not find the exact orange colour of my coat here, so I have been obliged to satisfy myself with the next best—a cardinal red with more of yellow.

The coat will be ready in a few days.

Got about $70 the other day by lecturing at Waldorf. And hope to get some more by tomorrow's lecture.

From 7th to 19th there are engagements in Boston, but they pay very little.

Yesterday I bought a pipe for $13—meerschaum do not tell it to Father Pope [Mr. George Hale, for whom the pipe was bought]. The coat will cost $30. I am all right getting food, drink and money enough. Hope very soon to put something in the bank after the coming lecture.

I have eaten ... just now because in the evening I am going to speak in a vegetarian dinner! Well, I am a vegetarian for all that because I prefer it when I can get it. I have another invitation to lunch with Lyman Abbott day after tomorrow. After all, I am having very nice time and hope to have very nice time in Boston—only that nasty nasty lecturing—disgusting. However as soon as 19th is over—one leap from Boston ... to Chicago ... and then I will have a long long breath and rest, rest for two three weeks. I will simply sit down and talk—talk and smoke.

By the by, your New York people are very good—only more money than brains.

I am going to speak to the students of the Harvard University. Three lectures at Boston, three at Harvard—all arranged by Mrs. Breed. They are arranging something here too, so that I will, on my way to Chicago, come to New York once more—give them a few hard raps and pocket the boodle and fly to Chicago....

I hate only one thing in the world—hypocrisy.[30]

Boston, May, 1894 · We are to give up and not to take. Had I not the "Fad" in my head, I would never have come over here. And it was with a hope that it would help my cause that I joined the Parliament of Religions—having always refused it when our people wanted to send me for it. I came over telling them—"that I may or may not join that assembly—and you may send me over if you like." They sent me over leaving me quite free....

I do not care for the attempts of the old missionary; but the fever of jealousy which attacked Mazoomdar gave me a terrible shock, and I pray that he would know better—for he is a great and good man who has tried all his life to do good. But this proves one of my Master's sayings, "Living in a room covered with black soot—however careful you may be—some spots must stick to your clothes." So, however one may try to be good and holy, so long he is in the world, some part of his nature must gravitate downwards.

The way to God is the opposite to that of the world. And to few, very few, are given to have God and mammon at the same time.

I was never a *missionary*, nor ever would be one—my place is in the Himalayas. I have satisfied myself so far that I can with a full conscience say, "My God, I saw terrible misery amongst my brethren; I searched and discovered the way out of it, tried my best to apply the remedy, but failed. So Thy will be done."[31]

Boston, 14 May 1894 · Oh, they are so, so dry—even girls talk dry metaphysics. Here is like our Benares where all is dry, dry metaphysics!! Nobody here understands "my Beloved." Religion to these people is reason, and horribly stony at that. I do not care for anybody who cannot love my "Beloved"....

Our people so much dislike the Brahmo Samaj that they only want an opportunity to show it to them. I dislike it. Any amount of enmity to certain persons cannot efface the good works of a life. And then they were only children in Religion. They never were much of religious men—

i.e. they only wanted to talk and reason, and did not struggle to see the Beloved; and until one does that I do not say that he has any religion. He may have books, forms, doctrines, words, reasons, etc., etc., but not religion; for that begins when the soul feels the necessity, the want, the yearning after the "Beloved," and never before.[32]

Chicago, 24 May 1894 · Herewith I forward to you a letter from one of our ruling princes of Rajputana, His Highness the Maharaja of Khetri, and another from the opium commissioner, late minister of Junagad ... These I hope would convince you of my being no fraud....

I am bound, my dear friend, to give you every satisfaction of my being a genuine Sannyasin, but to you alone. I do not care what the rabbles say or think about me.

"Some would call you a saint, some a Chandala; some a lunatic, others a demon. Go on then straight to thy work without heeding either"—thus saith one of our great Sannyasins, an old emperor of India, King Bhartrihari, who joined the order in old times.[33]

Chicago, 28 May 1894 · I was whirling to and fro from New York to Boston ... I do not know when I am going back to India. It is better to leave everything in the hands of Him who is at my back directing me.... I have done a good deal of lecturing here.... The expenses here are terrible; money has to fly, although I have been almost always taken care of everywhere by the nicest and the highest families.[34]

Chicago, 18 June 1894 · I am going to New York in a week ... Mrs. Bagley seems to be unsettled by that article in the Boston paper against me. She sent me over a copy from Detroit and has ceased correspondence with me. Lord bless her. She has been very kind to me....

This is a queer place—this world of ours. On the whole I am very very thankful to the Lord for the amount of kindness I have received at the hands of the people of this country—I, a complete stranger here without even "credentials." Everything works for the best.[35]

Chicago, Spring, 1894 · Money can be raised in this country by lecturing for two or three years. But I have tried a little, and although there is much public appreciation of my work, it is thoroughly uncongenial and demoralising to me.[36]

Chicago, 20 June 1894 · The backbiters, I must tell you, have not indirectly benefited me; on the other hand, they have injured me immensely in view of the fact that our Hindu people did not move a finger to tell the Americans that I represented them. Had our people sent some words thanking the American people for their kindness to me and stating that I was representing them? On the other hand Mazoomdar, Bombay's Nagarkar, and a Christian woman named Sorabji have been telling the American people that I have donned the Sannyasin's garb only in America and that I was a cheat, bare and simple. So far as reception goes, it has no effect on the American nation; but so far as helping me with funds goes, it has a terrible effect in making them take off their helping hands from me. And it is one year since I have been here, and not one man of note from India has thought it fit to make the Americans know that I am no cheat. There again the missionaries are always seeking for something against me, and they are busy picking up anything said against me by the Christian papers of India and publishing it here. Now you must know that the people here know very little of the distinction in India between the Christian and the Hindu....

[A] God-man ... was born in India. He was the great Ramakrishna Paramahamsa, and round him this band [of Sannyasins] is slowly gathering. They will do the work. Now ... this requires an organisation, money—a little at least to set the wheel in motion. Who would have given us money in India?—so ... I crossed over to America. You may remember I begged all the money from the poor, and the offers of the rich I would not accept because they could not understand my ideas. Now lecturing for a year in this country, I could not succeed at all (of course, I have no wants for myself) in my plan for raising some funds for setting up my work. First, this year is a very bad year in America; thousands of their poor are without work. Secondly, the missionaries and the Brahmo Samajists try to thwart all my views. Thirdly, a year has rolled by, and our countrymen could not even do so much for me as to say to the American people that I was a real Sannyasin and no cheat, and that I represented the Hindu religion. Even this much, the expenditure of a few words, they could not do! Bravo, my countrymen!...

Human help I spurn with my foot. He who has been with me through hills and dales, through deserts or forests, will be with me, I hope; if not, some heroic soul would arise some time or other in India, far abler than myself, and carry it out.... I am sincere to the backbone, and my greatest fault is that I love my country only too, too well.[37]

Chicago, 28 June 1894 · Now as to my prospects here—it is well-nigh zero. Why, because although I had the best purpose, it has been made null and void by these causes. All that I get about India is from Madras letters. Your letters say again and again how I am being praised in India. But that is between you and me, for I never saw a single Indian paper writing about me, except the three square inches sent to me by Alasinga. On the other hand, everything that is said by Christians in India is sedulously gathered by the missionaries and regularly published, and they go from door to door to make my friends give me up. They have succeeded only too well, for there is not one word for me from India. Indian Hindu papers may laud me to the skies, but not a word of that ever came to America, so that many people in this country think me a fraud. In the face of the missionaries and with the jealousy of the Hindus here to back them, I have not a word to say.

I now think it was foolish of me to go to the Parliament on the strength of the urging of the Madras boys. They are boys after all. Of course, I am eternally obliged to them, but they are after all enthusiastic young men without any executive abilities. I came here without credentials. How else to show that I am not a fraud in the face of the missionaries and the Brahmo Samaj?... There has not been one voice for me in one year and every one against me, for whatever you may say of me in your homes, who knows anything of it here? More than two months ago I wrote to Alasinga about this. He did not even answer my letter. I am afraid his heart has grown lukewarm.... On the other hand, my brethren foolishly talk nonsense about Keshab Sen; and the Madrasis, telling the Theosophists anything I write about them, are creating only enemies.... Oh! If only I had one man of some true abilities and brains to back me in India! But His will be done. I stand a fraud in this country. It was my foolishness to go to the Parliament without any credentials, hoping that there would be many for me. I have got to work it out slowly.

... After all, I must work my Karma out. So far as pecuniary circumstances go I am all right and will be all right....

Every moment I expected something from India. No, it never came. Last two months especially I was in torture at every moment. No, not even a newspaper from India! My friends waited—waited month after month; nothing came, not a voice. Many consequently grew cold and at last gave me up. But it is the punishment for relying upon man ...

My thanks eternal to the Madras young men. May the Lord bless them for ever.... I am always praying for their welfare, and I am not in the least displeased with them, but I am not pleased with myself. I committed a terrible error—of calculating upon others' help—once in my life—and I have paid for it. It was my fault and not theirs. Lord bless all the Madras people.... I have launched my boat in the waves, come what may. Regarding my brutal criticisms, I have really no right to make them.... I must bear my own Karma, and that without a murmur.[38]

New York, 1 July 1894 · I do not know what I am going to do next. Patiently wait and resign myself unto His guidance—that is my motto.[39]

New York, 11 July 1894 · We will do great things yet! Last year I only sowed the seeds; this year I mean to reap....

In the Detroit lecture I got $900, i.e. Rs. 2,700. In other lectures, I earned in one, $2,500, i.e. Rs. 7,500 in one hour, but got only 200 dollars! I was cheated by a roguish Lecture Bureau. I have given them up. I spent a good deal here; only about $3,000 remains.[40]

Beacon, New York, 17 July 1894 · I came yesterday to this place, and shall remain here a few days. I received in New York a letter from you but did not receive any *Interior*, for which I am glad, because I am not perfect yet, and knowing the "unselfish love" the Presbyterian priests, especially the *Interior*, has for "me," I want to keep aloof from rousing bad feelings towards these "sweet Christian gentlemen" in my heart.

Our religion teaches that anger is a great sin, even if it is "righteous." Each must follow his own religion. I could not for my soul distinguish ever the distinction between "religious anger" and "commonplace anger," "religious killing" and "commonplace killing," "religious slandering and irreligious," and so forth. Nor may that "fine" ethical distinction ever enter into the ethics of our nation! Jesting apart... I do not care the least for the gambols these men play, seeing as I do through and through the insincerity, the hypocrisy, and love of self and name that is the only motive power in these men....

I am bearing the heat very well here. I had an invitation to Swampscott on the sea from a very rich lady whose acquaintance I made last winter in New York, but I declined with thanks. I am very careful not to take the hospitality of anybody here, especially the rich. I had a few other invitations from some very rich people here. I refused; I have by this time seen the whole business through.[41]

Fishkill-on-the-Hudson, New York, 19 July 1894 · It is a lovely summer place, this Cedar Lawn of the Guernseys. Miss Guernsey has gone on a visit to Swampscott. I had also an invitation there, but I thought [it] better to stay here in the calm and silent place full of trees and with the beautiful Hudson flowing by and mountain in the background....

Most probably I will go to England very soon. But between you and me, I am a sort of mystic and cannot move without *orders*, and that has not come yet....

As for me, you need not be troubled in the least. My whole life is that of a vagabond—homeless, roving tramp; any fare, good or bad, in any country, is good enough for me.[42]

Swampscott, Massachusetts, 26 July 1894 · I had a beautiful letter from sister Mary. See how I am getting the dash, sister Jeany teaches me all that. She can jump and run and play and swear like a devil and talk slang at the rate of 500 a minute; only she does not much care for religion, only a little. She is gone today home, and I am going to Greenacre. I had been to see Mrs. Breed. Mrs. Stone was there, with whom is residing Mrs. Pullman and all the golden bugs, my old friends hereabouts. They are kind as usual. On my way back from Greenacre I am going to Annisquam to see Mrs. Bagley for a few days.

Darn it, forget everything. I had duckings in the sea like a fish. I am enjoying every bit of it. What nonsense was the song Harriet taught me "dans la plaine" the deuce take it. I told it to a French scholar and he laughed and laughed till the fellow was well-nigh burst at my wonderful translation. That is the way you would have taught me French! You are a pack of fools and heathens, I tell you. Now are you gasping for breath like a huge fish stranded? I am glad that you are sizzling. Oh! how nice and cool it is here, and it is increased a hundred-fold when I think about the gasping, sizzling, boiling, frying four old maids [the Hale sisters], and how cool and nice I am here. Whooooo!

Miss Phillips has a beautiful place somewhere in N.Y. State—mountain, lake, river, forest altogether—what more? I am going to make a Himalayas there and start a monastery as sure as I am living—I am not going to leave this country without throwing one more apple of discord into this already roaring, fighting, kicking, mad whirlpool of American religion.[43]

Greenacre Inn, Eliot, Maine, 26 July 1894 · This is a big inn and farm-house where the Christian Scientists are holding a session. Last spring in New York I was invited by the lady projector of the meeting to come here, and after all I am here. It is a beautiful and cool place, no doubt, and many of my old friends of Chicago are here. Mrs. Mills, Miss Stockham, and several other ladies and gentlemen live in tents which they have pitched on the open ground by the river. They have a lively time and sometimes all of them wear what you call your scientific dress the whole day. They have lectures almost every day. One Mr. Colville from Boston is here; he speaks every day, it is said, under spirit control. The Editor of the *Universal Truth* has settled herself down here. She is conducting religious services and holding classes to heal all manner of diseases, and very soon I expect them to be giving eyes to the blind, and the like! After all, it is a queer gathering. They do not care much about social laws and are quite free and happy. Mrs. Mills is quite brilliant, and so are many other ladies.... Another lady from Detroit—very cultured and with beautiful black eyes and long hair—is going to take me to an island fifteen miles out at sea. I hope we shall have a nice time.... I may go over to Annisquam from here, I suppose. This is a beautiful and nice place and the bathing is splendid. Cora Stockham has made a bathing dress for me, and I am having as good a time in the water as a duck....

There is here Mr. Wood of Boston who is one of the great lights of your sect [Christian Science]. But he objects to belong to the sect of Mrs. Whirlpool [Mary Baker Eddy]. So he calls himself a mental healer of metaphysico-chemico-physico-religiosio what not! Yesterday there was a tremendous cyclone which gave a good "treatment" to the tents. The big tent under which they had the lectures had developed so much spirituality, under the "treatment," that it entirely disappeared from mortal gaze, and about two hundred chairs were dancing about the grounds under spiritual ecstasy! Mrs. Figs of Mills company gives a class every morning; and Mrs. Mills is jumping all about the place; they are all in high spirits. I am especially glad for Cora, for they have suffered a good deal last winter and a little hilarity would do her good. You will be astounded with the liberty they enjoy in the camps, but they are very good and pure people there—a little erratic and that is all. I shall be here till Saturday next....

The other night the camp people went to sleep beneath a pine tree under which I sit every morning *à la* Hindu and talk to them. Of course I went with them, and we had a nice night under the stars, sleeping on the lap of mother earth, and I enjoyed every bit of it. I cannot describe to you that night's glories—after a year of brutal life that I have led, to sleep on the ground, to meditate under the tree in the forest! The inn people are more or less well-to-do, and the camp people are healthy, young, *sincere*, and holy men and women. I teach them Shivo'ham, Shivo'ham, and they all repeat it, innocent and pure as they are and brave beyond all bounds. And so I am happy and glorified. Thank God for making me poor, thank God for making these children in the tents poor. The Dudes and Dudines are in the Hotel, but iron-bound nerves and souls of triple steel and spirits of fire are in the camp. If you had seen them yesterday, when the rain was falling in torrents and the cyclone was overturning everything, hanging by their tent strings to keep them from being blown down, and standing on the majesty of their souls—these brave ones—it would have done your hearts good. I will go a hundred miles to see the like of them. Lord bless them! I hope you are enjoying your nice village life. Never be anxious for a moment. I will be taken care of, and if not, I will know my time has come and shall pass out.

"Sweet One! Many people offer to You many things, I am poor—but I have the body, mind, and soul. I give them over to You. Deign to accept, Lord of the Universe, and refuse them not"—so have I given over my life and soul once for all. One thing—they are a dry sort of people here—and as to that very few in the whole world are there that are not. They do not understand "Madhava," the Sweet One. They are either intellectual or go after faith cure, table turning, witchcraft, etc., etc. Nowhere have I heard so much about "love, life, and liberty" as in this country, but nowhere is it less understood. Here God is either a terror or a healing power, vibration, and so forth. Lord bless their souls! And these parrots talk day and night of love and love and love![44]

Greenacre, Maine, 11 August 1894 · I have been all this time in Greenacre. I enjoyed this place very much. They have been all very kind to me. One Chicago lady, Mrs. Pratt of Kenilworth, wanted to give me $500; she became so much interested in me; but I refused. She has made me promise that I would send word to her whenever I need money, which I hope the Lord will never put me in. His help alone is sufficient for me....

I will be in New York next fall. New York is a grand and good place. The New York people have a tenacity of purpose unknown in any other city.[45]

Annisquam, Massachusetts, 20 August 1894 · I want a little quiet, but it is not the will of the Lord, it seems. At Greenacre I had to talk on an average 7 to 8 hours a day—that was rest, if it ever was. But it was of the Lord, and that brings vigour along with it.[46]

Annisquam, 20 August 1894 · I am with the Bagleys once more. They are kind as usual. Professor Wright was not here. But he came day before yesterday and we have very nice time together. Mr. Bradley of Evanston, whom you have met at Evanston, was here. His sister-in-law had me sit for a picture several days and had painted me. I had some very fine boating and one evening overturned the boat and had a good drenching—clothes and all.

I had very very nice time at Greenacre. They were all so earnest and kind people....

From here I think I will go back to New York. Or I may go to Boston to Mrs. Ole Bull. Perhaps you have heard of Mr. Ole Bull, the great violinist of this country. She is his widow. She is a very spiritual lady. She lives in Cambridge and has a fine big parlour made of woodwork brought all the way from India. She wants me to come over to her any time and use her parlour to lecture. Boston of course is the great field for everything, but the Boston people as quickly take hold of anything as give it up; while the New Yorkers are slow, but when they get hold of anything they do it with a mortal grip.

I have kept pretty good health all the time and hope to do in the future. I had no occasion yet to draw on my reserve, yet I am rolling on pretty fair. And I have given up all money-making schemes and will be quite satisfied with a bite and a shed and work on....

Perhaps I did not tell you in my last how I slept and lived and preached under the trees and for a few days at least found myself once more in the atmosphere of heaven.[47]

Annisquam, 23 August 1894 · This public life is such a botheration. I am nearly daft. Where to fly? In India I have become horribly public—crowds will follow me and take my life out.... Every ounce of fame can only be bought at the cost of a pound of peace and holiness. I never thought of that before. I have become entirely disgusted with this blazoning. I am disgusted with myself. Lord will show me the way to peace and purity. Why, Mother, I confess to you: no man can live in an atmosphere of public life, even in religion, without the devil of competition now and then thrusting his head into the serenity of his heart. Those who are trained to preach a doctrine never feel it, for they never knew religion. But those that are after God, and not after the world, feel at once that every bit of name and fame is at the cost of their purity. It is so much gone from that ideal of perfect unselfishness, perfect disregard of gain or name or fame. Lord help me.... I am very much disgusted with myself. Oh, why the world be so that one cannot do anything without putting himself to the front; why cannot one act hidden and unseen and unnoticed? The world has not gone one step beyond idolatry yet. They cannot act from ideas, they cannot be led by ideas. But they want the person, the man. And any man that wants to do something must pay the penalty—no hope. This nonsense of the world. Shiva, Shiva, Shiva.

By the by, I have got such a beautiful edition of Thomas à Kempis. How I love that old monk. He caught a wonderful glimpse of the "behind the veil"—few ever got such. My, that is religion. No humbug of the world. No shilly-shallying, tall talk, conjecture—I presume, I believe, I think. How I would like to go out of this piece of painted humbug they call the beautiful world with Thomas à Kempis—beyond, beyond, which can only be felt, never expressed.

That is religion. Mother, there is God. There all the saints, prophets and incarnations meet. Beyond the Babel of Bibles and Vedas, creeds and crafts, dupes and doctrines—where is all light, all love, where the miasma of this earth can never reach. Ah! who will take me thither?... My soul is groaning now under the hundred sorts of bondage I am placing on it. Whose India? Who cares? Everything is His. What are we? Is He dead? Is He sleeping? He, without whose command a leaf does not fall, a heart does not beat, who is nearer to me than my own self. It is bosh and nonsense—to do good or do bad or do fuzz. We do nothing. We are not. The world is not. He is, He is. Only He is. None else is. He is.

Om, the one without a second. He in me, I in Him. I am like a bit of glass in an ocean of light. I am not, I am not. He is, He is, He is.

Om, the one without a second.[48]

Magnolia, Massachusetts, 28 August 1894 · I have written to India not to bother me with constant letters. Why, when I am travelling in India nobody writes to me. Why should they spend all their superfluous energy in scrawling letters to me in America? My whole life is to be that of a wanderer—here or there or anywhere. I am in no hurry. I had a foolish plan in my head unworthy of a Sannyasin. I have given it up now and mean to take life easy. No indecent hurry.... You must always remember ... that I cannot settle down even at the North Pole, that wander about I must—that is my vow, my religion. So India or North Pole or South Pole—don't care where. Last two years I have been travelling among races whose language even I cannot speak. "I have neither father nor mother nor brothers nor sisters nor friends nor foes, nor home nor country—a traveller in the way of eternity, asking no other help, seeking no other help but God."[49]

Annisquam, Massachusetts, 31 August 1894 · You know the greatest difficulty with me is to keep or even to touch money. It is disgusting and debasing.... I have friends here who take care of all my monetary concerns.... It will be a wonderful relief to me to get rid of horrid money affairs.[50]

Boston, 12 September 1894 · I do not think the Lord will allow his servant to be inflated with vanity at the appreciation of his countrymen. I am glad that they appreciate me—not for my sake, but that I am firmly persuaded that a man is never improved by abuse but by praise, and so with nations. Think how much of abuse has been quite unnecessarily hurled at the head of my devoted, poor country, and for what? They never injured the Christians or their religion or their preachers. They have always been friendly to all. So you see, Mother, every good word a foreign nation says to them has such an amount of power for good in India. The American appreciation of my humble work here has really done a good deal of benefit to them. Send a good word, a good thought—at least to the downtrodden, vilified, poor millions of India instead of abusing them day and night. That is what I beg of every nation. Help them if you can; if you cannot, at least cease from abusing them.[51]

Boston, 13 September 1894 · I have been in this hotel for about a week. I will remain in Boston some time yet. I have plenty of gowns already, in fact, more than I can carry with ease. When I had that drenching in Annisquam, I had on that beautiful black suit you appreciate so much, and I do not think it can be damaged any way; it also has been penetrated with my deep meditations on the Absolute.... I am vagabondising. I was very much amused the other day at reading Abe Hue's description of the vagabond lamas of Tibet—a true picture of our fraternity. He says they are queer people. They come when they will, sit at everybody's table, invitation or no invitation, live where they will, and go where they will. There is not a mountain they have not climbed, not a river they have not crossed, not a nation they do not know, not a language they do not talk. He thinks that God must have put into them a part of that energy which makes the planets go round and round eternally. Today this vagabond lama was seized with a desire of going right along scribbling, and so I walked down and entering a store bought all sorts of writing material and a beautiful portfolio which shuts with a clasp and has even a little wooden inkstand. So far it promises well. Hope it will continue. Last month I had mail enough from India and am greatly delighted with my countrymen at their generous appreciation of my work. Good enough for them. I cannot find anything more to write. Prof. Wright, his wife, and children were as good as ever. Words cannot express my gratitude to them.

Everything so far is not going bad with me except that I had a bad cold. Now I think the fellow is gone. This time I tried Christian Science for insomnia and really found it worked very well.[52]

Boston, 19 September 1894 · I am at present lecturing in several places in Boston. What I want is to get a place where I can sit down and write down my thoughts. I have had enough of speaking; now I want to write. I think I will have to go to New York for it. Mrs. Guernsey was so kind to me, and she is ever willing to help me. I think I will go to her and sit down and write my book.[53]

Boston, 21 September 1894 · I have been continuously travelling from place to place and working incessantly, giving lectures, holding classes, etc. I have not been able to write a line yet for my proposed book. Perhaps I may be able to take it in hand later on. I have made some nice friends here amongst the liberal people, and a few amongst the orthodox. I hope to return soon to India—I have had enough of this country, and especially as too much work is making me nervous. The giving of too many public lectures and constant hurry have brought on this nervousness. I do not care for this busy, meaningless, money-making life. So you see, I will soon return. Of course, there is a growing section with whom I am very popular, and who will like to have me here all the time. But I think I have had enough of newspaper blazoning and humbugging of a public life. I do not care the least for it.

There is no hope for money for our project here. It is useless to hope. No large number of men in any country do good out of mere sympathy.... The Westerners are miserly in comparison to our race. I sincerely believe that the Asians are the most charitable race in the world, only they are very poor.[54]

Boston (?), 25 September 1894 · Here in summer they go to the seaside: I also did the same. They have got almost a mania for boating and yachting. The yacht is a kind of light vessel which everyone, young and old, who has the means, possesses. They set sail in them every day to the sea, and return home, to eat and drink and dance—while music continues day and night. Pianos render it a botheration to stay indoors!

I shall now tell you something of the Hales to whose address you direct my letters. He and his wife are an old couple, having two daughters, two nieces, and a son. The son lives abroad where he earns a living. The daughters live at home. In this country, relationship is through the girls. The son marries and no longer belongs to the family, but the daughter's husband pays frequent visits to his father-in-law's house. They say,

"Son is son till he gets a wife; The daughter is daughter all her life."

All the four are young and not yet married. Marriage is a very troublesome business here. In the first place, one must have a husband after one's heart. Secondly, he must be a moneyed man.... They will probably live unmarried; besides, they are now full of renunciation through my contact and are busy with thoughts of Brahman!

The two daughters are blondes, that is, have golden hair, while the two nieces are brunettes, that is, of dark hair. They know all sorts of occupations. The nieces are not so rich, they conduct a kindergarten school; but the daughters do not earn. Many girls of this country earn their living. Nobody depends upon others. Even millionaires' sons earn their living; but they marry and have separate establishments of their own. The daughters call me brother; and I address their mother as mother. All my things are at their place; and they look after them, wherever I may go. Here the boys go in search of a living while quite young; and the girls are educated in the universities. So you will find that in a meeting there will be ninety-nine percent of girls. The boys are nowhere in comparison with them.

There are a good many spiritualists in this country. The medium is one who induces the spirit. He goes behind a screen; and out of this come ghosts of all sizes and all colours. I have witnessed some cases, but they seemed to be a hoax. I shall test some more before I come to a final conclusion. Many of the spiritualists respect me.

Next comes Christian Science. They form the most influential party, nowadays, figuring everywhere. They are spreading by leaps and bounds, and causing heart-burn to the orthodox. They are Vedantins; I mean, they have picked up a few doctrines of the Advaita and grafted them upon the Bible. And they cure diseases by proclaiming "So'ham So'ham"—"I am He! I am He!"—through strength of mind. They all admire me highly.

Nowadays the orthodox section of this country are crying for help. "Devil worship"* is but a thing of the past. They are mortally afraid of me and exclaim, "What a pest! Thousands of men and women follow him! He is going to root out orthodoxy!" Well, the torch has been applied and the conflagration that has set in through the grace of the Guru will not be put out. In course of time the bigots will have their breath knocked out of them....

The Theosophists have not much power. But they, too, are dead set against the orthodox section.

The Christian Science is exactly like our Kartabhaja sect [a Bengali Vaishnava sect]: Say, "I have no disease," and you are whole; and say, "I am He—So'ham"—and you are quits—be at large. This is a thoroughly materialistic country. The people of this Christian land will recognise religion if only you can cure diseases, work miracles, and open up avenues to money; and they understand little of anything else. But there are honourable exceptions....

---

* The orthodox Christians brand Hindus and people of other religions with this name and look upon them with scorn.

People here have found a new type of man in me. Even the orthodox are at their wit's end. And people are now looking up to me with an eye of reverence. Is there a greater strength than that of Brahmacharya—purity, my boy?... They are good-natured, kind, and truthful. All is right with them, but that enjoyment is their God. It is a country where money flows like a river, with beauty as its ripple and learning its waves, and which rolls in luxury....

They look with veneration upon women, who play a most prominent part in their lives.... Well, I am almost at my wit's end to see the women of this country! They take me to the shops and everywhere, as if I were a child. They do all sorts of work—I cannot do even a sixteenth part of what they do.[55]

Boston (?), 27 September 1894 · One thing I find in the books of my speeches and sayings published in Calcutta. Some of them are printed in such a way as to savour of political views; whereas I am no politician or political agitator. I care only for the Spirit—when that is right everything will be righted by itself.... So you must warn the Calcutta people that no political significance be ever attached falsely to any of my writings or sayings. What nonsense!... I heard that Rev. Kali Charan Banerji in a lecture to Christian missionaries said that I was a political delegate. If it was said publicly, then publicly ask the Babu for me, to write to any of the Calcutta papers and prove it, or else take back his foolish assertion. This is their trick! I have said a few harsh words in honest criticism of Christian governments in general, but that does not mean that I care for, or have any connection with politics or that sort of thing. Those who think it very grand to print extracts from those lectures and want to prove that I am a political preacher, to them I say, "Save me from my friends."

... Tell my friends that a uniform silence is all my answer

to my detractors. If I give them tit for tat, it would bring us down to a level with them. Tell them that truth will take care of itself, and that they are not to fight anybody for me....

This nonsense of public life and newspaper blazoning has disgusted me thoroughly. I long to go back to the Himalayan quiet.[56]

Chicago, September 1894 (?) · I have been travelling all over this country all this time and seeing everything. I have come to this conclusion that there is only one country in the world which understands religion—it is India; that with all their faults the Hindus are head and shoulders above all other nations in morality and spirituality; and that with proper care and attempt and struggle of all her disinterested sons, by combining some of the active and heroic elements of the West with the calm virtues of the Hindus, there will come a type of men far superior to any that have ever been in this world.

I do not know when I come back; but I have seen enough of this country, I think, and so soon will go over to Europe and then to India.[57]

New York, 9 October (?) *1894* [*Swami Vivekananda writes about the Calcutta meeting held in his honour on 5 September 1894*] · Glory unto Jagadamba [Mother of the Universe]! I have gained beyond expectations. The prophet has been honoured and with a *vengeance*. I am weeping like a child at His mercy—he never leaves His servant, sisters. The letter I send you will explain all, and the printed things are coming to the American people. The names there are the very flower of our country. The President was the chief *nobleman* of Calcutta, and the other man Mahesh Chandra Nyayaratna is the principal of the Sanskrit College and the chief Brahmin in all India and recognised by the Government as such. The letter will tell you all. O sisters! What a rogue am I that in the face of such mercies sometimes the faith totters—seeing every moment that I am in His hands. Still the mind sometimes gets despondent. Sister, there is a God—a Father—a *Mother* who never leaves His children, never, never, never. Put uncanny theories aside and becoming children take refuge in Him. I cannot write more—I am weeping like a woman.

Blessed, blessed art Thou, Lord God of my soul![58]

Washington DC, 23 October 1894 · By this time I have become one of their own teachers. They all like me and my teachings.... I travel all over the country from one place to another, as was my habit in India, preaching and teaching. Thousands and thousands have listened to me and taken my ideas in a very kindly spirit. It is the most expensive country, but the Lord provides for me everywhere I go.[59]

Washington DC, November 1894 · I have been very well treated here and am doing very well. Nothing extraordinary in the meantime except I got vexed at getting loads of newspapers from India; so after sending a cart-load to Mother Church and another to Mrs. Guernsey, I had to write them to stop sending their newspapers. I have had "boom" enough in India. Alasinga writes that every village all over the country now has heard of me. Well, the old peace is gone for ever and no rest anywhere from heretofore. These newspapers of India will be my death, I am sure. They will now talk what I ate on such and such a date and how I sneezed. Lord bless them, it was all my foolery. I really came here to raise a little money secretly and go over but was caught in the trap and now no more of a reserved life.[60]

U.S.A., 1894 · Last winter I travelled a good deal in this country although the weather was very severe. I thought it would be dreadful, but I did not find it so after all.[61]

New York, 19 November 1894 · Nothing else is necessary but these—love, sincerity, and patience. What is life but growth, i.e. expansion, i.e. love? Therefore all love is life, it is the only law of life; all selfishness is death, and this is true here or hereafter. It is life to do good, it is death not to do good to others. Ninety percent of human brutes you see are dead, are ghosts—for none lives, my boys, but he who loves. Feel, my children, feel; feel for the poor, the ignorant, the downtrodden; feel till the heart stops and the brain reels and you think you will go mad—then pour the soul out at the feet of the Lord, and then will come power, help, and indomitable energy.

Struggle, struggle, was my motto for the last ten years. Struggle, still say I. When it was all dark, I used to say, struggle; when light is breaking in, I still say, struggle. Be not afraid, my children. Look not up in that attitude of fear towards that infinite starry vault as if it would crush you. Wait! In a few hours more, the whole of it will be under your feet. Wait, money does not pay, nor name; fame does not pay, nor learning. It is love that pays; it is character that cleaves its way through adamantine walls of difficulties....

I have depended always on the Lord, always on Truth broad as the light of day. Let me not die with stains on my conscience for having played Jesuitism to get up name or fame, or even to do good.[62]

Cambridge, Massachusetts, 6 December 1894 · I have sent part of my money to India and intend sending nearly the whole of it very soon. Only, I will keep enough for the passage back.[63]

Cambridge, 26 December 1894 · In reference to me every now and then attacks are made in missionary papers (so I hear), but I never care to see them.[64]

Chicago, 1894 · Through the Lord's will, the desire for name and fame has not yet crept into my heart, and I dare say never will. I am an instrument, and He is the operator. Through this instrument He is rousing the religious instinct in thousands of hearts in this far-off country. Thousands of men and women here love and revere me.... I am amazed at His grace. Whichever town I visit, it is in an uproar. They have named me "the cyclonic Hindu." Remember, it is His will—I am a voice without a form.[65]

Chicago, 3 January 1895 · At present I find I have a mission in this country also.... I do not know when I shall go over to India. I obey the leading of the Lord. I am in His hands.[66]

Chicago, 3 January 1895 · I lectured at Brooklyn last Sunday. Mrs. Higgins gave a little reception the evening I arrived, and some of the prominent members of the Ethical Society including Dr. Janes were there. Some of them thought that such Oriental religious subjects will not interest the Brooklyn public.

But the lecture, through the blessings of the Lord, proved a tremendous success. About 800 of the elite of Brooklyn were present, and the very gentlemen who thought it would not prove a success are trying for organising a series in Brooklyn....

I am trying to get a new gown here. The old gown is here, but it is so shrunken by constant washings that it is unfit to wear in public. I am almost confident of finding the exact thing in Chicago.[67]

Chicago, 11 January 1895 · I have been running all the time between Boston and New York, two great centres of this country, of which Boston may be called the brain, and New York, the purse. In both, my success is more than ordinary.

I am indifferent to the newspaper reports, and you must not expect me to send any of them to you. A little boom was necessary to begin work....

I want to teach the truth; I do not care whether here or elsewhere....

I shall work incessantly until I die, and even after death I shall work for the good of the world....

Thousands of the best men do care for me ... I am slowly exercising an influence in this land greater than all the newspaper blazoning of me can do. The orthodox feel it, but they cannot help it. It is the force of character, of purity, and of truth—of personality. So long as I have these things, you can feel easy; no one will be able to injure a hair of my head. If they try, they will fail, saith the Lord.... The Lord is giving me a deeper and deeper insight every day....

I do not care whether they are Hindus or Mohammedans or Christians, but those that love the Lord will always command my service.

... I like to work on calmly and silently, and the Lord is always with me.[68]

Chicago, 12 January 1895 · Now know once and for all that I do not care for name or fame, or any humbug of that type. I want to preach my ideas for the good of the world.... My life is more precious than spending it in getting the admiration of the world. I have no time for such foolery.[69]

New York, 24 January 1895 · My last lecture was not very much appreciated by the *men* but awfully so by *vemen* [women]. You know this Brooklyn is the centre of anti-women's rights movements; and when I told them that women deserve and are fit for everything, they did not like it of course. Never mind, the women were in ecstasies.[70]

New York, 1 February 1895 · I just received your beautiful note.... Well, sometimes it is a good discipline to be forced to work for work's sake, even to the length of not being allowed to enjoy the fruits of one's labour.... I am very glad of your criticisms and am not sorry at all. The other day at Miss Thursby's I had an excited argument with a Presbyterian gentleman, who, as usual, got very hot, angry, and abusive. However, I was afterwards severely reprimanded by Mrs. Bull for this, as such things hinder my work. So, it seems, is your opinion.

I am glad you write about it just now, because I have been giving a good deal of thought to it. In the first place, I am not at all sorry for these things—perhaps that may disgust you—it may. I know full well how good it is for one's worldly prospects to be *sweet*. I do everything to be *sweet*, but when it comes to a horrible compromise with the truth within, then I stop. I do not believe in *humility*. I believe in *Samadarshitva*—same state of mind with regard to all. The duty of the ordinary man is to obey the commands of his "God," society; but the children of light never do so. This is an eternal law. One accommodates himself to surroundings and social opinion and gets all good things from society, the giver of all good to such. The other stands alone and draws society up towards him. The accommodating man finds a path of roses; the non-accommodating, one of thorns. But the worshippers of "Vox populi" go to annihilation in a moment; the children of truth *live for ever*.

I will compare truth to a corrosive substance of infinite power. It burns its way in wherever it falls—in soft substance at once, hard granite slowly, but it must. What is writ is writ. I am so, so sorry, Sister, that I cannot make myself sweet and accommodating to every black falsehood. But I cannot. I have suffered for it all my life. But I cannot. I have essayed and essayed. But I cannot. At last I have given it up. The Lord is great. He will not allow me to become a hypocrite. Now let what is in come out. I have not found a way that will please all, and I cannot but be what I am, true to my own self. "Youth and beauty vanish, life and wealth vanish, name and fame vanish, even the mountains crumble into dust. Friendship and love vanish. Truth alone abides." God of Truth, be Thou alone my guide! I am too old to change now into milk and honey. Allow me to remain as I am. "Without fear—without shopkeeping, caring neither for friend nor foe, do thou hold on to Truth, Sannyasin, and from this moment give up this world and the next and all that are to come—their enjoyments and their vanities. Truth, be thou alone my guide." I have no desire for wealth or name or fame or enjoyments, Sister—they are dust unto me. I wanted to help my brethren. I have not the *tact to earn money*, bless the Lord. What reason is there for me to conform to the vagaries of the world around me and not obey the voice of Truth within? The mind is still weak, Sister, it sometimes mechanically clutches at earthly help. But I am not afraid. Fear is the greatest sin my religion teaches.

The last fight with the Presbyterian priest and the long fight afterwards with Mrs. Bull showed me in a clear light what Manu says to the Sannyasin, "Live alone, walk alone." All friendship, all love, is only limitation. There never was a friendship, especially of women, which was not exacting. O great sages! You were right. One cannot serve the God of Truth who leans upon somebody. Be still, my soul! Be alone! and the Lord is with you. Life is nothing! Death is a delusion! All this is not, God alone is! Fear not, my soul! Be alone. Sister, the way is long, the time is short, evening is approaching. I have to go home soon. I have no time to give my manners a finish. I cannot find time to deliver my message. You are good, you are so kind, I will do anything for you;

and do not be angry, I see you all are mere children.

Dream no more! Oh, dream no more, my soul! In one word, I have a message to give, I have no time to be sweet to the world, and every attempt at sweetness makes me a hypocrite. I will die a thousand deaths rather than lead a jelly-fish existence and yield to every requirement of this foolish world, no matter whether it be my own country or a foreign country. You are mistaken, utterly mistaken, if you think I have a *work*, as Mrs. Bull thinks; I have no *work* under or beyond the sun. I have a message, and I will give it after my own fashion. I will neither Hinduise my message, nor Christianise it, nor make it any "ise" in the world. I will only my-ise it, and that is all. *Liberty*, Mukti, is all my religion, and everything that tries to curb it, I will avoid by fight or flight. Pooh! I try to pacify the priests!! Sister, do not take this amiss. But you are babies and babies must submit to be taught. You have not yet drunk of that fountain which makes "reason unreason, mortal immortal, this world a zero, and of man a God." Come out if you can of this network of foolishness they call this *world*. Then I will call you indeed brave and free. If you cannot, cheer those that dare dash this false God, society, to the ground and trample on its unmitigated hypocrisy; if you cannot cheer them, pray, be silent, but do not try to drag them down again into the mire with such false nonsense as *compromise* and becoming nice and sweet.

I hate this world, this dream, this horrible nightmare, with its churches and chicaneries, its books and black-guardisms, its fair faces and false hearts, its howling righteousness on the surface and utter hollowness beneath, and, above all, its sanctified shopkeeping. What! measure my soul according to what the bond-slaves of the world say?—pooh! Sister, you do not know the Sannyasin. "He stands on the heads of the Vedas!" say the Vedas, because he is free from churches and sects and religions and prophets and books and all of that ilk! Missionary or no missionary, let them howl and attack me with all they can, I take them as Bhartrihari says, "Go thou thy ways, Sannyasin! Some will say, 'Who is this mad man?' Others, 'Who is this Chandala?' Others will know thee to be a sage. Be glad at the prattle of the worldlings." But when they attack, know that, "The elephant passing through the marketplace is always beset by curs, but he cares not. He goes straight on *his own way*. So it is always, when a great soul appears there will be numbers to bark after him." [Tulasidasa.]

I am living with Landsberg at 54 W. 33rd Street. He is a brave and noble soul, Lord bless him. Sometimes I go to the Guernseys' to sleep.[71]

New York, 9 February 1895 · In this dire winter I have travelled across mountains and over snows at dead of night and collected a little fund; and I shall have peace of mind when a plot is secured for Mother [Sri Sarada Devi].[72]

New York, 14 February 1895 · According to Manu, collecting funds even for a good work is not good for a Sannyasin, and I have begun to feel that the old sages were right. "Hope is the greatest misery, despair is the greatest happiness." It appears like a hallucination. I am getting out of them. I was in these childish ideas of doing this and doing that.

"Give up all desire and be at peace. Have neither friends nor foes, and live alone. Thus shall we travel having neither friends nor foes, neither pleasure nor pain, neither desire nor jealousy, injuring no creatures, being the cause of injury to no creatures—from mountain to mountain, from village to village, preaching the name of the Lord."

"Seek no help from high or low, from above or below. Desire nothing—and look upon this vanishing panorama as a witness and let it pass."

Perhaps these mad desires were necessary to bring me over to this country. And I thank the Lord for the experience.

I am very happy now. Between Mr. Landsberg and me, we cook some rice and lentils or barley and quietly eat it, and write something or read or receive visits from poor people who want to learn something, and thus I feel I am more a Sannyasin now than I ever was in America.

"In wealth is the fear of poverty, in knowledge the fear of ignorance, in beauty the fear of age, in fame the fear of backbiters, in success the fear of jealousy, even in body is the fear of death. Everything in this earth is fraught with fear. He alone is fearless who has given up everything." [Bhartrihari, *Vairāgya-śaṭakam* 31]

I went to see Miss Corbin the other day, and Miss Farmer and Miss Thursby were also there. We had a nice half-hour and she wants me to hold some classes in her home from next Sunday.

I am no more seeking for these things. If they come, the Lord be blessed, if not, blessed more be He.[73]

New York, 18 February 1895 · I am doing very well. Only some of these big dinners kept me late, and I returned home at 2 o'clock in the morning several days. Tonight I am going to one of these. This will be the last of its kind. So much keeping up the night is not good for me. Every day from 11 to 1 o'clock I have classes in my rooms and I talk [to] them till they [grow] tired. The Brooklyn course ended yesterday. Another lecture I have there next Monday.

Bean soup and rice or barley is now my general diet. I am faring well. Financially I am making the ends meet and nothing more because I do not charge anything for the classes I have in my rooms. And the public lectures have to go through so many hands. I have a good many lectures planned ahead in New York, which I hope to deliver by and by....

Between swells and Delmonico and Waldorf dinners, my health was going to be injured. So I quickly turned a thorough vegetarian to avoid all invitations. The rich are really the salt of this world—they are neither food nor drink.[74]

I have myself been told by some of the best Western scientific minds of the day, how wonderfully rational the conclusions of the Vedanta are. I know one of them personally who scarcely has time to eat his meal or go out of his laboratory, but who yet would stand by the hour to attend my lectures on the Vedanta; for, as he expresses it, they are so scientific, they so exactly harmonise with the aspirations of the age and with the conclusions to which modern science is coming at the present time.[75]

While I was in America I had certain wonderful powers developed in me. By looking into people's eyes I could fathom in a trice the contents of their minds. The workings of everybody's mind would be patent to me, like a fruit on the palm of one's hand. To some I used to give out these things, and of those to whom I communicated these, many would become my disciples; whereas those who came to mix with me with some ulterior motive would not, on coming across this power of mine, even venture into my presence any more.

When I began lecturing in Chicago and other cities, I had to deliver every week some twelve or fifteen or even more lectures at times. This excessive strain on the body and mind would exhaust me to a degree. I seemed to run short of subjects for lectures and was anxious where to find new topics for the morrow's lecture. New thoughts seemed altogether scarce. One day, after the lecture, I lay thinking of what means to adopt next. The thought induced a sort of slumber, and in that state I heard as if somebody standing by me was lecturing—many new ideas and new veins of thought, which I had scarcely heard or thought of in my life. On awaking I remembered them and reproduced them in my lecture. I cannot enumerate how often this phenomenon took place. Many, many days did I hear such lectures while lying in bed. Sometimes the lecture would be delivered in such a loud voice that the inmates of adjacent rooms would hear the sound and ask me the next day, "With whom, Swamiji, were you talking so loudly last night?" I used to avoid the question somehow. Ah, it was a wonderful phenomenon.[76]

When people began to honour me, then the Padris were after me. They spread many slanders about me by publishing them in the newspapers. Many asked me to contradict these slanders. But I never took the slightest notice of them. It is my firm conviction that no great work is accomplished in this world by low cunning; so without paying any heed to these vile slanders, I used to work steadily at my mission. The upshot I used to find was that often my slanderers, feeling repentant afterwards, would surrender to me and offer apologies, by themselves contradicting the slanders in the papers. Sometimes it so happened that learning that I had been invited to a certain house, somebody would communicate those slanders to my host, who hearing them, would leave home, locking his door. When I went there to attend the invitation, I found it was deserted and nobody was there. Again a few days afterwards, they themselves, learning the truth, would feel sorry for their previous conduct and come to offer themselves as disciples. The fact is ... this whole world is full of mean ways of worldliness. But men of real moral courage and discrimination are never deceived by these. Let the world say what it chooses, I shall tread the path of duty—know this to be the line of action for a hero. Otherwise, if one has to attend day and night to what this man says or that man writes, no great work is achieved in this world.... "Let those who are versed in the ethical codes praise or blame, let Lakshmi, the goddess of Fortune, come or go wherever she wisheth, let death overtake him today or after a century, the wise man never swerves from the path of rectitude." [Bhartrihari's *Nitisataka*] [77]

I stand for truth. Truth will never ally itself with falsehood. Even if all the world should be against me, Truth must prevail in the end.[78]

Missionaries and others could not do much against me in this country [America]. Through the Lord's grace the people here like me greatly and are not to be tricked by the opinions of any particular class. They appreciate my ideas ... [79]

When I was in America, I heard once the complaint made that I was preaching too much of Advaita, and too little of dualism. Ay, I know what grandeur, what oceans of love, what infinite, ecstatic blessings and joy there are in the dualistic love-theories of worship and religion. I know it all. But this is not the time with us to weep even in joy; we have had weeping enough; no more is this the time for us to become soft. This softness has been with us till we have become like masses of cotton and are dead. What our country now wants are muscles of iron and nerves of steel, gigantic wills which nothing can resist, which can penetrate into the mysteries and the secrets of the universe, and will accomplish their purpose in any fashion even if it meant going down to the bottom of the ocean and meeting death face to face. That is what we want, and that can only be created, established, and strengthened by understanding and realising the ideal of the Advaita, that ideal of the oneness of all.... To preach the Advaita aspect of the Vedanta is necessary to rouse up the hearts of men, to show them the glory of their souls. It is, therefore, that I preach this Advaita; and I do so not as a sectarian, but upon universal and widely acceptable grounds.[80]

When I was a boy I thought that fanaticism was a great element in work, but now, as I grow older, I find out that it is not.... My experience comes to this, that it is rather wise to avoid all sorts of fanatical reforms.[81]

To make a man take up everything and believe it, would be to make him a lunatic. I once had a book sent me, which said I must believe everything told in it. It said there was no soul, but that there were gods and goddesses in heaven, and a thread of light going from each of our heads to heaven! How did the writer know all these things? She had been inspired, and wanted me to believe it too; and because I refused, she said, "You must be a very bad man; there is no hope for you!" This is fanaticism.[82]

No, I do not believe in the occult. If a thing be unreal, it is not. What is unreal does not exist. Strange things are natural phenomena. I know them to be matters of science. Then they are not occult to me. I do not believe in occult societies. They do no good, and can never do good.[83]

New York, 27 March 1895 · This is a wonderful country for cheating, and 99.9 per cent have some *motive* in the background to take advantage of others. If anyone just but closes his eyes for a moment, he is *gone*!!... I have been so well handled by the people here that I look round me for hours before I take a step....

Mrs. Bull has been greatly benefited by [Mrs. Adams's] lessons. I also took a few, but no use; the ever increasing load in front does not allow me to bend forward as Mrs. Adams wants it. If I try to bend forward in walking, the centre of gravity comes to the surface of the stomach, and so I go cutting front somersaults....

My classes are full of women.... Life goes on the same old ruts. Sometimes I get disgusted with eternal lecturings and talkings, want to be silent for days and days.[84]

New York, 11 April 1895 · I am going away to the country tomorrow to see Mr. Leggett for a few days. A little fresh air will do me good, I hope.

I have given up the project of removing from this house just now, as it will be too expensive, and moreover it is not advisable to change just now. I am working it up slowly....

[Miss Hamlin] wants me to be introduced to the "right kind of people." This is the second edition of the "Hold yourself steady" business, I am afraid. The only "right sort of people" are those whom the Lord sends—that is what I understand in my life's experience. They alone can and will help me. As for the rest, Lord help them in a mass and save me from them.

Every one of my friends thought it would end in nothing, this my getting up quarters all by myself, and that no *ladies would ever come here.* Miss Hamlin especially thought that "she" or "her right sort of people" were *way up* from such things as to go and listen to a man who lives by himself in a poor lodging. But the "right kind" came for all that, day and night, and she too. Lord! how hard it is for man to believe in Thee and Thy mercies! Shiva! Shiva! Where is the right kind and where is the bad, mother? It is all *He*! In the tiger and in the lamb, in the saint and sinner all *He*! In Him I have taken my refuge, body, soul, and Atman. Will He leave me now after carrying me in His arms all my life? Not a drop will be in the ocean, not a twig in the deepest forest, not a crumb in the house of the god of wealth, if the Lord is not merciful. Streams will be in the desert and the beggar will have plenty, if He wills it. He seeth the sparrow's fall. Are these but words, mother, or literal, actual life?

Truce to this "right sort of presentation." Thou art my right, Thou my wrong, my Shiva. Lord, since a child I have taken refuge in Thee. Thou wilt be with me in the tropics or at the poles, on the tops of mountains or in the depth of oceans. My stay—my guide in life—my refuge—my friend—my teacher—my God—my real Self, Thou wilt never leave me, *never*. I know it for sure. Sometimes I become weak, being alone and struggling against odds, my God; and I think of human help. Save Thou me for ever from these weaknesses, and may I never, never seek for help from any being but Thee. If a man puts his trust in another good man, he is never betrayed, never forsaken. Wilt Thou forsake me, Father of all good, Thou who knowest that *all* my life I am Thy servant and Thine alone? Wilt Thou give me over to be played upon by others, or dragged down by evil?

He will never leave me, I am sure, mother.[85]

New York, 23 April 1895 · I have just arrived home. The trip did me good, and I enjoyed the country and the hills, and especially Mr. Leggett's country-house in New York State. Poor Landsberg has gone from this house. Neither has he left one his address. May the Lord bless Landsberg wherever he goes! He is one of the few sincere souls I have had the privilege in this life to come across.

All is for good. All conjunctions are for subsequent disjunction. I hope I shall be perfectly able to work alone. The less help from men, the more from the Lord! Just now I received a letter from an Englishman in London who had lived in India in the Himalayas with two of my brethren. He asks me to come to London.[86]

New York, 24 April 1895 · I am going on pretty nearly in the same old fashion. Talking when I can and silent when forced to be. I do not know whether I will go to Greenacre this summer. I saw Miss Farmer the other day. She was in a hurry to go away, so I had but very little talk with her. She is a noble, noble lady....

Landsberg has gone away to live in some other place, so I am left alone. I am living mostly on nuts and fruits and milk, and find it very nice and healthy too. I hope to lose about 30 to 40 lbs. this summer. That will be all right for my size. I am afraid I have forgotten all about Mrs. Adams's lessons in walking. I will have to renew them when she comes again to N.Y....

This year I could hardly keep my head up, and I did not go about lecturing. The three great commentaries on the Vedanta philosophy belonging to the three great sects of dualists, qualified dualists, and monists are being sent to me from India. Hope they will arrive safe. Then I will have an intellectual feast indeed. I intend to write a book this summer on the Vedanta philosophy. This world will always be a mixture of good and evil, of happiness and misery; this wheel will ever go up and come down; dissolution and resolution is the inevitable law. Blessed are those who struggle to go beyond.[87]

New York, 24 April 1895 · I am perfectly aware that although some truth underlies the mass of mystical thought which has burst upon the Western world of late, it is for the most part full of motives, unworthy, or insane. For this reason, I have never had anything to do with these phases of religion, either in India or elsewhere, and mystics as a class are not very favourable to me....

I quite agree with you that only the Advaita philosophy can save mankind, whether in East or West, from "devil worship" and kindred superstitions, giving tone and strength to the very nature of man. India herself requires this, quite as much or even more than the West. Yet it is hard uphill work, for we have first to create a taste, then teach, and lastly proceed to build up the whole fabric.

Perfect sincerity, holiness, gigantic intellect, and an all-conquering will. Let only a handful of men work with these, and the whole world will be revolutionised. I did a good deal of platform work in this country last year, and received plenty of applause, but found that I was only working for myself. It is the patient upbuilding of character, the intense struggle to realise the truth, which alone will tell in the future of humanity. So this year I am hoping to work along this line—training up to practical Advaita realisation a small band of men and women. I do not know how far I shall succeed.... I agree perfectly as to your idea of a magazine. But I have no business capacity at all to do these things. I can teach and preach, and sometimes write. But I have intense faith in Truth. The Lord will send help and hands to work with me. Only let me be perfectly pure, perfectly sincere, and perfectly unselfish.[88]

New York, 25 April 1895 · I cannot go to Greenacre now; I have arranged to go to the Thousand Islands, wherever that may be. There is a cottage belonging to Miss Dutcher, one of my students, and a few of us will be there in rest and peace and seclusion. I want to manufacture a few "Yogis" out of the materials of the classes, and a busy farm like Greenacre is the last place for that, while the other is quite out of the way, and none of the curiosity-seekers will dare go there.

I am very glad that Miss Hamlin took down the names of the 130 persons who come to the Jnana-Yoga class. There are 50 more who come to the Wednesday Yoga class and about 50 more to the Monday class. Mr. Landsberg had all the names;

and they will come anyhow, names or no names.... If they do not, others will, and so it will go on—the Lord be praised.

Taking down names and giving notices is a big task, no doubt, and I am very thankful to both of them for doing that for me. But I am thoroughly persuaded that it is laziness on my part, and therefore immoral, to depend on others, and always evil comes out of laziness. So henceforth I will do it all myself.... However, I will be only too glad to take in any one of Miss Hamlin's "right sort of persons," but unfortunately for me, not one such has as yet turned up. It is the duty of the teacher always to turn the "right sort" out of the most "unrighteous sort" of persons. After all, though I am very, very grateful to the young lady, Miss Hamlin, for the great hope and encouragement she gave me of introducing me to the "right sort of New Yorkers" and for the practical help she has given me, I think I had better do my little work with my own hands....

I am only glad that you [Mrs. Ole Bull] have such a great opinion about Miss Hamlin. I for one am glad to know that you will help her, for she requires it. But, Mother, through the mercy of Ramakrishna, my instinct "sizes up" almost infallibly a human face as soon as I see it, and the result is this: you may do anything you please with my affairs, I will not even murmur;—I will be only too glad to take Miss Farmer's advice, in spite of ghosts and spooks. Behind the spooks I see a heart of immense love, only covered with a thin film of laudable ambition—even that is bound to vanish in a few years. Even I will allow Landsberg to "monkey" with my affairs from time to time; but here I put a full stop. Help from any other persons besides these frightens me. That is all I can say. Not only for the help you have given me, but from my instinct (or, as I call it, inspiration of my Master), I regard you as my mother and will always abide by any advice you may have for me—but only personally. When you select a medium, I will beg leave to exercise my choice. That is all.[89]

New York, 5 May 1895 · What I expected has come. I always thought that although Prof. Max Müller in all his writings on the Hindu religion adds in the last a derogatory remark, he must see the whole truth in the long run. As soon as you can, get a copy of his last book *Vedantism*; there you will find him swallowing the whole of it—reincarnation and all....

Many points you will find smack of my paper in Chicago.

I am glad now the old man has seen the truth, because that is the only way to have religion in the face of modern research and science.[90]

New York, 6 May 1895 · I did not come to seek name and fame; it was forced upon me. I am the one man who dared defend his country, and I have given them such ideas as they never expected from a Hindu. There are many who are against me, but I will never be a coward ...

I have a firm footing in New York, the very centre of American life, and so my work will go on. I am taking several of my disciples to a summer retreat to finish their training in Yoga and Bhakti and Jnana, and then they will be able to help carry the work on....

I am to create a new order of humanity here who are sincere believers in God and care nothing for the world.[91]

New York, May 1895 · My pupils have come round me with help, and the classes will go on nicely now no doubt.

I was so glad at it because teaching has become a part of my life, as necessary to my life as eating or breathing.[92]

New York, 16 May 1895 · I do not know whether I will be able to come over to Chicago or not. I am trying to get a free pass;

in case I succeed I will come, else not. Financially this winter's work was no success at all—I could barely keep myself up—but spiritually very great.[93]

New York, 28 May 1895 · I have succeeded in doing something in this country at last.[94]

Percy, New Hampshire, 7 June 1895 · I am here at last with Mr. Leggett. This is one of the most beautiful spots I have ever seen. Imagine a lake, surrounded with hills covered with a huge forest, with nobody but ourselves. So lovely, so quiet, so restful! And you may imagine how glad I am to be here after the bustle of cities.

It gives me a new lease of life to be here. I go into the forest alone and read my Gita and am quite happy. I will leave this place in about ten days and go to the Thousand Island Park. I will meditate by the hour there and be all alone to myself. The very idea is ennobling.[95]

Thousand Island Park, New York, 18 June 1895 · We are having a nice time here except, as an old Hindu proverb says, that "a pestle must pound even if it goes to heaven." I have to work hard all the same.[96]

Thousand Island Park, 26 June 1895 · [In] the articles by Prof. Max Müller on the "Immortality of the Soul"... the old man has taken in Vedanta, bones and all, and has boldly come out....

I am asked again and again ... in the letters from India, to go over. They are getting desperate. Now if I go to Europe, I will go as the guest of Mr. Francis Leggett of N.Y. He will travel all over Germany, England, France, and Switzerland for six weeks. From there I shall go to India, or I may return to America. I have a seed planted here and wish it to grow. This winter's work in N.Y. was splendid, and it may die if I suddenly go over to India, so I am not sure about going to India soon.

Nothing noticeable has happened during this visit to the Thousand Islands. The scenery is very beautiful and I have some of my friends here with me to talk about God and soul ad libitum. I am eating fruits and drinking milk and so forth, and studying huge Sanskrit books on Vedanta which they have kindly sent me from India....

My reply to Madras ... has produced a tremendous effect there. A late speech by the President of the Madras Christian College, Mr. Miller, embodies a large amount of my ideas and declares that the West is in need of Hindu ideas of God and man and calls upon the young men to go and preach to the West. This has created quite a furore of course amongst the Missions....

Travelling is the best thing in life. I am afraid I shall die if made to stick to one place for a long time. Nothing like a nomadic life!

The more the shades around deepen, the more the ends approach and the more one understands the true meaning of life, that it is a dream; and we begin to understand the failure of everyone to grasp it, for they only attempted to get meaning out of the meaningless. To get reality out of a dream is boyish enthusiasm. "Everything is evanescent, everything is changeful"—knowing this, the sage gives up both pleasure and pain and becomes a witness of this panorama (the universe) without attaching himself to anything.[97]

Thousand Island Park, 28 (?) June 1895 · I am enjoying this place immensely. Very little eating and [a] good deal of thinking and talking and study. A wonderful calmness is coming over my soul. Every day I feel I have no duty to do; I am always in eternal rest and peace. It is He that works. We are only the instruments. Blessed be His name! The threefold bondage of lust and gold and fame is, as it were, fallen from me for the time being, and once more, even here, I feel what sometimes I felt in India, "From me all difference has fallen, all right or wrong, all delusion and ignorance has vanished, I am walking in the path beyond the qualities." What law I obey, what disobey? From that height the universe looks like a mud-puddle. Hari Om Tat Sat. He exists; nothing else does. I in Thee and Thou in me. Be Thou Lord my eternal refuge! Peace, Peace, Peace![98]

Thousand Island Park, 9 July 1895 · I am ... a man of dogged perseverance. I have planted a seed in this country; it is already a plant, and I expect it to be a tree very soon. I have got a few hundred followers. I shall make several Sannyasins, and then I go to India, leaving the work to them. The more the Christian priests oppose me, the more I am determined to leave a permanent mark on their country.... I have already some friends in London. I am going there by the end of August.... Each work has to pass through these stages—ridicule, opposition, and then acceptance. Each man who thinks ahead of his time is sure to be misunderstood. So opposition and persecution are welcome, only I have to be steady and pure and must have immense faith in God, and all these will vanish.[99]

Thousand Island Park, 30 July 1895 · Oh, Mother, my heart is so, so sad. The letters bring the news of the death of Dewanji. Haridas Viharidas has left the body. He was as a father to me. Poor man, he was the last five years seeking the retirement from business life, and at last he got it but could not enjoy it long. I pray that he may never come back again to this dirty hole they call the Earth. Neither may he be born in heaven or any other horrid place. May he never again wear a body—good or bad, thick or thin. What a humbug and illusion this world is, Mother, what a mockery this life. I pray constantly that all mankind will come to know the reality, i.e. God, and this "Shop" here be closed for ever. My heart is too full to write more.[100]

Thousand Island Park, August (?) 1895 · I have done my duty to my people fairly well. Now for the world that gave me this body—the country that gave me the ideas, the humanity which allows me to be one of them!

The older I grow, the more I see behind the idea of the Hindus that man is the greatest of all beings.[101]

New York, August 1895 · I have done a good deal of work this year and hope to do a good deal more in the next. Don't bother about the missionaries. It is quite natural that they should cry. Who does not when his bread is dwindling away? The missionary funds have got a big gap the last two years, and it is on the increase. However, I wish the missionaries all success.... My ideas are going to work in the West better than in India.... I believe in truth, the Lord sends me workers by the scores wherever I go ... they are ready to give up their lives for their Guru. Truth is my God, the universe my country. I do not believe in duty. Duty is the curse of the Samsari [householder], not for the Sannyasin. Duty is humbug. I am free, my bonds are cut; what care I where this body goes or does not go?... I have a truth to teach, I, the child of God. And He that gave me the truth will send me fellow workers from the earth's bravest and best.[102]

New York, August 1895 · I am going to Paris first with a friend and start for Europe on the 17th of August. I will however remain in Paris only a week to see my friend married, and then I go over to London....

I have many strong friends here, but unfortunately they are

most of them poor. So the work here must be slow. Moreover it requires a few months more of work in New York to carry it to some visible shape: as such I will have to return to New York early this winter, and in summer I will return to London again. So far as I see now I can stay only a few weeks in London. But if the Lord wills, that small time may prove to be the beginning of great things. From Paris I will inform you by wire when I arrive in England.

Some Theosophists came to my classes in New York, but as soon as human beings perceive the glory of the Vedanta, all abracadabras fall off of themselves. This has been my uniform experience. Whenever mankind attains a higher vision, the lower vision disappears of itself. Multitude counts for nothing. A few heart-whole, sincere, and energetic men can do more in a year than a mob in a century. If there is heat in one body, then those others that come near it must catch it. This is the law. So success is ours, so long as we keep up the heat, the spirit of truth, sincerity, and love. My own life has been a very chequered one, but I have always found the eternal words verified: "Truth alone triumphs, not untruth. Through truth alone lies the way to God."[103]

New York, 9 August 1895 · The names of those who will wish to injure us will be legion. But is not that the surest sign of our having the truth? The more I have been opposed, the more my energy has always found expression. I have been driven and worshipped by princes. I have been slandered by priests and laymen alike. But what of it? Bless them all! They are my very Self, and have they not helped me by acting as a spring-board from which my energy could take higher and higher flights?... I have discovered one great secret—I have nothing to fear from *talkers* of religion. And the great ones who realise—they become enemies to none! Let talkers talk! They know no better! Let them have their fill of name and fame and money and woman. Hold we on to realisation, to being Brahman, to becoming Brahman. Let us hold on to truth unto death, and from life to life. Let us not pay the least attention to what others say, and if, after a lifetime's effort, one soul, only one, can break the fetters of the world and be free, we have done our work. Hari Om!... One word more. Doubtless I do love India. But every day my sight grows clearer. What is India, or England, or America to us? We are the servants of that God who by the ignorant is called MAN.[104]

Paris, 9 September 1895 · If the people in India want me to keep strictly to my Hindu diet, please tell them to send me a cook and money enough to keep him. This silly bossism without a mite of real help makes me laugh. On the other hand, if the missionaries tell you that I have ever broken the two great vows of the Sannyasin—chastity and poverty—tell them that they are big liars.[105]

In England

No one ever landed on English soil with more hatred in his heart for a race than I did for the English ... but the more I lived among them and saw how the machine was working—the English national life—and mixed with them, I found where the heartbeat of the nation was, and the more I loved them.[106]

London, September 1895 · I arrived safe in London, found my friend, and am all right in his home. It is beautiful. His wife is surely an angel, and his life is full of India. He has been years there—mixing with the Sannyasins, eating their food, etc., etc.; so you see I am very happy. I found already several retired Generals from India; they were very civil and polite to me.... Nobody even stares at me in the street.

I am very much more at home here than anywhere out of India. The English people know us, we know them. The standard of education and civilisation is very high here—that makes a great change, so does the education of many generations....

My friend being a Sanskrit scholar, we are busy working on the great commentaries of Shankara etc. Nothing but philosophy and religion here.[107]

It is taught here in the West that society began eighteen hundred years ago, with the New Testament. Before that there was no society. That may be true with regard to the West, but it is not true as regards the whole world. Often, while I was lecturing in London, a very intellectual and intelligent friend of mine would argue with me, and one day after using all his weapons against me, he suddenly exclaimed, "But why did not your Rishis come to England to teach us?" I replied, "Because there was no England to come to. Would they preach to the forests?"[108]

Caversham, England, 24 September 1895 · I do not seek to know people; if people are thrown in my way by the Lord all right. It is my principle not to force myself on others.... I am waiting for the next wave. "Avoid not and seek not—wait for what the Lord sends," is my motto.[109]

Caversham, 4 October 1895 · I am now in England.... Mr. Sturdy has taken initiation from me, and is a very enterprising and good man....

[Sri Ramakrishna] is protecting us, forsooth—I see it before my eyes.... Is it through my own strength that beauty like that of fairies, and hundreds of thousands of rupees, lose their attraction and appear as nothing to me? Or is it he who is protecting me?[110]

Caversham, October 1895 · I am enjoying England very much. I am living with my friend on *philosophy*, leaving a little margin for eating and smoking. We are getting nothing else but Dualism and Monism and all the rest of them....

The Englishmen here are very friendly. Except a few Anglo-Indians, they do not hate black men at all. Not even do they hoot at me in the streets. Sometimes I wonder whether my face has turned white, but the mirror tells the truth. Yet they are all so friendly here.

Again, the English men and women who love India are more Hindu than the Hindus themselves. I am getting plenty of vegetables cooked, you will be surprised to hear, *à la Indienne* perfectly. When an Englishman takes up a thing, he goes to its very depths.[111]

Caversham, October 1895 · Mr. Sturdy is known to Tarakda [Swami Shivananda]. He has brought me to his place, and we are both trying to create a stir in England. I shall this year leave again in November for America.[112]

Caversham, October 1895 · I have to work day and night, and am always whirling from place to place besides.... Here, as in our country, one has to spend from one's own pocket to give lectures, but one can make good the expenses if one lives long enough and makes a reputation. Another thing, my incessant lecturing tours are making my constitution very nervous, causing insomnia and other troubles. Over and above that, I have to work single-handed.[113]

England, October 1895 · Individuality is my motto, I have no ambition beyond training individuals up.... As for me, I again repeat—I form no sect, nor organization—I know very little and that little I teach without reserve. Where I am ignorant I confess it as such and never never am I so glad as when I find people being helped by Theosophists or Christians or Mohammedans or anybody in the world. I am a Sannyasin, as such I hold myself as a servant not as a master in this world. Yet if people love me, they are welcome, if they hate they are also very welcome.

Each one will have to save himself, each one to do his own work. I *seek* no help, I reject *none*; nor have I any right in the world to be helped. Whosoever has helped me or will help, it will be their mercy to me, not my right, and as such I am eternally grateful.

I am very sorry your circumstances are so bad—but you know, *ma chère fille* [my dear girl], I am in a worse plight. In this country I have everything to spend and nothing to gain, the rooms in London alone cost me £3 a week, then many other necessities. To whom shall I complain? It is my own Karma that will have to be worked out, and when I became a Sannyasin I consciously took the step, knowing that perhaps this body will have to die of starvation. What of that? *A Sannyasin must never complain.* In this world he is a traveller. Come what may, a blessing on all.... I am a beggar, my friends are poor. I love the poor. I welcome poverty. I am glad that I sometimes have to starve. I ask help of none. What is the use? Truth will preach itself, it will not die for the want of the helping hand of me!! "Making happiness and misery the same, making success or failure the same, fight thou on"—Gita. It is that eternal love, unruffled equanimity under all circumstances, and above all perfect freedom from jealousy or animosity that will tell, that alone will tell—nothing else....

There is only one friend in all England who gives me food and shelter when I am in need.[114]

London, 23 October 1895 · My teaching is my own interpretation of our ancient books, in the light which my Master shed upon them. I claim no supernatural authority. Whatever in my teaching may appeal to the highest intelligence and be accepted by thinking men, the adoption of that will be my reward. All religions have for their object the teaching either of devotion, knowledge, or Yoga, in a concrete form. Now, the philosophy of Vedanta is the abstract science which embraces all these methods, and this it is that I teach, leaving each one to apply it to his own concrete form. I refer each individual to his own experiences, and where reference is made to books, the latter are procurable, and may be studied by each one for himself. Above all, I teach no authority proceeding from hidden beings speaking through visible agents, any more than I claim learning from hidden books or manuscripts. I am the exponent of no occult societies, nor do I believe that good can come of such bodies. Truth stands on its own authority, and truth can bear the light of day....

I teach only the Self, hidden in the heart of every individual and common to all. A handful of strong men knowing that Self and living in Its light would revolutionise the world, even today, as has been the case by single strong men before, each in his day....

I represented the Hindu religion at the Parliament of Religions held at Chicago in 1893. Since then I have been travelling and lecturing in the United States. The American people have proved most interested audiences and sympathetic friends, and my work there has so taken root that I must shortly return to that country....

I propound a philosophy which can serve as a basis to every possible religious system in the world, and my attitude towards all of them is one of extreme sympathy—my teaching is antagonistic to none. I direct my attention to the individual, to make him strong, to teach him that he himself is divine, and I call upon men to make themselves conscious of this divinity within. That is really the ideal—conscious or unconscious—of every religion....

My hope is to imbue individuals with the teachings to which I have referred, and to encourage them to express these to others in their own way; let them modify them as they will; I do not teach them as dogmas; truth at length must inevitably prevail.

The actual machinery through which I work is in the hands of one or two friends....

I am prepared to follow any course that opens—to attend meetings in people's drawing-rooms or elsewhere, to answer letters, or discuss personally. In a mercenary age I may venture to remark that none of my activities are undertaken for a pecuniary reward.[115]

London, 24 October 1895 · It is a queer life, mine—always travelling, no rest. Rest will be my death—such is the force of habit. Little success here, little there—and a good deal of bumping. Saw Paris a good [deal]. Miss Josephine MacLeod, a New York friend, showed it all over to me for a month. Even there, the kind American girl! Here in England they know us more. Those that do not like the Hindus, they hate them; those that like, they worship them.

It is slow work here, but sure. Not frothy, not superficial. English women as a rule are not as highly educated as the American women, nor are so beautiful. They are quite submissive wives or hidden away daughters or church going mothers—the embodiments of crystallized conventionality....

Sometimes—and generally when I score a success—I feel a despondence; I feel as if everything is vain—as if this life has no meaning, as if it is a waking dream. Love, friendship, religion, virtue, kindness—everything, a momentary state of mind. I seem to long to go; in spite of myself I say, how far—O

ow far! Yet the body and mind will have to work its Karma
ut. I hope it will not be bad....

Yet the life seems to grow deep and at the same time lose
s hold on itself.

Not disgust, nor joy for life, but a sort of indifference—
nings will take their course; who can resist—only stand
y and look on. Well, I will not talk about myself so much.
gregious egotist! I always was that, you know.... Great fun
his life, isn't it?...

A calm, restful, settled married life is good for the majority
f mankind. Mr. Sturdy, the friend with whom I am living
ow, was in India several times. He mixed with our monks
nd is very ascetic in his habits, but he is married at last and
as settled down. And [he] has got a beautiful little baby.
heir life is very nice. The wife, of course, doesn't much care
bout metaphysics or Sanskrit, but her whole life is in her
usband—and husband's soul is in Sanskrit metaphysics! Yet
t is a good combination of theory and practice, I think.[116]

ngland, October or November 1895 · One must prevail over
hese people by dint of learning, or one will be blown off at
 puff. They understand neither Sadhus nor your Sannyasins,
or the spirit of renunciation. What they do understand is
he vastness of learning, the display of eloquence and tre-
nendous activity.[117]

London, 18 November 1895 · In England my work is really splendid, I am astonished myself at it. The English people do not
alk much in the newspapers, but they work silently. I am
ure of more work in England than in America. Bands and
bands come, and I have no room for so many; so they squat
on the floor, ladies and all. I tell them to imagine that they
are under the sky of India, under a spreading banyan, and
hey like the idea. I shall have to go away next week, and

they are so sorry. Some think my work here will be hurt little if I go away so soon. I do not think so. I do not depend on men or things. The Lord alone I depend upon—and He works through me....

I have no time even to die, as the Bengalis say. I work, work, work, and earn my own bread and help my country, and this all alone, and then get only criticism from friends and foes for all that! Well ... I shall have to bear everything. I have sent for a Sannyasin from Calcutta and shall leave him to work in London. I want one more for America—I want my own man... I am really tired from incessant work. Any other Hindu would have died if he had to work as hard as I have to.... I want to go to India for a long rest.[118]

S.S. Britannic [*On board ship*], *29 November 1895* · So far the journey has been very beautiful. The purser has been very kind to me and gave me a cabin to myself. The only difficulty is the food—meat, meat, meat. Today they have promised to give me some vegetables.

We are standing at anchor now. The fog is too thick to allow the ship to proceed. So I take this opportunity to write a few letters.

It is a queer fog almost impenetrable though the sun is shining bright and cheerful.[119]

Back to the U.S.A.

I have a message to the West as Buddha had a message to the East.[120]

Ingersoll once said to me: "I believe in making the most out of this world, in squeezing the orange dry, because this world is all we are sure of." I replied: "I know a better way to squeeze the orange of this world than you do, and I get more out of

. I know I cannot die, so I am not in a hurry; I know there is no fear, so I enjoy the squeezing. I have no duty, no bondage of wife and children and property; I can love all men and women. Everyone is God to me. Think of the joy of loving man as God! Squeeze your orange this way and get ten thousandfold more out of it. Get every single drop."[121]

In the West, people often used to ask me, "How could you know the questions that were agitating our minds?" This knowledge does not happen to me so often, but with Sri Ramakrishna it was almost always there.[122]

New York, 8 December 1895 · After ten days of a most tedious and rough voyage I safely arrived in New York. My friends had already engaged some rooms at the above where I am living now and intend to hold classes ere long. In the meanwhile the Theosophists have been alarmed very much and are trying their best to hurt me; but they and their followers are of no consequence whatever.

I went to see Mrs. Leggett and other friends, and they are as kind and enthusiastic as ever.[123]

New York, 8 December 1895 · After 10 days of the most disastrous voyage I ever had I arrived in New York. I was so so sick for days together.

After the clean and beautiful cities of Europe, New York appears very dirty and miserable. I am going to begin work next Monday.[124]

New York, 8 December 1895 · I am once more on American Soil and have taken lodgings at 228 W. 39, where I begin work from Monday next. Sometime after Christmas I intend to make a tour through Detroit and Chicago.

I do not care for public lecturings at all—and do not think I shall have any more public lectures charging admission. If you will see Mrs. Phelps and others of our friends and arrange some classes (strictly on nonpayment basis), it will facilitate things a good deal.[125]

New York, 10 December 1895 · I had a splendid success in England and have left a *nucleus* there to work till my arrival next summer. You will be astonished to learn that some of my strongest friends are big "guns" of the Church of England....

Give Mrs. Phelps my love and kindly arrange the classes [in Detroit] with her. The best thing is to arrange for a public lecture where I give out my general plan of work. The Unitarian church is available; and if the lecture is free, there will be a big crowd. The collection most possibly will cover the expenses. Then out of this we will get the materials of a big class and then hurry them through, leaving Mrs. Phelps and you [Christina Greenstidel] and Mrs. Funke to work on with them.

This plan is entirely feasible and if Mrs. Phelps and Mrs. Bagley desire it, they can work it out very quickly.[126]

New York, 16 December 1895 · The classes I had here were six in the week, besides a question class. The general attendance varies between 70 to 120. Besides every Sunday I have a public lecture. The last month my lectures were in a small hall holding about 600. But 900 will come as a rule, 300 standing, and about 300 going off, not finding room. This week therefore I have a bigger hall, with a capacity of holding 1200 people.

There is no admission charged in these lectures, but a collection covers the rent. The newspapers have taken me up this week, and altogether I have stirred up New York considerably this year. If I could have remained here this summer and organised a summer place, the work would be going on sure foundations here. But as I intended to come over in May to England, I shall have to leave it unfinished....

Again, I am afraid my health is breaking down under constant work. I want some rest. We are so unused to these Western methods, especially the keeping to time.... The Brahmavadin is going on here very satisfactorily. I have begun to write articles on Bhakti ... Some friends here are publishing my Sunday lectures....

Next month I go to Detroit, then to Boston, and Harvard University. Then I shall have a rest, and then I come to England ...[127]

New York, 23 December 1895 · I have a strong hatred for child-marriage. I have suffered terribly from it, and it is the great sin for which our nation has to suffer. As such, I would hate myself if I help such a diabolical custom directly or indirectly.... Emotional natures like mine are always preyed upon by relatives and friends. This world is merciless. This world is our friend when we are its slaves and no more. This world is broad enough for me. There will always be a corner found for me somewhere. If the people of India do not like me, there will be others who do. I must set my foot to the best of my ability upon this devilish custom of child-marriage.... I am sorry, very sorry, I cannot have any partnership with such doings as getting husbands for babies. Lord help me, I never had and never will have.... I can kill the man who gets a husband for a baby. The upshot of the whole thing is—I want bold, daring, adventurous spirits to help me. Else I will work alone. I have a mission to fulfil. I will work it out alone. I do not care who comes or who goes.... At least I am pleased with myself for having tried my best to discharge the duties laid on me by my Guru, and well done or ill, I am glad that I tried.... I want no help from any human being in any country.[128]

I got thoroughly used to the interviewer in America. Because it is not the fashion in my country, that is no reason why I should not use means existing in any country I visit, for spreading what I desire to be known! There I was representative of the Hindu religion at the World's Parliament of Religions at Chicago in 1893. The Raja of Mysore and some other friends sent me there. I think I may lay claim to having had some success in America. I had many invitations to other great American cities besides Chicago; my visit was a very long one, for, with the exception of a visit to England last summer... I remained about three years in America. The American civilisation is, in my opinion, a very great one. I find the American mind peculiarly susceptible to new ideas; nothing is rejected because it is new. It is examined on its own merits, and stands or falls by these alone....

It might convey a more definite idea to call [my teaching] the kernel of all forms of religion, stripping from them the nonessential, and laying stress on that which is the real basis.[129]

New York, 23 December 1895 · The work here is going on splendidly. I have been working incessantly at two classes a day since my arrival. Tomorrow I go out of town with Mr. Leggett for a week's holiday. Did you know Madame Antoinette Sterling, one of your greatest singers? She is very much interested in the work.

I have made over all the secular part of the work to a committee and am free from all that botheration. I have no aptitude for organising. It nearly breaks me to pieces....

I have now taken up the Yoga-Sutras and take them up one by one and go through all the commentators along with them. These talks are all taken down, and when completed will form the fullest annotated translation of Patanjali in English.[130]

New York, 6 January 1896 · I have been in the midst of the genuine article in England. The English people received me with open arms, and I have very much toned down my ideas about the English race. First of all, I found that those fellows as Lund etc. who came over from England to attack me were nowhere. Their existence is simply ignored by the English people. None but a person belonging to the English Church is thought to be genteel. Again, some of the best men of England belonging to the English Church and some of the highest in position and fame became my truest friends. This was quite another sort of experience from what I met in America, was it not?

The English people laughed and laughed when I told them about my experience with the Presbyterians and other fanatics here and my reception in hotels etc. I also found at once the difference in culture and breeding between the two countries and came to understand why American girls go in shoals to be married to Europeans. Everyone was kind to me there, and I have left many noble friends of both sexes anxiously waiting my return in the spring.

As to my work there, the Vedantic thought has already permeated the higher classes of England. Many people of education and rank, and amongst them not a few clergymen, told me that the conquest of Rome by Greece was being re-enacted in England....

I had eight classes a week apart from public lectures, and they were so crowded that a good many people, even ladies of high rank, sat on the floor and did not think anything of it. In England I find strong-minded men and women to take up the work and carry it forward with the peculiar English grip and energy. This year my work in New York is going on splendidly. Mr. Leggett is a very rich man of New York and very much interested in me. The New Yorker has more steadiness than any other people in this country, so I have determined to make my centre here. In this country my teachings are thought to be queer by the "Methodist" and "Presbyterian" aristocracy. In England it is the highest philosophy to the English Church aristocracy.

Moreover those talks and gossips, so characteristic of the American woman, are almost unknown in England. The English woman is slow; but when she works up to an idea, she will have a hold on it sure; and they are regularly carrying on my work there and sending every week a report—think of that! Here if I go away for a week, everything falls to pieces.[131]

New York, 16 January 1896 · I have begun my Sunday lectures here and also the classes. Both are very enthusiastically received. I make them all free and take up a collection to pay the hall etc. Last Sunday's lecture was very much appreciated and is in the press....

As my friends have engaged a stenographer [Mr. J.J. Goodwin], all these class lessons and public lectures are taken down....

I have a chance of getting a piece of land in the country, and some buildings on it, plenty of trees and a river, to serve as a summer meditation resort. That, of course, requires a committee to look after it in my absence, as also the handling of money and printing and other matters.

I have separated myself entirely from money questions, yet without it the movement cannot go on. So necessarily I have to make over everything executive to a committee, which will look after these things in my absence.[132]

New York, 25 January 1896 · This year, I am afraid, I am getting overworked, as I feel the strain. I want a rest badly....

Tomorrow will be the last Sunday lecture of this month. The first Sunday of next month there will be a lecture in Brooklyn; the rest, three in New York, with which I will close this year's New York lectures....

I have no anxiety about anything. I am also getting tired

of lecturing and having classes. After a few months' work in England I will go to India and hide myself absolutely for some years or for ever.... I hope the Lord will give me freedom from this preaching and adding good bondages.

"If you have known the Atman as the one existence and that nothing else exists, for whom, for what desire, do you trouble yourself?" Through Maya all this doing good etc. came into my brain—now they are leaving me. I get more and more convinced that there is no other object in work except the purification of the soul—to make it fit for knowledge. This world with its good and evil will go on in various forms. Only the evil and good will take new names and new seats. My soul is hankering after peace and rest eternal undisturbed.

"Live alone, live alone. He who is alone never comes into conflict with others—never disturbs others, is never disturbed by others." I long, oh! I long for my rags, my shaven head, my sleep under the trees, and my food from begging! India is the only place where, with all its faults, the soul finds its freedom, its God. All this Western pomp is only vanity, only bondage of the soul. Never more in my life I realised more forcibly the vanity of the world. May the Lord break the bondage of all—may all come out of Maya—is the constant prayer of Vivekananda.[133]

New York, 6 February 1896 · My health has nearly broken down. I have not slept even one night soundly in New York since I came; and this year there is incessant work, both with the pen and the mouth. The accumulated work and worry of years is on me now, I am afraid. Then a big struggle awaits me in England. I wish to go to the bottom of the sea and have a good, long sleep....

So far I have tried to work conscientiously—let the fruits belong to the Lord. If they were good they will sprout up sooner or later; if bad, the sooner they die the better. I am quite satisfied with my task in life. I have been much more active than a Sannyasin ought to be. Now I will disappear from society altogether. The touch of the world is degenerating me, I am sure, so it is time to be off. Work has no more value beyond purifying the heart. My heart is pure enough; why shall I bother my head about doing good to others? "If you have known the Atman as the one, only existence and nothing else exists, desiring what?—for whose desire you trouble yourself?" This universe is a dream, pure and simple. Why bother myself about a dream? The very atmosphere of the world is poison to the Yogi, but I am waking up. My old iron heart is coming back—all attachments of relatives, friends, disciples are vanishing fast. "Neither through wealth nor through progeny, but by giving up everything as chaff is that immortality attained"—the Vedas. I am so tired of talking too; I want to close my lips and sit in silence for years. All talk is nonsense.[134]

New York, 17 February 1896 · I have succeeded now in rousing the very heart of the American civilisation, New York, but it has been a terrific struggle.... I have spent nearly all I had on this New York work and in England. Now things are in such a shape that they will go on. Just as I am writing to you, every one of my bones is paining after last afternoon's long Sunday public lecture.... It is hard work, my boy, hard work! To keep one's self steady in the midst of this whirl of Kamakanchana and hold on to one's own ideals, until disciples are moulded to conceive of the ideas of realisation and perfect renunciation, is indeed difficult work, my boy. Thank God, already there is great success. I cannot blame the missionaries and others for not understanding me—they hardly ever saw a man who did not care in the least about women and money.

At first they could not believe it to be possible ... People are now flocking to me. Hundreds have now become convinced that there are men who can really control their bodily desires; and reverence and respect for these principles are growing. All things come to him who waits.[135]

New York, 29 February 1896 · One book, the *Karma-Yoga*, has been already published; the *Raja-Yoga*, a much bigger one, is in the course of publication; the *Jnana-Yoga* may be published later on. These will be popular books, the language being that of talk ... The stenographer, who is an Englishman named Goodwin, has become so interested in the work that I have now made him a Brahmacharin, and he is going round with me ...[136]

Boston, 23 March 1896 · One of my new Sannyasins is indeed a woman.... The others are men. I am going to make some more in England and take them over to India with me....

My success is due to my popular style—the greatness of a teacher consists in the simplicity of his language....

I am afraid I have worked too much; my nerves are almost shattered by this long-continued work. I don't want you to sympathise, but only I write this so that you may not expect much from me now. Work on, the best way you can. I have very little hope of being able to do great things now. I am glad, however, that a good deal of literature has been created by taking down stenographic notes of my lectures. Four books are ready.... Well, I am satisfied that I have tried my best to do good, and shall have a clear conscience when I retire from work and sit down in a cave.[137]

Simplicity is the secret. My ideal of language is my Master's language, most colloquial and yet most expressive. It must express the thought which is intended to be conveyed.[138]

Second Visit to England

Reading, England, 20 April 1896 · The voyage has been pleasant and no sickness this time. I gave myself treatment to avoid it. I made quite a little run through Ireland and some of the old English towns and now am once more in Reading amidst Brahma and Maya and Jiva, the individual and the universal soul, etc. The other monk [Swami Saradananda] is here; he is one of the nicest of men I see, and is quite a learned monk too. We are busy editing books now. Nothing of importance happened on the way. It was dull, monotonous, and prosaic as my life. I love America more when I am out of it. And, after all, those years there have been some of the best I have yet seen.[139]

Reading, April (?) 1896 · This City of London is a sea of human heads—ten or fifteen Calcuttas put together. One is apt to be lost in the mazes unless he arranges for somebody to meet him on arrival.[140]

London, May 1896 · In London once more. The climate now in England is nice and cool. We have fire in the grate. We have a whole house to ourselves ... It is small but convenient, and in London they do not cost so much as in America.... Some old friends are here, and Miss MacLeod came over from the Continent. She is good as gold, and as kind as ever. We have a nice little family, in the house, with another monk [Swami Saradananda] from India.... I have had two classes already—they will go on for four or five months and after that to India I go. But it is to Amerique—there where the heart is. I love the Yankee land. I like to see new things. I do not care a fig to loaf about old ruins and mope a life out about old histories and keep sighing about the ancients. I have too much vigour in my blood for that. In America is the place, the people, the opportunity for everything. I have become horribly radical. I am just going to India to see what I can do in that awful mass of conservative jelly-fish, and start a new thing, entirely new—simple, strong, new and fresh as the first born baby.

The eternal, the infinite, the omnipresent, the omniscient is a principle, not a person. You, I, and everyone are but embodiments of that principle, and the more of this infinite principle is embodied in a person, the greater is he, and all in the end will be the perfect embodiment of that, and thus all will be one, as they are now essentially. This is all there is of religion, and the practice is through this feeling of oneness that is love. All old fogy forms are mere old superstitions. Now, why struggle to keep them alive? Why give thirsty people ditch-water to drink whilst the river of life and truth flows by? This is only human selfishness, nothing else. Life is short—time is flying—that place and people where one's ideas work best should be the country and the people for everyone. Ay, for a dozen bold hearts, large, noble, and sincere!

I am very well indeed and enjoying life immensely.[141]

London, 30 May 1896 · I had a beautiful visit with Prof. Max Müller. He is a saint—a Vedantist through and through. What think you? He has been a devoted admirer of my old Master for years. He has written an article on my Master in *The Nineteenth Century*, which will soon come out. We had long talk on Indian things. I wish I had half his love for India....

I am having classes here just now. I begin Sunday lectures from next week. The classes are very big and are in the house. We have rented it for the season. Last night I made a dish. It was such a delicious mixture of saffron, lavender, mace, nutmeg, cubebs, cinnamon, cloves, cardamom, cream, limejuice, onions, raisins, almonds, pepper, and rice, that I myself could not eat it. There was no asafoetida, though that would have made it smoother to swallow.[142]

London, 6 June 1896 · What an extraordinary man is Prof. Max Müller! I paid a visit to him a few days ago. I should say, that I went to pay my respects to him, for whosoever loves Sri Ramakrishna, whatever be his or her sect, or creed, or nationality, my visit to that person I hold as a pilgrimage. "*Madbhaktānāṁ ca ye bhaktāḥ te me bhaktatamā matāḥ*—They who are devoted to those who love Me—they are My best devotees." Is that not true?... The Professor was kindness itself, and asked Mr. Sturdy and myself to lunch with him. He showed us several colleges in Oxford and the Bodleian library. He also accompanied us to the railway station; and all this he did because, as he said, "It is not every day one meets a disciple of Ramakrishna Paramahamsa."

The visit was really a revelation to me. That nice little house in its setting of a beautiful garden, the silver-headed sage, with a face calm and benign, and forehead smooth as a child's in spite of seventy winters, and every line in that face speaking of a deep-seated mine of spirituality somewhere behind; that noble wife, the helpmate of his life through his long and arduous task of exciting interest, overriding opposition and contempt, and at last creating a respect for the thoughts of the sages of ancient India—the trees, the flowers, the calmness, and the clear sky—all these sent me back in imagination to the glorious days of Ancient India, the days of our Brahmarshis and Rājarshis, the days of the great Vānaprasthas, the days of Arundhatis and Vasishthas.

It was neither the philologist nor the scholar that I saw, but a soul that is every day realising its oneness with Brahman, a heart that is every moment expanding to reach oneness with the Universal. Where others lose themselves in the desert of dry details, he has struck the well-spring of life. Indeed his heartbeats have caught the rhythm of the Upanishads—"*Tamevaikaṁ jānatha ātmānam anyā vāco vimuñcatha*—Know the Atman alone, and leave off all other talk"....

And what love he bears towards India! I wish I had a hundredth part of that love for my own motherland! Endued with an extraordinary, and at the same time intensely active mind, he has lived and moved in the world of Indian thought for fifty years or more, and watched the sharp interchange of light and shade in the interminable forest of Sanskrit literature with deep interest and heartfelt love, till they have all sunk into his very soul and coloured his whole being.[143]

My impression is that it is Sāyana who is born again as Max Müller to revive his own commentary on the Vedas. I have had this notion for long. It became confirmed in my mind, it seems, after I had seen Max Müller. Even here in this country [India], you don't find a scholar so persevering, and so firmly grounded in the Vedas and the Vedanta. Over and above this, what a deep, unfathomable respect for Sri Ramakrishna! Do you know, he believes in his Divine Incarnation! And what great hospitality towards me when I was his guest! Seeing the old man and his lady, it seemed to me that they were living their home-life like another Vasishtha and Arundhati! At the time of parting with me, tears came into the eyes of the old man....

What are Varnāshrama and caste divisions to one who is the commentator of the Vedas, the shining embodiment of knowledge? To him they are wholly meaningless, and he can assume human birth wherever he likes for doing good to mankind. Specially, if he did not choose to be born in a land which excelled both in learning and wealth, where would he secure the large expenses for publishing such stupendous volumes?

Didn't you hear that the East India Company paid nine lakhs of rupees in cash to have the Rig-Veda published? Even this money was not enough. Hundreds of Vedic Pandits had to be employed in this country on monthly stipends. Has anybody seen in this age, here in this country, such profound yearning for knowledge, such prodigious investment of money for the sake of light and learning? Max Müller himself has written it in his preface, that for twenty-five years he prepared only the manuscripts. Then the printing took another twenty years! It is not possible for an ordinary man to drudge for forty-five years of his life with one publication. Just think of it! Is it an idle fancy of mine to say he is Sāyana himself?[144]

The biggest guns of the English Church told me that I was putting Vedantism into the Bible.[145]

In England, there was not one missionary or anybody who said anything against me; not one who tried to make a scandal about me. To my astonishment, many of my friends belong to the Church of England.[146]

I have visited a good deal of Europe, including Germany and France, but England and America were the chief centres of my work. At first I found myself in a critical position, owing to the hostile attitude assumed against the people of this country [India] by those who went there from India. I believe the Indian nation is by far the most moral and religious nation in the whole world, and it would be a blasphemy to compare the Hindus with any other nation. At first, many fell foul of me, manufactured huge lies against me by saying that I was a fraud, that I had a harem of wives and half a regiment of children. But my experience of these missionaries opened my eyes as to what they are capable of doing in the name of religion. Missionaries were nowhere in England. None came to fight me. Mr. Lund went over to America to abuse me behind my back, but people would not listen to him. I was very popular with them. When I came back to England, I thought this missionary would be at me, but the Truth silenced him. In England the social status is stricter than caste is in India. The English Church people are all gentlemen born, which many of the missionaries are not. They greatly sympathised with me. I think that about thirty English Church clergymen agree entirely with me on all points of religious discussion. I was agreeably surprised to find that the English clergymen, though they differed from me, did not abuse me behind my back and stab me in the dark. There is the benefit of caste and hereditary culture.

A great number of people sympathised with me in America—much more than in England. Vituperation by the low-caste missionaries made my cause succeed better. I had no money, the people of India having given me my bare passage-money, which was spent in a very short time. I had to live just as here on the charity of individuals. The Americans are very hospitable people. In America one-third of the people are Christians, but the rest have no religion, that is they do not belong to any of the sects, but amongst them are to be found the most spiritual persons. I think the work in England is sound. If I die tomorrow and cannot send any more Sannyasins, still the English work will go on. The Englishman is a very good man. He is taught from his childhood to suppress all his feelings. He is thick-headed, and is not so quick as the Frenchman or the American. He is immensely practical. The American people are too young to understand renunciation.

England has enjoyed wealth and luxury for ages. Many people there are ready for renunciation. When I first lectured in England I had a little class of twenty or thirty, which was kept going when I left, and when I went back from America

I could get an audience of one thousand. In America I could get a much bigger one, as I spent three years in America and only one year in England. I have two Sannyasins—one in England and one in America, and I intend sending Sannyasins to other countries.[147]

London, 7 June 1896 · My ideal indeed can be put into a few words and that is: to preach unto mankind their divinity, and how to make it manifest in every movement of life.

This world is in chains of superstition. I pity the oppressed, whether man or woman, and I pity more the oppressors.

One idea that I see clear as daylight is that misery is caused by ignorance and nothing else. Who will give the world light? Sacrifice in the past has been the Law; it will be, alas, for ages to come. The earth's bravest and best will have to sacrifice themselves for the good of many, for the welfare of all. Buddhas by the hundred are necessary with eternal love and pity.

Religions of the world have become lifeless mockeries. What the world wants is character. The world is in need of those whose life is one burning love, selfless. That love will make every word tell like thunderbolt....

Bold words and bolder deeds are what we want. Awake, awake, great ones! The world is burning with misery. Can you sleep? Let us call and call till the sleeping gods awake, till the god within answers to the call. What more is in life? What greater work? The details come to me as I go. I never make plans. Plans grow and work themselves. I only say, awake, awake![148]

London 7 July 1896 · The work here progressed wonderfully. I had one monk here from India. I have sent him to the U.S.A. and sent for another from India. The season is closed; the classes, therefore, and the Sunday lectures are to be closed on the 16th next. And on the 19th I go for a month or so for quiet and rest in the Swiss Mountains to return next autumn to London and begin again. The work here has been very satisfactory. By rousing interest here I really do more for India than in India.... I am going with three English friends to the Swiss Hills. Later on, towards the end of winter, I expect to go to India with some English friends who are going to live in my monastery there, which, by the by, is in the air yet. It is struggling to materialise somewhere in the Himalayas.[149]

London, 6 July 1896 · This British Empire with all its drawbacks is the greatest machine that ever existed for the dissemination of ideas. I mean to put my ideas in the centre of this machine, and they will spread all over the world. Of course, all great work is slow, and the difficulties are too many, especially as we Hindus are the conquered race. Yet, that is the very reason why it is bound to work, for spiritual ideals have always come from the downtrodden. Jews overwhelmed the Roman Empire with their spiritual ideals. You will be pleased to know that I am also learning my lessons every day in patience and, above all, in sympathy. I think I am beginning to see the Divine, even inside the high and mighty Anglo-Indians. I think I am slowly approaching to that state when I should be able to love the very "Devil" himself, if there were any.

At twenty years of age I was the most unsympathetic, uncompromising fanatic; I would not walk on the footpath on the theatre side of the streets in Calcutta. At thirty-three, I can live in the same house with prostitutes and never would think of saying a word of reproach to them. Is it degenerate? Or is it that I am broadening out into the Universal Love which is the Lord Himself? Again I have heard that if one does not see the evil round him he cannot do good work—he lapses into a sort of fatalism. I do not see that. On the other hand, my power of work is immensely increasing and becoming immensely effective. Some days I get into a sort of ecstasy. I feel that I must bless every one, everything, love and embrace everything, and I do see that evil is a delusion. I am in one of these moods now, dear Francis, and am actually shedding tears of joy at the thought of you and Mrs. Leggett's love and kindness to me. I bless the day I was born. I have had so much of kindness and love here, and that Love Infinite that brought me into being has guarded every one of my actions, good or bad, (don't be frightened), for what am I, what was I ever, but a tool in His hands, for whose service I have given up everything, my beloved ones, my joys, my life? He is my playful darling, I am His playfellow. There is neither rhyme nor reason in the universe! What reason binds Him? He the playful one is playing these tears and laughters over all parts of the play! Great fun, great fun, as Joe says.

It is a funny world, and the funniest chap you ever saw is He—the Beloved Infinite! Fun, is it not? Brotherhood or playmatehood—a school of romping children let out to play in this playground of the world! Isn't it? Whom to praise, whom to blame, it is all His play. They want explanations, but how can you explain Him? He is brainless, nor has He any reason. He is fooling us with little brains and reason, but this time He won't find me napping.

I have learnt a thing or two: Beyond, beyond reason and learning and talking is the feeling, the "Love," the "Beloved." Ay, *saké*, fill up the cup and we will be mad.[150]

Switzerland

Saas-grund, Switzerland, 25 July 1896 · I want to forget the world entirely at least for the next two months and practise hard. That is my rest.... The mountains and snow have a beautifully quieting influence on me, and I am getting better sleep here than for a long time.[151]

Valais, Switzerland, 4 August 1896 · I am reading a little, starving a good deal, and practising a good deal more. The strolls in the woods are simply delicious. We are now situated under three huge glaciers, and the scenery is very beautiful.

By the by, whatever scruples I may have had as to the Swiss-lake origin of the Aryans have been taken clean off my mind.[152]

Saas Fee, Switzerland, 4 (?) August 1896 · I went to the glacier of Monte Rosa yesterday and gathered a few hardy flowers growing almost in the midst of eternal snow.[153]

Saas Fee, 5 August 1896 · Surrounded on all sides by eternal snow peaks, sitting on the grass in a beautiful wood, my thoughts go to those I love—so I write.

I am in Switzerland—constantly on the move—getting a much needed rest. It is a miniature Himalayas, and has the same effect of raising the mind up to the Self and driving away all earthly feelings and ties. I am intensely enjoying it. I feel so, so uplifted. I cannot write, but I wish you will have the same for ever—when your feet do not want, as it were, to touch the material earth—when the soul finds itself floating, as it were, in an ocean of spirituality.[154]

Saas Fee, 8 August 1896 · I am now taking rest....

I am much refreshed now. I look out of the window and see the huge glaciers just before me and feel that I am in the Himalayas. I am quite calm. My nerves have regained their accustomed strength; and little vexations, like those you write of, do not touch me at all. How shall I be disturbed by this child's play? The whole world is a mere child's play—preaching, teaching, and all included. "Know him to be the

Sannyasin who neither hates not desires" (Gita, 5.3). And what is there to be desired in this little mud-puddle of a world, with its ever-recurring misery, disease, and death? "He who has given up all desires, he alone is happy."

This rest, eternal, peaceful rest, I am catching a glimpse of now in this beautiful spot. "Having once known that the Atman alone, and nothing else, exists, desiring what, or for whose desire, shall you suffer misery about the body?" (*Brihadaranyaka*, 4.4.12.)

I feel as if I had my share of experience in what they call "work." I am finished, I am longing now to get out. "Out of thousands, but one strives to attain the Goal. And even of those who struggle hard, but few attain" (Gita, 7.3); for the senses are powerful, they drag men down.[155]

Saas Fee, 12 August 1896 · I haven't yet written anything nor read anything. I am indeed taking a good rest.... I had a letter from the Math stating that the other Swami [Swami Abhedananda] is ready to start. He will, I am sure, be just the man you want. He is one of the best Sanskrit scholars we have ... and as I hear, he has improved his English much. I had a number of newspaper cuttings from America about Saradananda—I hear from them that he has done very well there. America is a good training ground to bring out all that is in a man.[156]

Lucerne, Switzerland, 23 August 1896 · I am very glad to hear that Saradananda and Goodwin are doing good work in the U.S. As for me, I do not lay any claim to that £500 for any work. I think I have worked enough. I am now going to retire. I have sent for another man from India who will join me next month. I have begun the work, let others work it out. So you see, to set the work going I had to touch money and property, for a time. Now I am sure my part of the work is done, and I have no more interest in Vedanta or any philosophy in the world or the work itself. I am getting ready to depart to return no more to this hell, this world. Even its religious utility is beginning to pall me. May Mother gather me soon to Herself never to come back any more! These works, and doing good, etc., are just a little exercise to cleanse the mind. I had enough of it. This world will be world ever and always. What we are, so we see it. Who works? Whose work? There is no world. It is God Himself. In delusion we call it world. Neither I nor thou nor you—it is all He the Lord, all One. So I do not want anything to do about money matters from this time....

I have given up the bondage of iron, the family tie—I am not to take up the golden chain of religious brotherhood. I am free, must always be free. I wish everyone to be free—free as the air.... As for me, I am as good as retired. I have played my part in the world.[157]

Schaffhausen, Switzerland, 26 August 1896 · I have just now got your letter. I am on the move. I have been doing a great deal of mountain-climbing and glacier-crossing in the Alps. Now I am going to Germany. I have an invitation from Prof. Deussen to visit him at Kiel.[158]

Kiel, Germany, 10 September 1896 · I have at last seen Prof. Deussen.... The whole of yesterday was spent very nicely with the Professor, sight-seeing and discussing about the Vedanta.

He is what I should call "a warring Advaitist." No compromise with anything else. "Ishwara" is his bug-bear. He would have none of it if he could.[159]

I have seen professors of Sanskrit in America and in Europe. Some of them are very sympathetic towards Vedantic thought.

I admire their intellectual acumen and their lives of unselfish labour. But Paul Deussen—or as he prefers to be called in Sanskrit, Deva-Sena—and the veteran Max Müller have impressed me as being the truest friends of India and Indian thought. It will always be among the most pleasing episodes in my life—my first visit to this ardent Vedantist at Kiel, his gentle wife who travelled with him in India, and his little daughter, the darling of his heart—and our travelling together through Germany and Holland to London, and the pleasant meetings we had in and about London.[160]

Back to England

London, 17 September 1896 · Today I reached London, after my two months of climbing and walking and glacier seeing in Switzerland. One good it has done me—a few pounds of unnecessary adipose tissue have returned back to the gaseous state. Well, there is no safety even in that, for the solid body of this birth has taken a fancy to outstrip the mind towards infinite expansion. If it goes on this way, I would have soon to lose all personal identity even in the flesh—at least to all the rest of the world....

I had a pleasant visit with Prof. Deussen in Germany. I am sure you have heard of him as the greatest living German philosopher. He and I travelled together to England and today came together to see my friend here with whom I am to stop for the rest of my stay in England. He (Deussen) is very fond of talking Sanskrit and is the only Sanskrit scholar in the West who can talk in it. As he wants to get practice, he never talks to me in any other language but Sanskrit.[161]

London, 7 October 1896 · Once more in London ... and the classes have begun already.... For me, ever-increasing mad work ... My natural tendency is to go into a cave and be quiet, but a fate behind pushes me forward and I go. Whoever could resist fate?...

We have a hall now, a pretty big one holding about 200 or more. There is a big corner which will be fitted up as the Library. I have another man from India now to help me [Swami Abhedananda]....

I now live mostly on fruits and nuts. They seem to agree with me well.... I have lost a good deal of my fat. But on days I lecture, I have to go on solid food....

I met Madam Sterling in the street today. She does not come any more for my lectures, good for her. Too much of philosophy is not good.... That lady who used to come to every meeting too late to hear a word but button-holed me immediately after and kept me talking, till a battle of Waterloo would be raging in my internal economy through hunger—she came. They are all coming and more. That is cheering.[162]

London, 28 October 1896 · The new Swami delivered his maiden speech yesterday at a friendly society's meeting. It was good and I liked it; he has the making of a good speaker in him, I am sure.... Goodwin is going to become a Sannyasin. He of course will travel with me. It is he to whom we owe all our books. He took shorthand notes of my lectures, which enabled the books to be published.[163]

London, 20 November 1896 · I am leaving England on the 16th of December for Italy, and shall catch the North German Lloyd S.S. Prinz Regent Luitpold at Naples. The steamer is due at Colombo on the 14th of January next.

I intend to see a little of Ceylon, and shall then go to Madras. I am being accompanied by three English friends—Capt. and Mrs. Sevier and Mr. Goodwin. Mr. Sevier and his wife are going to start a place near Almora in the Himalayas which I intend to make my Himalayan Centre, as well as a place for Western disciples to live as Brahmacharins and Sannyasins. Goodwin is an unmarried young man who is going to travel and live with me; he is like a Sannyasin....

My present plan of work is to start two centres, one in Calcutta and the other in Madras, in which to train up young preachers. I have funds enough to start the one in Calcutta, which being the scene of Sri Ramakrishna's life-work, demands my first attention. As for the Madras one, I expect to get funds in India.

We will begin work with these three centres; and later on, we will get to Bombay and Allahabad. And from these points, if the Lord is pleased, we will invade not only India, but send over bands of preachers to every country in the world. That should be our first duty.... You must not forget that my interests are *international* and not Indian alone.[164]

London, 28 November 1896 · The work in London has been a roaring success.... Capt. and Mrs. Sevier and Mr. Goodwin are going to India with me to work and spend their own money on it....

Now I am going to start a centre in Calcutta and another in the Himalayas. The Himalayan one will be an entire hill about 7,000 ft. high—cool in summer, cold in winter. Capt. and Mrs. Sevier will live there ... [165]

London, 3 December 1896 · Things are in a "hum" here just now; the big hall for the class, 39 Victoria, is full and yet more are coming.

Well, the good old country now calls me; I must go. So good-bye to all projects of visiting Russia this April.

I just set things a-going a little in India and am off again for the ever beautiful U.S. and England etc....

The coming of Goodwin was very opportune, as it captured

the lectures here which are being published in a periodical form....

Three lectures next week, and my London work is finished for this season. Of course, everybody here thinks it foolish to give it up just now the "boom" is on, but the Dear Lord says, "Start for Old India." I obey.[166]

Dampfer, "Prinz-regent Leopold" [On board ship], 3 January 1897 · We are nearing Port Said after four days of frightfully bad sailing from Naples. The ship is rolling as hard as she can, and you must pardon my scrawls under such circumstances.

From Suez begins Asia. Once more Asia. What am I? Asiatic, European, or American? I feel a curious medley of personalities in me....

I land in a few days at Colombo and mean to "do" Ceylon a bit....

I enjoyed Rome more than anything in the West, and after seeing Pompeii I have lost all regard for the so-called "Modern Civilisation." With the exception of steam and electricity they had everything else and infinitely more art conceptions and executions than the Moderns.[167]

I had a curious dream on my return voyage from England. While our ship was passing through the Mediterranean Sea, in my sleep, a very old and venerable-looking person, Rishi-like in appearance, stood before me and said, "Do ye come and effect our restoration. I am one of that ancient order of Theraputtas [Theraputae] which had its origin in the teachings of the Indian Rishis. The truths and ideals preached by us have been given out by Christians as taught by Jesus; but for the matter of that, there was no such personality by the name of Jesus ever born. Various evidences testifying to this fact will be brought to light by excavating here." "By excavating which place can those proofs and relics you speak of be found?" I asked. The hoary-headed one, pointing to a locality in the vicinity of Turkey, said, "See here." Immediately after, I woke up, and at once rushed to the upper deck and asked the Captain, "What neighbourhood is the ship in just now?" "Look yonder," the Captain replied, "there is Turkey and the Island of Crete."[168]

I had to work till I am at death's door and had to spend nearly the whole of that energy in America, so that the Americans may learn to be broader and more spiritual. In England I worked only six months. There was not a breath of scandal save one, and that was the working of an American woman, which greatly relieved my English friends—not only no attacks but many of the best English Church clergymen became my firm friends, and without asking I got much help for my work.[169]

From first to last [my experience of America] was very good.... The Americans are most hospitable, kind-hearted, generous, and good-natured.[170]

All the social upheavalists [in America and England], at least the leaders of them, are trying to find that all their communistic or equalising theories must have a spiritual basis, and that spiritual basis is in the Vedanta only. I have been told by several leaders, who used to attend my lectures, that they required the Vedanta as the basis of the new order of things....

Many times I was near being mobbed in America and England, only on account of my dress. But I never heard of such a thing in India as a man being mobbed because of peculiar dress.[171]

The little tendency that remained in me for taking to European ways vanished, thanks to the Americans. I was sorely troubled by an overgrown beard, but no sooner did I peep into a hair-cutting saloon than somebody called out, "This is no place for such shabby-looking people as you." I thought that perhaps seeing me so quaintly dressed in turban and Gerua [ochre] cloak, the man was prejudiced against me. So I should go and buy an English coat and hat. I was about to do this when fortunately I met an American gentleman who explained to me that it was much better that I was dressed in my Gerua cloak, for now the gentlemen would not take me amiss, but if I dressed in European fashion, everybody would chase me away. I met the same kind of treatment in one or two other saloons. After which I began the practice of shaving with my own hands. Once I was burning with hunger, and went into a restaurant, and asked for a particular thing, whereupon the man said, "We do not stock it." "Why, it is there." "Well, my good man, in plain language it means there is no place here for you to sit and take your meal." "And why?" "Because nobody will eat at the same table with you, for he will be outcasted." Then America began to look agreeable to me, somewhat like my own caste-ridden country.[172]

[*Swami Vivekananda acknowledged that he had "maybe more" than three thousand initiated disciples in the West. He continued*] · My disciples are all Brahmins. I quite admit the truth of the words that none except the Brahmins has the right to Pranava. But the son of a Brahmin is not necessarily always a Brahmin; though there is every possibility of his being one, he may not become so.... The Brahmin caste and the Brahmanya qualities are two distinct things. In India, one is held to be a Brahmin by one's caste, but in the West, one should be known as such by one's Brahmanya qualities.[173]

I am at heart a mystic ... all this reasoning is only apparent. I am really always on the lookout for signs and things—and so I never bother about the fate of my initiations. If [my disciples] want to be sannyasins badly enough I feel that the rest is not my business. Of course it has its bad side. I have to pay dearly for my blunder sometimes—but it has one advantage. It has kept me still a sannyasin through all this.[174]

I do not meddle with my workers at all. The man who can work has an individuality of his own, which resists against any pressure. This is my reason for leaving workers entirely free.[175]

The Hindus visit foreign countries—Rangoon, Java, Hong Kong, Madagascar, Suez, Aden, Malta—and they take with them Ganga water and the Gita.

The Gita and the sacred waters of the Ganga constitute the Hinduism of the Hindus. Last time I went to the West, I also took a little of it with me, fearing it might be needed, and whenever opportunities occurred I used to drink a few drops of it. And every time I drank, in the midst of the stream of humanity, amid that bustle of civilisation, that hurry of frenzied footsteps of millions of men and women in the West, the mind at once became calm and still, as it were. That stream of men, that intense activity of the West, that clash and competition at every step, those seats of luxury and celestial opulence—Paris, London, New York, Berlin, Rome—all would disappear and I used to hear that wonderful sound of "Hara, Hara," to see that lonely forest on the sides of the Himalayas, and feel the murmuring heavenly river coursing through the heart and brain and every artery of the body and thundering forth, "Hara, Hara, Hara!"[176]

When I take a retrospective view of my past life, I feel no remorse. From country to country I have travelled teaching something, however little, to people, and in exchange for that have partaken of their slices of bread. If I had found I had done no work, but simply supported myself by imposing upon people, I would have committed suicide today.[177]

People there in the West think that the more a man is religious, the more demure he must be in his outward bearing—no word about anything else from his lips! As the priests in the West would on the one hand be struck with wonder at my liberal religious discourses, they would be as much puzzled on the other hand when they found me, after such discourses, talking frivolities with my friends. Sometimes they would speak out to my face: "Swami, you are a priest, you should not be joking and laughing in this way like ordinary men. Such levity does not look well in you." To which I would reply, "We are children of bliss, why should we look morose and sombre?" But I doubt if they could rightly catch the drift of my words.[178]

I have been asked many times, "Why do you laugh so much and make so many jokes?" I become serious sometimes—when I have stomach-ache! The Lord is all blissfulness. He is the reality behind all that exists, He is the goodness, the truth in everything. You are His incarnations. That is what is glorious. The nearer you are to Him, the less you will have occasions to cry or weep. The further we are from Him, the more will long faces come. The more we know of Him, the more misery vanishes. If one who lives in the Lord becomes miserable, what is the use of living in Him? What is the use of such a God? Throw Him overboard into the Pacific Ocean! We do not want Him![179]

CHAPTER SEVEN

RETURN TO INDIA

I AM PERSUADED THAT a leader is not made in one life. He has to be born for it. For the difficulty is not in organisation and making plans; the test, the real test of the leader, lies in holding widely different people together along the line of their common sympathies. And this can only be done unconsciously, never by trying.[1]

I was asked by an English friend on the eve of my departure, "Swami, how do you like now your motherland after four years' experience of the luxurious, glorious, powerful West?" I could only answer, "India I loved before I came away. Now the very dust of India has become holy to me, the very air is now to me holy; it is now the holy land, the place of pilgrimage, the Tirtha."[2]

We must electrify society, electrify the world....

Let character be formed and then I shall be in your midst....

A huge spiritual tidal wave is coming—he who is low shall become noble, and he who is ignorant shall become the teacher of great scholars—through HIS grace. "*Uttiṣṭhata jāgrata prāpya varān nibodhata*—Arise! Awake! and stop not till the goal is reached"....

Arise! Arise! A tidal wave is coming! Onward! Men and women, down to the Chandala—all are pure in his eyes. Onward! Onward! There is no time to care for name, or fame, or Mukti, or Bhakti! We shall look to these some other time. Now in this life let us infinitely spread his lofty character, his sublime life, his infinite soul. This is the only work—there is nothing else to do. Wherever his name will reach, the veriest worm will attain divinity, nay, is actually attaining it; you have got eyes, and don't you see it? Is it a child's play? Is it silly prattle? Is it foolery? *"Uttiṣṭhata jāgrata*—Arise! Awake!" Great Lord! He is at our back. I cannot write any more—onward! I only tell you this, that whoever reads this letter will imbibe my spirit! Have faith! Onward! Great Lord!... I feel as if somebody is moving my hand to write in this way. Onward! Great Lord! Everyone will be swept away! Take care, he is coming! Whoever will be ready to serve him—no, not him but his children—the poor and the downtrodden, the sinful and the afflicted, down to the very worm—who will be ready to serve these, in them he will manifest himself. Through their tongue the Goddess of Learning Herself will speak, and the Divine Mother—the Embodiment of all Power—will enthrone Herself in their hearts.[3]

We shall crush the stars to atoms, and unhinge the universe. Don't you know who we are? We are the servants of Sri Ramakrishna.[4]

My children must plunge into the breach, must renounce the world—then the firm foundation will be laid....

Work unto death—I am with you, and when I am gone, my spirit will work with you. This life comes and goes—wealth, fame, enjoyments are only of a few days. It is better, far better to die on the field of duty, preaching the truth, than to die like a worldly worm. Advance![5]

You have heard that Christ said, "My words are spirit and they are life." So are my words spirit and life; they will burn their way into your brain and you will never get away from them![6]

From Columbo to Almora

Pamban, 26 January 1897 · It is impossible for me to express my gratitude to H. H. the Raja of Ramnad for his love towards me. If any good work has been done by me and through me, India owes much to this good man, for it was he who conceived the idea of my going to Chicago, and it was he who put that idea into my head and persistently urged me on to accomplish it.[7]

Ramnad, 30 January 1897 · Things are turning out most curiously for me. From Colombo in Ceylon, where I landed, to Ramnad, the nearly southernmost point of the Indian continent where I am just now as the guest of the Raja of Ramnad, my journey has been a huge procession—crowds of people, illuminations, addresses, etc., etc. A monument forty feet high is being built on the spot where I landed. The Raja of Ramnad has presented his address to "His most Holiness" in a huge casket of solid gold beautifully worked. Madras and Calcutta are on the tiptoe of expectation as if the whole nation is rising to honour me. So you see ... I am on the very height of my destiny, yet the mind turns to quietness and peace, to the days we had in Chicago, of rest, of peace, and love.[8]

Once I was preaching at Anuradhapuram [in Sri Lanka] among the Hindus—not Buddhists—and that in an open maidan, not on anybody's property—when a whole host of Buddhist monks and laymen, men and women, came out beating drums and cymbals and set up an awful uproar. The lecture had to stop, of course, and there was the imminent risk of bloodshed. With great difficulty I had to persuade the

Hindus that we at any rate might practise a bit of non-injury, if they did not. Then the matter ended peacefully.[9]

Madras, 9 February 1897 · With all my faults, I think I have a little bit of boldness.... I want, before going into the subject of the day, to speak a few bold words to you all. There have been certain circumstances growing around me, tending to thwart me, oppose my progress, and crush me out of existence if they could. Thank God they have failed, as such attempts will always fail. But there has been, for the last three years, a certain amount of misunderstanding, and so long as I was in foreign lands, I held my peace and did not even speak one word; but now, standing upon the soil of my motherland, I want to give a few words of explanation. Not that I care what the result will be of these words—not that I care what feeling I shall evoke from you by these words. I care very little, for I am the same Sannyasin that entered your city about four years ago with this staff and Kamandalu; the same broad world is before me....

Now I come to the reform societies in Madras.... Some of these societies, I am afraid, try to intimidate me to join them. That is a strange thing for them to attempt. A man who has met starvation face to face for fourteen years of his life, who has not known where he will get a meal the next day and where to sleep, cannot be intimidated so easily. A man, almost without clothes, who dared to live where the thermometer registered thirty degrees below zero, without knowing where the next meal was to come from, cannot be so easily intimidated in India. This is the first thing I will tell them—I have a little will of my own. I have my little experience too; and I have a message for the world which I will deliver without fear and without care for the future. To the reformers I will point out that I am a greater reformer than any one of them.

They want to reform only little bits. I want root-and-branch reform. Where we differ is in the method. Theirs is the method of destruction, mine is that of construction. I do not believe in reform; I believe in growth. I do not dare to put myself in the position of God and dictate to our society, "This way thou shouldst move and not that." I simply want to be like the squirrel in the building of Rama's bridge, who was quite content to put on the bridge his little quota of sand-dust. That is my position....

This I have to tell to the social reformers of Madras that I have the greatest respect and love for them. I love them for their great hearts and their love for their country, for the poor, for the oppressed. But what I would tell them with a brother's love is that their method is not right; it has been tried a hundred years and failed. Let us try some new method....

Vain is it to attempt the lines of action that foreign societies have engrafted upon us; it is impossible. Glory unto God, that it is impossible, that we cannot be twisted and tortured into the shape of other nations. I do not condemn the institutions of other races; they are good for them, but not for us. What is meat for them may be poison for us. This is the first lesson to learn. With other sciences, other institutions, and other traditions behind them, they have got their present system. We, with our traditions, with thousands of years of Karma behind us, naturally can only follow our own bent, run in our own grooves; and that we shall have to do....

What is my plan then? My plan is to follow the ideas of the great ancient Masters....

I did not go to America, as most of you know, for the Parliament of Religions, but this demon of a feeling was in me and within my soul. I travelled twelve years all over India, finding no way to work for my countrymen, and that is why I went to America. Most of you know that, who knew me then. Who cared about this Parliament of Religions? Here was my own flesh and blood sinking every day, and who cared for them? This was my first step.[10]

Madras, 12 February 1897 · I am to start by S.S. Mombasa next Sunday. I had to give up invitations from Poona and other places on account of bad health. I am very much pulled down by hard work and heat.[11]

Alambazar Math, Calcutta, 25 February 1897 · I have not a moment to die as they say, what with processions and tomtomings and various other methods of reception all over the country; I am almost dead. As soon as the Birthday [celebration of Sri Ramakrishna] is over I will fly off to the hills.... I am so, so tired. I do not know whether I would live even six months more or not, unless I have some rest.

Now I have to start two centres, one in Madras, the other in Calcutta....

The country is full of persons, jealous and pitiless, who would leave no stones unturned to pull my work to pieces.

But as you know well, the more the opposition, the more the demon in me is roused. My duty would not be complete if I die without starting the two places.[12]

[*Referring to the public reception accorded him in Calcutta*] I wished rather that a great enthusiasm should be stirred up. Don't you see, without some such thing how would the people be drawn towards Sri Ramakrishna and be fired in his name? Was this ovation done for me personally, or was not his name glorified by this? See how much thirst has been created in the minds of men to know about him! Now they will come to know of him gradually, and will not that be conducive to the good of the country? If the people do not know him who came for the welfare of the country, how can good befall them? When they know what he really was, then men—real men—will be made ... So I say that I rather desired that there should be some bustle and stir in Calcutta, so that the public might be inclined to believe in the mission of Sri Ramakrishna; otherwise what was the use of making so much fuss for my sake? What do I care for it? Have I become any greater now?... I am the same now as I was before.[13]

Darjeeling, 26 March 1897 · The demonstrations and national jubilations over me are over—at least I had to cut them short, as my health broke completely down. The result of this steady work in the West and the tremendous work of a month in India upon the Bengali constitution is "diabetes." It is a hereditary foe and is destined to carry me off, at best, in a few years' time. Eating only meat and drinking no water seems to be the only way to prolong life—and, above all, perfect rest for the brain. I am giving my brain the needed rest in Darjeeling.[14]

Darjeeling, 6 April 1897 · To meet the expenses of my reception, the people of Calcutta made me deliver a lecture and sold tickets![15]

Darjeeling, 20 April 1897 · My illness is now much less—it may even be cured completely, if the Lord wills.[16]

Darjeeling, 28 April 1897 · The whole country here rose like one man to receive me. Hundreds of thousands of persons, shouting and cheering at every place, Rajas drawing my carriage, arches all over the streets of the capitals with blazing mottoes etc.!... But unfortunately I was already exhausted by hard work in England; and this tremendous exertion in the heat of Southern India prostrated me completely. I had of course to give up the idea of visiting other parts of India and fly up to the nearest hill station, Darjeeling. Now I feel much better, and a month more in Almora would complete the cure....

I have just lost a chance of coming over to Europe. Raja Ajit Singh and several other Rajas start next Saturday for England. Of course, they wanted hard to get me to go over with them. But unfortunately the doctors would not hear of my undertaking any physical or mental labour just now. So with the greatest chagrin I had to give it up, reserving it for a near future....

This Darjeeling is a beautiful spot with a view of the glorious Kanchenjanga (28,146 ft.) now and then when the clouds permit it, and from a near hilltop one can catch a glimpse of Gauri Shankar [Mt. Everest] (29,000 ft?) now and then. Then, the people here too are picturesque, the Tibetans and Nepalese and, above all, the beautiful Lepcha women. Do you know one Colston Turnbull of Chicago? He was here a few weeks before I reached India. He seems to have had a great liking for me, with the result that Hindu people all liked him very much....

My hair is turning grey in bundles, and my face is getting wrinkled up all over; that losing of flesh has given me twenty years of age more. And now I am losing flesh rapidly, because I am made to live upon meat and meat alone—no bread, no rice, no potatoes, not even a lump of sugar in my coffee!...

I am very well here, for life in the plains has become a torture. I cannot put the tip of my nose out into the streets, but there is a curious crowd!! Fame is not all milk and honey!! I am going to train a big beard; now it is turning grey. It gives a venerable appearance and saves one from American scandalmongers! O thou white hair, how much thou canst conceal, all glory unto thee, Hallelujah![17]

Baghbazar, Calcutta, 1 May 1897 · The conviction has grown in my mind after all my travels in various lands that no great cause can succeed without an organisation....

Let this Association be named after him, in whose name, indeed, we have embraced the monastic life, with whom as your Ideal in life you all toil on the field of work from your station in family life, within twenty years of whose passing away a wonderful diffusion of his holy name and extraordinary life has taken place both in the East and the West. We are the servants of the Lord. Be you all helpers in this cause....

Well, how do you know that all this is not on Sri Ramakrishna's lines? He had an infinite breadth of feeling, and dare you shut him up within your own limited views of life? I will break down these limits and scatter broadcast over the earth his boundless inspiration. He never instructed me to introduce any rites of his own worship. We have to realise the teachings he has left us about religious practice and devotion, concentration and meditation, and such higher ideas and truths, and then preach these to all men. The infinite number of faiths are only so many paths. I haven't been born to found one more sect in a world already teeming with sects. We have been blessed with obtaining refuge at the feet of the Master, and we are born to carry his message to the dwellers of the three worlds.[18]

Calcutta, 1 May 1897 · The impulse is constantly coming nowadays to my mind to do this and to do that, to scatter broadcast on earth the message of Sri Ramakrishna and so on. But I pause again to reflect, lest all this give rise to another sect in India. So I have to work with a good deal of caution. Sometimes I think, what if a sect does grow up. But then again the thought comes, "No. Sri Ramakrishna never disturbed anybody's own spiritual outlook; he always looked at the inner sameness." Often do I restrain myself with this thought....

I think we do things according to our own will. Yet, that in misfortunes and adversities, in times of want and poverty, he reveals himself to us and guides us along the true path—this I have been able to realise. But alas, I still fail to comprehend in any way the greatness of his power.[19]

Calcutta, May 1897 · When one attains Bhakti, one's heart and nerves become so soft and delicate that they cannot bear even the touch of a flower!... I cannot think or talk of Sri Ramakrishna long, without being overwhelmed. So I am trying and trying always to keep down the rush of Bhakti welling within me. I am trying to bind and bind myself with the iron chain of Jnana, for still my work to my motherland is unfinished, and my message to the world not yet fully delivered. So, as soon as I find that Bhakti feelings are coming up to sweep me off my feet, I give them a hard knock and make myself adamant by bringing up austere Jnana. Oh, I have work to do! I am a slave of Ramakrishna, who left his work to be done by me, and will not give me rest till I have finished it! And, oh, how shall I speak of him! Oh, his love for me![20]

Alambazar Math, Calcutta, 5 May 1897 · I have been to Darjeeling for a month to recuperate my shattered health. I am very much better now. The disease disappeared altogether in Darjeeling. I am going tomorrow to Almora, another hill station, to perfect this improvement.

Things are looking not very hopeful here ... though the whole nation has risen as one man to honour me and people went almost mad over me!... The price of the land has gone up very much near Calcutta. My idea at present is to start three centres at three capitals. These would be my normal schools, from thence I want to invade India....

I am perfectly convinced that what they call modern Hinduism with all its ugliness is only stranded Buddhism. Let the Hindus understand this clearly, and then it would be easier for them to reject it without murmur. As for the ancient form which the Buddha preached, I have the greatest respect for it, as well as for His person. And you well know that we Hindus worship Him as an Incarnation. Neither is the Buddhism of Ceylon any good. My visit to Ceylon has entirely disillusioned me ... The real Buddhism, I once thought, would yet do much good. But I have given up the idea entirely, and I clearly see the reason why Buddhism was driven out of India ...

I was one man in America and another here. Here the whole nation is looking upon me as their authority—there I was a much reviled preacher. Here Princes draw my carriage, there I would not be admitted to a decent hotel. My utterances here, therefore, must be for the good of the race, my people—however unpleasant they might appear to a few. Acceptance, love, toleration for everything sincere and honest—but never for hypocrisy....

India is already Ramakrishna's and for a purified Hinduism I have organised my work here a bit.[21]

Alambazar Math, Calcutta, 5 May 1897 · There are moments when one feels entirely despondent, no doubt—especially when one has worked towards an ideal during a whole life's time and just when there is a bit of hope of seeing it partially accomplished, there comes a tremendous thwarting blow. I do not care for the disease, but what depresses me is that my ideals have not had yet the least opportunity of being worked out. And you know, the difficulty is money.

The Hindus are making processions and all that, but they cannot give money. The only help I got in the world was in England, from Miss Muller, and Mr. Sevier. I thought there that a thousand pounds was sufficient to start at least the principal centre in Calcutta, but my calculation was from the experience of Calcutta ten or twelve years ago. Since then the prices have gone up three or four times.

The work has been started anyhow. A rickety old little house has been rented for six or seven shillings, where about twenty-four young men are being trained. I had to go to Darjeeling for a month to recover my health, and I am glad to tell you I am very much better, and would you believe it, without taking any medicine, only by the exercise of mental healing! I am going again to another hill station tomorrow, as it is very hot in the plains.... The London work is not doing well at all, I hear, and that was the main reason why I would not come to England just now—although some of our Rajas going for the Jubilee tried their best to get me with them—as I would have to work hard again to revive the interest in Vedanta. And that would mean a good deal more trouble physically.

I may come over for a month or so very soon however. Only if I could see my work started here, how gladly and freely would I travel about!...

Mr. and Mrs. Hammond wrote two very kind and nice letters and Mr. Hammond a beautiful poem in the *Brahmavadin*, although I did not deserve it a bit.[22]

Almora, 20 May 1897 · Even now money is floating on the waters, as it were ... but it will surely come. When it comes, buildings, land, and a permanent fund—everything will come all right. But one can never rest assured until the chickens are hatched; and I am not now going down to the hot plains within two or three months. After that I shall make a tour and shall certainly secure some money....

On account of the great heat in Almora, I am now in an excellent garden twenty miles from there. This place is comparatively cool, but still warm. The heat does not seem to be particularly less than that of Calcutta....

The feverishness is all gone. I am trying to go to a still cooler place. Heat or the fatigue of walking, I find, at once produces trouble of the liver. The air here is so dry that there is a burning sensation in the nose all the time, and the tongue becomes, as it were, a chip of wood.[23]

Almora, 29 May 1897 · I began to take a lot of exercise on horseback, both morning and evening. Since that I am very much better indeed... I really began to feel that it was a pleasure to have a body. Every movement made me conscious of strength—every movement of the muscles was pleasurable.... You ought to see me, Doctor, when I sit meditating in front of the beautiful snow peaks and repeat from the Upanishads: "*Na tasya rogo na jarā na mṛtyuḥ prāptasya yogāgnimayaṁ śarīram*—he has neither disease, nor decay, nor death; for, verily, he has obtained a body full of the fire of Yoga."[24]

Almora, 2 June 1897 · I have been very, very bad indeed; now recovering a bit—hope to recover very soon.

What about the work in London? I am afraid it is going to pieces....

I am living in a beautiful garden belonging to a merchant of Almora—a garden abutting several miles of mountains and forests. Night before last a leopard came here and took away a goat from the flock kept in this garden. It was a frightful din the servants made and the barking of the big Tibet watchdogs. These dogs are kept chained at a distance all night since I am here, so that they may not disturb my sleep with their deep barks. The leopard thus found his opportunity and got a decent meal, perhaps, after weeks. May it do much good to him!...

Before me, reflecting the afternoon's glow, stand long, long lines of huge snow peaks. They are about twenty miles as the crow flies from here, and forty through the circuitous mountain roads....

Sleep, eat, and exercise; exercise, eat, and sleep—that is

what I am going to do some months yet. Mr. Goodwin is with me. You ought to have seen him in his Indian clothes. I am very soon going to shave his head and make a full-blown monk of him.[25]

Almora, 20 June 1897 · I have not had any news of the work [in London] for so long.... I do not expect any help from India, in spite of all the jubilating over me. They are so poor!

But I have started work in the fashion in which I myself was trained—that is to say, under the trees, and keeping body and soul together anyhow. The plan has also changed a little. I have sent some of my boys to work in the famine districts. It has acted like a miracle. I find, as I always thought, that it is through the heart, and that alone, that the world can be reached....

A number of boys are already in training, but the recent earthquake has destroyed the poor shelter we had to work in, which was only rented, anyway. Never mind. The work must be done without shelter and under difficulties.... As yet it is shaven heads, rags, and casual meals. This must change, however, and will, for are we not working for it, head and heart?...

It is true in one way that the people here have so little to give up—yet renunciation is in our blood. One of my boys in training has been an executive engineer, in charge of a district. That means a very big position here. He gave it up like straw![26]

Almora, 20 June 1897 · I am all right now, with plenty of muscular strength, and no thirst.... The liver, too, acts well. I am not certain as to what effects Shashi [Babu]'s medicine had. So I have stopped using it. I am having plenty of mangoes. I am getting exceptionally adept in riding, and do not feel the least pain or exhaustion even after a run of twenty or thirty miles at a stretch. Milk I have altogether stopped for fear of corpulence.

Yesterday I came to Almora, and shall not go any more to the garden. Henceforth I am to have three meals a day in the English fashion, as Miss Muller's guest.[27]

Almora, 4 July 1897 · Although I am still in the Himalayas, and shall be here for at least a month more, I started the work in Calcutta before I came, and they write progress every week.

Just now I am very busy with the famine, and except for training a number of young men for future work, have not been able to put more energy into the teaching work. The "feeding work" is absorbing all my energy and means. Although we can work only on a very small scale as yet, the effect is marvellous. For the first time since the days of Buddha, Brahmin boys are found nursing by the bed-side of cholera-stricken Pariahs.

In India, lectures and teaching cannot do any good. What we want is Dynamic Religion. And that, "God willing," as the Mohammedans say, I am determined to show.[28]

Almora, 9 July 1897 · I had arranged to go with Ajit Singh to England; but the doctors not allowing, it fell through....

I had also a lot of cuttings from different American papers fearfully criticising my utterances about American women and furnishing me with the strange news that I had been outcasted! As if I had any caste to lose, being a Sannyasin!

Not only no caste has been lost, but it has considerably shattered the opposition to sea voyage—my going to the West.... A leading Raja of the caste to which I belonged before my entering the order got up a banquet in my honour, at which were most of the big bugs of that caste.... These feet have been washed and wiped and worshipped by the descendants of kings, and there has been a progress through the country which none ever commanded in India.

It will suffice to say that the police were necessary to keep order if I ventured out into the street! That is outcasting indeed!

I never planned anything. I have taken things as they came. Only one idea was burning in my brain—to start the machine for elevating the Indian masses—and that I have succeeded in doing to a certain extent. It would have made your heart glad to see how my boys are working in the midst of famine and disease and misery—nursing by the mat-bed of the cholera-stricken Pariah and feeding the starving Chandala—and the Lord sends help to me and to them all. "What are men?" He is with me, the Beloved, He was when I was in America, in England, when I was roaming about unknown from place to place in India. What do I care about what they talk—the babies, they do not know any better. What! I, who have realised the Spirit and the vanity of all earthly nonsense, to be swerved from my path by babies' prattle! Do I look like that?

I had to talk a lot about myself because I owed that to you. I feel my task is done—at most three or four years more of life are left. I have lost all wish for my salvation. I never wanted earthly enjoyments. I must see my machine in strong working order, and then knowing sure that I have put in a lever for the good of humanity, in India at least, which no power can drive back, I will sleep, without caring what will be next; and may I be born again and again, and suffer thousands of miseries so that I may worship the only God that exists, the only God I believe in, the sum total of all souls—and above all, my God the wicked, my God the miserable, my God the poor of all races, of all species, is the special object of my worship.

My time is short. I have got to unbreast whatever I have to say, without caring if it smarts some or irritates others. Therefore ... do not be frightened at whatever drops from my lips, for the power behind me is not Vivekananda but He the Lord, and He knows best. If I have to please the world, that will be injuring the world ... Every new thought must create opposition—in the civilised a polite sneer, in the vulgar savage howls and filthy scandals.[29]

Almora, 10 July 1897 · I am very busy from here directing work by my boys in some of the famine districts....

I have taken to the Himalayas, tired of lecturing and orating. I am so sorry the doctors would not allow my going over with the Raja of Khetri to England, and that has made Sturdy mad....

I had a great mind to go to Tibet this year; but they would not allow me, as the road is dreadfully fatiguing. However, I content myself with galloping hard over precipices on mountain ponies. (This is more exciting than your bicycle even, although I had an experience of that at Wimbledon.) Miles and miles of uphill and miles and miles of downhill, the road a few feet broad hanging over sheer precipices several thousand feet deep below....

Goodwin has gone to work in Madras on a paper [the *Brahmavadin*] to be started there soon.[30]

Almora, 13 July 1897 · Today my health is a little bad owing to this riding on horseback at breakneck speed in the sun. I took Shashi Babu's medicine for two weeks—I find no special benefit.... The pain in the liver is gone, and owing to plenty of exercise my hands and legs have become muscular, but the abdomen is distending very much. I feel suffocated while getting up or sitting down. Perhaps this is due to the taking of milk. Ask Shashi if I can give up milk. Previously I suffered from two attacks of sunstroke. From that time, my eyes become red if I expose myself to the sun, and the health continues to be bad for two or three days at a stretch.[31]

Almora, 25 July 1897 · I am having a good deal of riding and exercise, but I had to drink a lot of skimmed milk per prescription of the doctors, with the result that I am more to the front than back! I am always a forward man though—but do not want to be too prominent just now, and I have given up drinking milk....

By and by, I am glad to find that I am aging fast, my hair is turning grey. "Silver threads among the gold"—I mean black—are coming in fast.

It is bad for a preacher to be young, don't you think so? I do, as I did all my life. People have more confidence in an old man, and it looks more venerable. Yet the old rogues are the worst rogues in the world, isn't it? The world has its code of judgment which, alas, is very different from that of truth's....

I am so glad that you have been helped by Vedanta and Yoga. I am unfortunately sometimes like the circus clown who makes others laugh, himself miserable!...

Our difficulty in life is that we are guided by the present and not by the future. What gives us a little pleasure now drags us on to follow it, with the result that we always buy a mass of pain in the future for a little pleasure in the present.

I wish I had nobody to love, and I were an orphan in my childhood. The greatest misery in my life has been my own people—my brothers and sisters and mother etc. Relatives are like deadly clogs to one's progress, and is it not a wonder that people will still go on to find new ones by marriage!!!

He who is alone is happy. Do good to all, like everyone, but *do not love* anyone. It is a bondage, and bondage brings only misery. Live alone in your mind—that is happiness. To have nobody to care for and never minding who cares for one is the way to be free....

I am more of a woman than a man, you are more of a man

than woman. I am always dragging others' pain into me—for nothing, without being able to do any good to anybody—just as women, if they have no children, bestow all their love upon a cat!!!

Do you think this has any spirituality in it? Nonsense, it is all material nervous bondage—that is what it is. O! to get rid of the thraldom of the flesh!...

Sturdy's thermometer is now below zero, it seems. He seems to be greatly disappointed with my non-arrival in England this summer. What could I do?

We have started two Maths (monasteries) here, one in Calcutta, the other in Madras. The Calcutta Math (a wretched rented house) was awfully shaken in the late earthquake.

In a few days I am going down to the plains and from thence go to the Western parts of the mountains. When it is cooler in the plains, I will make a lecture tour all over and see what work can be done.[32]

Almora, 29 July 1897 · I am leaving this place the day after tomorrow—whether for Mussoorie Hills or somewhere else I shall decide later.

Yesterday I delivered a lecture in the circle of the local English people, and all were highly pleased with it. But I was very much pleased with the lecture in Hindi that I delivered the previous day—I did not know before that I could be oratorical in Hindi.[33]

Almora, 30 July 1897 · I am leaving this place next Monday.... Here I gave a lecture to a European audience in English, and another to the Indian residents in Hindi. This was my maiden speech in Hindi, but everyone liked it for all that.... Next Saturday there will be another lecture for the Europeans....

Monday next, trip to Bareilly, then to Saharanpur, next to Ambala, thence, most probably, to Mussoorie with Captain

Sevier, and as soon as it is a little cool, return to the plains and journey to Rajputana etc. Go on working at top speed. Never fear! I, too, have determined to work. The body must go, no mistake about that. Why then let it go in idleness? It is better to wear out than rust out. Don't be anxious—even when I die, my very bones will work miracles.[34]

Ambala, 19 August 1897 · I am now going to the hills at Dharamsala.... I intend to start work in the Punjab after a few days' more rest in the Punjab hills. The Punjab and Rajputana are indeed fields for work....

My health was very bad recently. Now I am very slowly recovering. It will be all right, if I stay in the hills for some more days.[35]

Amritsar, 2 September 1897 · Today I am leaving by the two o'clock train with all my party for Kashmir. The recent stay at Dharamsala Hills has improved my health much, and the tonsillitis, fever, etc. have completely disappeared.[36]

Srinagar, 13 September 1897 · Now Kashmir. The excellent accounts you heard of this place are all true. There is no place so beautiful as this; and the people also are fair and good-looking, though their eyes are not beautiful. But I have also never seen elsewhere villages and towns so horribly dirty. In Srinagar I am now putting up at the house of Rishibar Babu. He is very hospitable and kind.... In a few days I shall go out somewhere else on excursions; but while returning, I shall come by way of Srinagar ...

Since reaching Dharamsala I have been all right. I like the cold places; there the body keeps well. I have a desire either to visit a few places in Kashmir and then choose an excellent site and live a quiet life there, or to go on floating on the water. I shall do what the doctor advises.... In October I shall go down from here and shall deliver a few lectures in the Punjab. After that I may go via Sindh to Cutch, Bhuj, and Kathiawar—even down to Poona if circumstances are favourable; otherwise I go to Rajputana via Baroda. From Rajputana I go to the North-western Province, then Nepal, and finally Calcutta—this is my present programme. Everything, however, is in God's hands.[37]

Srinagar, 15 September 1897 · We are in Kashmir at last. I need not tell you of all the beauties of the place. It is the one land fit for Yogis, to my mind. But the land is now inhabited by a race who though possessing great physical beauty are extremely dirty. I am going to travel by water for a month seeing the sights and getting strong. But the city is very malarious just now, and Sadananda and Kristolal [Krishnalal] have got fever. Sadananda is all right today, but Kristolal has fever yet. The doctor came today and gave him a purgative. He will be all right by tomorrow, we hope; and we start also tomorrow. The State has lent me one of its barges, and it is fine and quite comfortable. They have also sent orders to the Tahsildars of different districts. The people here are crowding in banks to see us and are doing everything they can to make us comfortable.[38]

Srinagar, 30 September 1897 · Now I am returning from a visit to places in Kashmir. In a day or two I shall leave for the Punjab. As my health is now much better, I have decided to tour again in the same way as before. Not too much lecturing—one or two lectures, perhaps, in the Punjab, otherwise none. The people of our country have not yet offered me even as much as a pice for my travelling expenses ... It is also a matter of shame to have to draw upon only the English disciples. So, as before, I start out "with only a blanket."[39]

Kashmir, September (?) 1897 · This Kashmir is a veritable heaven on earth. Nowhere else in the world is such a country as this. Mountains and rivers, trees and plants, men and women, beasts and birds—all vie with one another for excellence.[40]

Srinagar, 1 October 1897 · I shall not try to describe Kashmir to you. Suffice it to say, I never felt sorry to leave any country except this Paradise on earth; and I am trying my best, if I can, to influence the Raja in starting a centre. So much to do here, and the material so hopeful![41]

Murree, 11 October 1897 · I feel I have been working as if under an irresistible impulse for the last ten days, beginning from Kashmir. It may be either a physical or a mental disease. Now I have come to the conclusion that I am unfit for further work.... Whatever of Mother's work was to be accomplished through me, She made me do, and has now flung me aside breaking down my body and mind. Her will be done!...

Now I retire from all this work. In a day or two I shall give up everything and wander out alone; I shall spend the rest of my life quietly in some place or other.... I have all along been like a hero—I want my work to be quick like lightning, and firm as adamant. Likewise shall I die also.... I have never retreated in a fight—shall I now?... There is success and failure in every work. But I am inclined to believe that one who is a coward will be born after death as an insect or a worm, that there is no salvation for a coward even after millions of years of penance. Well, shall I after all be born as a worm?... In my eyes this world is mere play—and it will always remain as such. Should one spend six long months brooding over the questions of honour and disgrace, gain and loss?... I am a man of action.... This life is not, in my view, such a sweet thing that I would long to live through so much care and caution and fear. Money, life, friends, and relatives, and the love of men and myself—if one wants to enter into work fully assured beforehand of all these—if one has to be so much ridden with fear, then one will get just what Gurudeva used to say, "The crow thinks itself very clever but ... [it cannot help eating filth.]"—well, he will get that....

When I fight, I fight with girded loins—that much I fully understand; and I also understand that man, that hero, that god, who says, "Don't care, be fearless. O brave one, here I am by your side!" To such a man-god I offer a million salutations. Their presence purifies the world, they are the saviours of the world. And the others who always wail, "Oh, don't go forward, there is this danger, there is that danger"—those dyspeptics—they always tremble with fear. But through the grace of the Divine Mother my mind is so strong that even the most terrible dyspepsia shall not make me a coward.... I am the child of the Divine Mother, the source of all power and strength. To me, cringing, fawning, whining, degrading inertia and hell are one and the same thing. O Mother of the Universe, O my Gurudeva, who would constantly say, "This is a hero!"—I pray that I may not have to die a coward. This is my prayer, O brother. "*Utpatsyate'sti mama ko'pi samānadharmā*—certainly there is, or there will be born one equal to me"; someone or other will certainly arise from these thousands of devotees of Sri Ramakrishna who will be like me, and who will be able to understand me.

O hero, awake, and dream no more. Death has caught you by the forelock ... still fear not. What I have never done—fleeing from the battle—well, will that happen today? For fear of defeat shall I retreat from the fight? Defeat is the ornament the hero adorns himself with. What, to acknowledge defeat without fighting! O Mother, Mother!... If Mother sends me men again in whose heart there is courage, in whose hands strength, in whose eyes there is fire, real children of the

Mother—if She gives me even one such, then I shall work again, then I shall return. Otherwise, I shall take it that, by Mother's will, this is the end. I am in a tremendous hurry, I want to work at hurricane speed, and I want fearless hearts.[42]

Lahore, 11 November 1897 · The lecture at Lahore is over somehow. I shall start for Dehra Dun in a day or two. I have now postponed my tour to Sindh ... Without regular exercise the body does not keep fit; talking, talking all the time brings illness—know this for certain.[43]

Lahore, 15 November 1897 · It is a matter of deep regret that in spite of my earnest wishes, I do not find it feasible to go to Karachi this time ... Owing to my kidney troubles I cannot count upon a long life. Even now it is one of my desires to start a Math in Calcutta, towards which as yet I could do nothing. Moreover, the people of my country have withheld the little help that they used to give to our Math of late. They have got a notion that I have brought plenty of money from England! Over and above that, it is impossible to celebrate Sri Ramakrishna's festival this year, for the proprietors of Rasmani's garden would not let me go there, as I am returned from the West! Hence my first duty lies in seeing the few friends we have in Rajputana and trying my best to have a centre in Calcutta. For these reasons I have been very sorry to postpone my tour to Sindh at present.[44]

Lahore, 15 November 1897 · My health is good; only I have to get up at night once or twice. I am having sound sleep; sleep is not spoiled even after exhausting lectures; and I am doing exercise every day.[45]

Dehra Dun, 24 November 1897 · Now Babu Raghunath Bhattacharya of Tehri is suffering very much from some pain in the neck; I also have been suffering for a long time from some pain at the back of my neck. If you can get hold of some very old ghee, then send some of it to him at Dehra Dun and some of it to me also at my Khetri address.[46]

Belur Math, 25 February 1898 · My health has not been all right of late; at present it is much better. Calcutta is unusually cool just now, and the American friends who are here are enjoying it ever so much. Today we take possession of the land we have bought, and though it is not practicable to have the Mahotsava [of Sri Ramakrishna's birthday] on it just now, I must have something on it on Sunday. Anyhow, Sriji's [Sri Ramakrishna's] relics must be taken to our place for the day and worshipped.... I have no money; every cent I had I have made over to Raja [Swami Brahmananda], as they all say I am a spendthrift and are afraid of keeping money with me....

By the by, we have once more started the dancing business here, and it would make your heart glad to see Hari and Sarada and my own good self in a waltz. How we keep balance at all is a wonder to me. [*Swamiji humorously alludes to the days with Sri Ramakrishna, in whose inspired company he and his brother-disciples used to sing and dance in ecstatic joy.*]

Sharat has come and is hard at work as usual. We have got some good furniture now, and a big jump from the old Chātāi [mat] in the old Math to nice tables and chairs and three Khāts [cots] ... I am going to America again with Mrs. Bull in a few months....

So the Math here is a *fait accompli*, and I am going over to get more help.... Work on with energy. India is a rotten corpse inside and outside. We shall revive it by the blessings of Sri Maharaj.[47]

Belur Math, 25 February 1898 · A friend to whom I owe much is here, presumably, to take me to his place in Darjeeling.

There are some American friends come, and every spare

moment is occupied in working for the new Math and several organisations therein, and I expect to leave India next month for America.[48]

Belur Math, 2 March 1898 · Well, it was in Southern India, when I came from London and when the people were fêting and feasting and pumping all the work out of me, that an old hereditary disease made its appearance. The tendency was always there, and excess of mental work made it "express" itself. Total collapse and extreme prostration followed, and I had to leave Madras immediately for the cooler North; a day's delay meant waiting for a week in that awful heat for another steamer. By the by, I learnt afterwards that Mr. Barrows arrived in Madras next day and was very much chagrined at not finding me as he expected, though I helped getting up an address for him and arranged for his reception. Poor man, he little knew I was at death's door then.

I have been travelling in the Himalayas all through last summer; and a cold climate, I found immediately, brought me round; but as soon as I come into the heat of the plains I am down again. From today the heat in Calcutta is becoming intense, and I will soon have to fly. This time to cool America as Mrs. Bull and Miss MacLeod are here. I have bought a piece of land for the institution on the river Ganga near Calcutta, on which is a little house where they are living now; within a stone's throw is the house where the Math is situated at present in which we live.

So I see them every day and they are enjoying it immensely *à L'Inde*. They intend making a trip to Kashmir in a month, and I am going with them as a guide and friend and philosopher perhaps, if they are willing. After that we all sail for the land of freedom and scandal.

You need not be alarmed with me as the disease will take two or three years at worst to carry me off. At best it may remain a harmless companion. I am content. Only I am working hard to set things all right and always so that the machine moves forward when I am off the stage. Death I have conquered long ago when I gave up life. My only anxiety is the work, and even that to the Lord I dedicate, and He knows best.[49]

Darjeeling, 23 April 1898 · My health was excellent on my return from Sandukphu (11,924 ft.) and other places; but after returning to Darjeeling, I had first an attack of fever, and after recovering from that, I am now suffering from cough and cold. I try to escape from this place every day; but they have been constantly putting it off for a long time. However, tomorrow, Sunday, I am leaving; after halting at Kharsana for a day I start again for Calcutta on Monday.[50]

Darjeeling, 29 April 1898 · I have had several attacks of fever, the last being influenza. It has left me now, only I am very weak yet. As soon as I gather strength enough to undertake the journey, I come down to Calcutta....

What enlightens your insides on a dark night when the fire God, Sun God, Moon God, and Star Goddesses have gone to sleep? It is hunger that keeps my consciousness up, I have discovered. Oh, the great doctrine of correspondence of light! Think how dark the world has been all these ages without it! And all this knowledge and love and work and all the Buddhas and Krishnas and Christs—vain, vain have been their lives and work, for they did not discover that "which keeps the inner light when the Sun and Moon were gone to the limbo" for the night! Delicious, isn't it?

If the plague comes to my native city, I am determined to make myself a sacrifice; and that I am sure is a "Darn sight, better way to Nirvana" than pouring oblations to all that ever twinkled.[51]

Almora, 20 May 1898 · After I reached Naini Tal, Baburam [Swami Premananda] went from here to Naini Tal on horseback against everybody's advice, and while returning, he also accompanied us on horseback. I was far behind as I was in a Dandi. When I reached the dak bungalow at night, I heard that Baburam had again fallen from the horse and had hurt one of his arms—though he had no fractures. Lest I should rebuke him, he stayed in a private lodging house. Because of his fall, Miss MacLeod gave him her Dandi and herself came on the horse. He did not meet me that night. Next day I was making arrangements for a Dandi for him, when I heard that he had already left on foot. Since then I have not heard of him. I have wired to one or two places, but no news. Perhaps he is putting up at some village. Very well! They are experts in increasing one's worries....

My health is much better, but the dyspepsia has not gone, and again insomnia has set in. It will be very helpful if you can soon send some good Ayurvedic medicine for dyspepsia....

The climate at Almora is excellent at this time. Moreover the bungalow rented by Sevier is the best in Almora. On the opposite side Annie Besant is staying in a small bungalow with Chakravarty.... One day I went to see him. Annie Besant told me entreatingly that there should be friendship between her organisation and mine all over the world, etc., etc. Today Besant will come here for tea. Our ladies are in a small bungalow near by and are quite happy. Only Miss MacLeod is a little unwell today. Harry Sevier is becoming more and more a Sadhu as the days pass by.[52]

Almora, June 1898 · With infinite sorrow I learn the sad news of Mr. Goodwin's departure from this life, the more so as it was terribly sudden and therefore prevented all possibilities of my being at his side at the time of death. The debt of gratitude I owe him can never be repaid, and those who think they have been helped by any thought of mine ought to know that almost every word of it was published through the untiring and most unselfish exertions of Mr. Goodwin. In him I have lost a friend true as steel, a disciple of never failing devotion, a worker who knew not what tiring was, and the world is less rich by one of those few who are born, as it were, to live only for others.[53]

Srinagar, 17 July 1898 · My health is all right. I have to get up seldom at night, even though I take twice a day rice and potatoes, sugar, or whatever I get. Medicine is useless—it has no action on the system of a knower of Brahman![54]

Amarnath, 2 August 1898 · I have enjoyed it so much! I thought the ice Linga was Shiva Himself. And there were no thievish Brahmins, no trade, nothing wrong. It was all worship. I never enjoyed any religious place so much![55]

Srinagar, 10 August 1898 · I have been to see Sri Amarnathji. It was a very enjoyable trip and the Darshana was glorious.

I will be here about a month more, then I return to the plains.[56]

Kashmir, 25 August 1898 · It is a lazy life I am leading for the last two months, floating leisurely in a boat, which is also my home, up and down the beautiful Jhelum, through the most gorgeous scenery God's world can afford, in nature's own park, where the earth, air, land, grass, plants, trees, mountains, snows, and the human form, all express, on the outside at least, the beauty of the Lord—with almost no possessions, scarcely a pen or an inkstand even, snatching up a meal whenever or wherever convenient, the very ideal of a Rip Van Winkle!...

Do not work yourself out. It is no use; always remember—"Duty is the midday sun whose fierce rays are burning the very vitals of humanity." It is necessary for a time as a discipline; beyond that, it is a morbid dream. Things go on all right whether we lend them our helping hands or not. We in delusion only break ourselves. There is a false sentiment which goes the extreme of unselfishness, only to injure others by its submission to every evil. We have no right to make others selfish by our unselfishness, have we?[57]

Srinagar, 28 August 1898 · I have been away a few days. Now I am going to join the ladies. The party then goes to a nice quiet spot behind a hill, in a forest, through which a murmuring stream flows, to have meditation deep and long under the deodars (trees of God) cross-legged *à la Buddha*.[58]

Kashmir, 6 October 1898 · No more "Hari Om!" It is all "Mother" now! All my patriotism is gone. Now it is only "Mother! Mother!" I have been very wrong. Mother said to me, "What, even if unbelievers should enter My temples, and defile My images! What is that to you? Do you protect Me? Or do I protect you?" So there is no more patriotism. I am only a little child![59] *

Kashmir, 12 October 1898 · It all came true, every word of it—
>Who dares misery love,
>Dance in Destruction's dance,
>And hug the form of death . . .

To *him* the Mother does indeed come. I have proved it. For I have hugged the form of Death![60]

---

* One day at Kshir-Bhavani, Swami Vivekananda had been pondering over the ruination and desecration of the temple wrought by the Muslim invaders. Distressed at heart he thought, "How could the people have permitted such sacrilege without offering strenuous resistance! If I were here then, I would never have allowed such things. I would have laid down my life to protect the Mother." Then the Mother spoke to him.

Lahore, October 1898 · I have three years more to live, and the only thought that disturbs me is whether I shall be able to give effect to all my ideas within this period.[61]

Belur Math, 20 October 1898 · Since visiting Amarnath, I feel as if Shiva is sitting on my head for twenty-four hours and would not come down.

I underwent great religious austerities at Amarnath and then in the temple of Kshir Bhavani....

On the way to Amarnath, I made a very steep ascent on the mountain. Pilgrims do not generally travel by that path. But the determination came upon me that I must go by that path, and so I did. The labour of the strenuous ascent has told on my body. The cold there is so biting that you feel it like pin-pricks....

I entered the cave with only my Kaupina on and my body smeared with holy ash; I did not then feel any cold or heat. But when I came out of the temple, I was benumbed by the cold....

I saw three or four white pigeons; whether they live in the cave or the neighbouring hills, I could not ascertain.... I have heard that the sight of the pigeons brings to fruition whatever desires one may have....

Since hearing that divine voice [at Kshir Bhavani], I cherish no more plans. The idea of building Maths etc. I have given up; as Mother wills, so it will be....

Whether it be internal or external, if you actually hear with your ears such a disembodied voice, as I have done, can you deny it and call it false? Divine Voices are actually heard, just as you and I are talking.[62]

Belur Math, 25 October 1898 · My health again failed badly. I had, therefore, to leave Kashmir in haste and come to Calcutta.

The doctors say I ought not go tramping again this winter. That is such a disappointment, you know. However, I am coming to the U.S. this summer. Mrs. Bull and Miss MacLeod enjoyed this year's trip to Kashmir immensely....

I am getting better every day—and then the long months before I can start for the U.S. Never mind, "Mother" knows what is best for us. She will show the way. I am now in Bhakti. As I am growing old, Bhakti is taking the place of Jnana.[63]

Belur Math, November 1898 · The other day, I was a guest of Babu Priyanath Mukherjee at Vaidyanath. There I had such a spell of asthma that I felt like dying. But from within, with every breath arose the deep-toned sound, "I am He, I am He." Resting on the pillow, I was waiting for the vital breath to depart, and observing all the time that from within was being heard the sound of "I am He, I am He!" I could hear all along "*Ekam evādvayaṁ brahma neha nānāsti kiñcana*—Brahman, the One without a second, alone exists, nothing manifold exists in the world."[64]

Calcutta, 12 November 1898 · Sri Mother [Sri Sarada Devi] is going this morning to see the new Math. I am also going there.[65]

Belur Math, 22 November 1898 · I have been ailing since my return.... This disease has been caused by nervous excitement; and no amount of change can do me good, unless the worry and anxiety and excitement are taken off me.

After trying these two years a different climate, I am getting worse every day and now almost at death's door.... I have one great sin rankling always in my breast, and that is [in order] to do a service to the world, I have sadly neglected my mother. Again, since my second brother has gone away, she has become awfully worn out with grief. Now my last desire is to make Seva [give service] and serve my mother, for some years at least. I want to live with my mother and get my younger brother married to prevent extinction of the family. This will certainly smoothen my last days as well as those of my mother. She lives now in a hovel. I want to build a little, decent home for her and make some provision for the youngest, as there is very little hope of his being a good earning man.[66]

Belur Math, 9 December 1898 · Sri Ramakrishna said to me [at Cossipore], "Wherever you will take me on your shoulders, there I will go and stay, be it under a tree or in a hut." It is therefore that I am myself carrying him on my shoulders to the new Math grounds. Know it for certain that Sri Ramakrishna will keep his seat fixed there, for the welfare of many, for a long time to come....

Each devotee colours Sri Ramakrishna in the light of his own understanding and each forms his own idea of him from his peculiar standpoint. He was, as it were, a great Sun, and each one of us is eyeing him, as it were, through a different kind of coloured glass and coming to look upon that one Sun as particoloured....

This Math that we are building will harmonise all creeds, all standpoints. Just as Sri Ramakrishna held highly liberal views, this Math too, will be a centre for propagating similar ideas. The blazing light of universal harmony that will emanate from here will flood the whole world....

Through the will of Sri Ramakrishna, his Dharmakshetra—sanctified spot—has been established today. A twelve years' anxiety is off my head. Do you know what I am thinking of at this moment?—this Math will be a centre of learning and spiritual discipline. Householders of a virtuous turn ... will build houses on the surrounding land and live there, and Sannyasins, men of renunciation, will live in the centre, while on that plot of land on the south of the Math, buildings will be erected for English and American disciples to live in....

Everything will come about in time. I am but laying the foundation. There will be lots of further developments in future. Some portion of it I shall live to work out.[67]

Belur Math, 15 December 1898 · The Mother is our guide and whatever happens or will happen is under Her ordination.[68]

Belur Math, 26 January 1899 · I was once more in the vale of death. The old diabetes has now disappeared. In its place has come what some doctors call asthma, others dyspepsia, owing to nervous prostration. However, it is a most worrying disease, giving one the sensation of suffocation—sometimes for days. I am best only in Calcutta; so I am here for rest and quiet and low diet. If I get well by March, I am going to start for Europe. Mrs. Bull and others are gone; sorry I could not accompany them owing to this disease....

Do not be the least anxious, dear. Things must be as "Mother" wishes. Ours is only to obey and work.[69]

Belur Math, April 1899 [*After the death of Swami Yogananda*] · I did not come to the temple these days because I was very angry with my Master for having deprived me of my dear brother. I love them so much because I have lived longer and more intimately with them than even with my own brothers.... But why should I be angry with my Master? Why should I expect that all things will be ordained according to my wishes? And why should I be sad at all? Am I not a hero? My Master used to say, laying his arm upon my shoulder, "Naren, you are a hero; the very sight of you inspires me with courage." Yes, I am a hero. Why should I then give way to grief?[70]

Belur Math, 11 April 1899 · Two years of physical suffering have taken away twenty years of my life. Well, but the soul changeth not, does it? It is there, the same madcap Atman, mad upon one idea, intent and intense.[71]

Belur Math, 16 April 1899 · If by the sacrifice of some specially cherished object of either myself or my brother-disciples many pure and genuinely patriotic souls come forward to help our cause ... we will not hesitate in the least to make that sacrifice nor shed a teardrop.... But up till now I have seen nobody coming forward to assist in this way. Only some have wished to put their own hobby in place of ours—that is all. If it really help our country or humanity—not to speak of giving up Guru-worship—believe me, we are prepared to commit any dire iniquity and suffer the eternal damnation of the Christians. But my hairs have turned grey since I began the study of man....

I have some doubts about those patriotic souls who can join with us if only we give up the worship of the Guru. Well, if, as they pose, they are indeed panting and struggling so much—almost to the point of dissolution from their body—to serve the country, how can the single accident of Guru-worship stop everything!...

Well, if this trifle of Guru-worship sticks in one's throat to choke one to death, we had better extricate him from this predicament.[72]

Belur Math, 10 May 1899 · I am getting better again. In my mind the whole of my complaint is bad assimilation of food and nervous exhaustion. The first, I am taking care of; the second will completely pass off when I meet you again. The great joy of meeting old, old friends, you know! Cheer up! There is no cause for anxiety. Do not believe a single desponding line I write now, because I am at times not myself. I get so nervous.

I start this summer for Europe anyway ...[73]

Calcutta, May (?) 1899 · Oh, the tremendous labour! Today the Americans out of love have given me this nice bed, and I have something to eat also. But alas—I have not been destined to enjoy physically—and lying on the mattress only aggravates my illness. I feel suffocated, as it were. I have to come down and lie on the floor for relief.[74]

Calcutta, May (?) 1899 · A very funny thing happened today. I went to a friend's house. He has had a picture painted, the subject of which is "Sri Krishna addressing Arjuna on the battlefield of Kurukshetra." Sri Krishna stands on the chariot, holding the reins in His hand and preaching the Gita to Arjuna. He showed me the picture and asked me how I liked it. "Fairly well," I said. But as he insisted on having my criticism on it, I had to give my honest opinion by saying, "There is nothing in it to commend itself to me; first, because the chariot of the time of Sri Krishna was not like the modern pagoda-shaped car, and also, there is no expression in the figure of Sri Krishna"....

Have you seen the chariots in the pictures of Grecian mythology? They have two wheels, and one mounts them from behind; we had that sort of chariot. What good is it to paint a picture if the details are wrong?...

Sri Krishna ought to be painted as He really was, the Gita personified; and the central idea of the Gita should radiate from His whole form as He was teaching the path of Dharma to Arjuna, who had been overcome by infatuation and cowardice.

[*Then Swami Vivekananda posed himself as Sri Krishna should be portrayed*] Look here, thus does he hold the bridle of the horses—so tight that they are brought to their haunches, with their forelegs fighting the air, and their mouths gaping. This will show a tremendous play of action in the figure of Sri Krishna. His friend, the world-renowned hero, casting aside his bow and arrows, has sunk down like a coward on the chariot, in the midst of the two armies. And Sri Krishna, whip in one hand and tightening the reins with the other, has turned Himself towards Arjuna, with his childlike face beaming with unworldly love and sympathy, and a calm and serene look—and is delivering the message of the Gita to his beloved comrade....

Ay, that's it! Intense action in the whole body, and withal a face expressing the profound calmness and serenity of the blue sky. This is the central idea of the Gita—to be calm and steadfast in all circumstances, with one's body, mind, and soul centred at His hallowed Feet![75]

CHAPTER EIGHT

THE PLAN OF WORK

Bold has been my message to the people of the West, bolder is my message to you, my beloved countrymen. The message of ancient India to new Western nations I have tried my best to voice—ill done or well done the future is sure to show; but the mighty voice of the same future is already sending forward soft but distinct murmurs, gaining strength as the days go by, the message of India that is to be to India as she is at present.

Many wonderful institutions and customs, and many wonderful manifestations of strength and power it has been my good fortune to study in the midst of the various races I have seen, but the most wonderful of all was to find that beneath all these apparent variations of manners and customs, of culture and power, beats the same mighty human heart under the impulse of the same joys and sorrows, of the same weakness and strength.

Good and evil are everywhere and the balance is wondrously even; but, above all, is the glorious soul of man everywhere which never fails to understand any one who knows how to speak its own language. Men and women are to be found in every race whose lives are blessings to humanity, verifying the words of the divine Emperor Ashoka: "In every land dwell Brahmins and Shramanas."

I am grateful to the lands of the West for the many warm hearts that received me with all the love that pure and disinterested souls alone could give; but my life's allegiance is to this my motherland; and if I had a thousand lives, every moment of the whole series would be consecrated to your service, my countrymen, my friends.

For to this land I owe whatever I possess, physical, mental, and spiritual; and if I have been successful in anything, the glory is yours, not mine. Mine alone are my weaknesses and failures, as they come through my inability of profiting by the mighty lessons with which this land surrounds one, even from his very birth....

We all hear so much about the degradation of India. There was a time when I also believed in it. But today standing on the vantage-ground of experience, with eyes cleared of obstructive predispositions, and above all, of the highly-coloured pictures of other countries toned down to their proper shade and light by actual contact, I confess in all humility that I was wrong. Thou blessed land of the Aryas, thou wast never degraded. Sceptres have been broken and thrown away, the ball of power has passed from hand to hand, but in India, courts and kings always touched only a few; the vast mass of the people, from the highest to the lowest, has been left to pursue its own inevitable course, the current of national life flowing at times slow and half-conscious, at others, strong and awakened. I stand in awe before the unbroken procession of scores of shining centuries, with here and there a dim link in the chain, only to flare up with added brilliance in the next, and there she is walking with her own majestic steps—my motherland—to fulfil her glorious destiny, which no power on earth or in heaven can check—the regeneration of man the brute into man the God.[1]

As to that ever blessed land which gave me this body, I look back with great veneration and bless the merciful being who permitted me to take birth in that holiest spot on earth. When the whole world is trying to trace its ancestry from men distinguished in arms or wealth, the Hindus alone are proud to trace their descent from saints.

That wonderful vessel which has been carrying for ages men and women across this ocean of life may have sprung small leaks here and there. And of that, too, the Lord alone knows how much is owing to themselves and how much to those who look down with contempt upon the Hindus.

But if such leaks there are, I, the meanest of her children, think it my duty to stop her from sinking even if I have to do it with my life. And if I find that all my struggles are in vain, still, as the Lord is my witness, I will tell them with my heartfelt benediction: "My brethren, you have done well—nay, better than any other race could have done under the same circumstances. You have given me all that I have. Grant me the privilege of being at your side to the last and let us all sink together."[2]

I am thoroughly convinced that no individual or nation can live by holding itself apart from the community of others, and whenever such an attempt has been made under the false ideas of greatness, policy, or holiness—the result has always been disastrous to the secluding one.

To my mind, the one great cause of the downfall and the degeneration of India was the building of a wall of custom—whose foundation was hatred of others—round the nation, and the real aim of which in ancient times was to prevent the Hindus from coming in contact with the surrounding Buddhistic nations.[3]

It has been one of the principles of my life not to be ashamed of my own ancestors. I am one of the proudest men ever born, but let me tell you frankly, it is not for myself, but on account of my ancestry. The more I have studied the past, the more I have looked back, more and more has this pride come to me, and it has given me the strength and courage of conviction, raised me up from the dust of the earth, and set me working out that great plan laid out by those great ancestors of ours.[4]

Here am I, one of the least of the Hindu race, yet proud of my race, proud of my ancestors. I am proud to call myself a Hindu, I am proud that I am one of your unworthy servants. I am proud that I am a countryman of yours, you the descendants of the sages, you the descendants of the most glorious Rishis the world ever saw. Therefore have faith in yourselves, be proud of your ancestors, instead of being ashamed of them.[5]

I believe in patriotism, and I also have my own ideal of patriotism. Three things are necessary for great achievements. First, feel from the heart. What is in the intellect or reason? It goes a few steps and there it stops. But through the heart comes inspiration. Love opens the most impossible gates; love is the gate to all the secrets of the universe. Feel, therefore, my would-be reformers, my would-be patriots! Do you feel? Do you feel that millions and millions of the descendants of gods and of sages have become next-door neighbours to brutes? Do you feel that millions are starving today, and millions have been starving for ages? Do you feel that ignorance has come over the land as a dark cloud? Does it make you restless? Does it make you sleepless? Has it gone into your blood, coursing through your veins, becoming consonant with your heartbeats? Has it made you almost mad? Are you seized with that one idea of the misery of ruin, and have you forgotten all about your name, your fame, your wives, your children, your property, even your own bodies? Have you done that? That is the first step to become a patriot, the very first step.[6]

For the last thousand years or more, you are told that you are weak, you are nobodies, you are good for nothing, and so on, and you have come to believe yourselves such. This body of mine was also born and bred on Indian soil, but I have never for a moment allowed such baneful ideas to enter my mind. I had tremendous faith in myself. It is because of that, by the grace of the Lord, that those who look down upon us as weak and low, regard me as their teacher. If you have the same faith in yourselves as I had, if you can believe that in you is infinite power, unbounded wisdom, indomitable energy, if you can rouse that power in yourselves, you will be like me, you will do wonders. You will say, "Where is that strength in us to be able to think like that, and where are the teachers to tell us not of weakness but of strength, and to rouse in us that faith?" It is to teach you that and to show you the way by my life that I have come to you. From me you must learn and realize that truth, and then go from town to town, from village to village, from door to door, and scatter the idea broadcast. Go and tell every Indian, "Arise, awake and dream no more. Rouse yourself and manifest the Divinity within." There is no want, there is no misery, that you cannot remove by the consciousness of the power of the Spirit within. Believe in these words and you will be omnipotent.[7]

I see it clear as daylight that you all have infinite power in you. Rouse that up; arise, arise—apply yourselves heart and soul, gird up your loins. What will you do with wealth and fame that are so transitory? Do you know what I think? I don't care for Mukti and all that. My mission is to arouse within you all such ideas; I am ready to undergo a hundred thousand rebirths to train up a single man.[8]

For my own part I will be incarnated two hundred times, if that is necessary, to do this work amongst my people that I have undertaken.[9]

I will have a lot of difficult work to do in this life. Compared with last time, there is much more to be done.... This time I will work up to the very last moment!...

I have just begun my work; in America I have raised only one or two waves; a tidal wave must be raised; society must be turned upside down; the world must be given a new civilization. The world will understand what that Power is and why I have come. Compared with the power I showed last time, it will be tremendous.[10]

The work of the Lord does not wait for the like of you or me. He can raise His workers from the dust by hundreds and by thousands. It is a glory and a privilege that we are allowed to work at all under Him.[11]

A bit of public demonstration was necessary for Guru Maharaj's work. It is done, and so far so good.[12]

India has suffered long, the Religion Eternal has suffered long. But the Lord is merciful. Once more He has come to help His children, once more the opportunity is given to rise to fallen India. India can only rise by sitting at the feet of Sri Ramakrishna. His life and his teachings are to be spread far and wide, are to be made to penetrate every pore of Hindu society.[13]

My Master used to say that these names, as Hindu, Christian, etc., stand as great bars to all brotherly feelings between man and man. We must try to break them down first. They have lost all their good powers and now only stand as baneful influences under whose black magic even the best of us behave like demons. Well, we will have to work hard and must succeed.

That is why I desire so much to have a centre. Organisation has its faults, no doubt, but without that nothing can be done....

One must work as the dictate comes from within, and then if it is right and good, society is bound to veer round, perhaps centuries after one is dead and gone. We must plunge heart and soul and body into the work. And until we be ready to sacrifice everything else to one Idea and to one alone, we never, never will see the light.

Those that want to help mankind must take their own pleasure and pain, name and fame, and all sorts of interests, and make a bundle of them and throw them into the sea, and then come to the Lord. This is what all the Masters said and did....

My *idea* and all my life with it—and to *God* for help; to none else! This is the only secret of success.[14]

Away back, where no recorded history, nay, not even the dim light of tradition, can penetrate, has been steadily shining the light, sometimes dimmed by external circumstances, at others effulgent, but undying and steady, shedding its lustre not only over India, but permeating the whole thought-world with its power, silent, unperceived, gentle, yet omnipotent, like the dew that falls in the morning, unseen and unnoticed, yet bringing into bloom the fairest of roses: this has been the thought of the Upanishads, the philosophy of the Vedanta.... This Vedanta, the philosophy of the Upanishads, I would make bold to state, has been the first as well as the final thought on the spiritual plane that has ever been vouchsafed to man....

In India ... in spite of all these jarring sects that we see today and all those that have been in the past, the one authority, the basis of all these systems, has yet been the Upanishads, the Vedanta.... All the Indian sects must bear allegiance to the Upanishads; but among these sects there are many apparent contradictions. Many times the great sages of yore themselves could not understand the underlying harmony of the Upanishads.... The time requires that a better interpretation should be given to this underlying harmony of the Upanishadic texts, whether they are dualistic, or non-dualistic, quasi-dualistic, or so forth.... I, through the grace of God, had the great good fortune to sit at the feet of one whose whole life was such an interpretation, whose life, a thousandfold more than whose teaching, was a living commentary on the texts of the Upanishads, was in fact the spirit of the Upanishads living in a human form. Perhaps I have got a little of that harmony; I do not know whether I shall be able to express it or not. But this is my attempt, my mission in life, to show that the Vedantic schools are not contradictory, that they all necessitate each other, all fulfil each other, and one, as it were, is the stepping-stone to the other, until the goal, the Advaita, the Tat Tvam Asi, is reached.[15]

[*Question: Why, if this is true, has it never been mentioned before by any of the great Masters?*] Because I was born for this, and it was left for me to do![16]

There is nothing higher than this knowledge of the Atman; all else is Maya, mere jugglery. The Atman is the one unchangeable Truth. This I have come to understand, and that is why I try to bring it home to you all.[17]

If there be a Hindu boy amongst us who is not ready to believe that his religion is pure spirituality, I do not call him a Hindu. I remember in one of the villages of Kashmir, while talking to an old Mohammedan lady, I asked her in a mild voice, "What religion is yours?" She replied in her own language, "Praise the Lord! By the mercy of God, I am a Mussalman." And then I asked a Hindu, "What is your religion?" He plainly replied, "I am a Hindu." I remember that grand word of the Katha Upanishad—Shraddhā or marvellous faith.... To preach the doctrine of Shraddhā or genuine faith is the mission of my life.... I do not care what philosophy you take up; only I am ready to prove here that throughout the whole of India, there runs a mutual and cordial string of eternal faith in the perfection of humanity, and I believe in it myself. And let that faith be spread over the whole land.[18]

My plan for India, as it has been developed and centralised, is this: I have told you of our lives as monks there, how we go from door to door, so that religion is brought to everybody without charge, except, perhaps, a broken piece of bread. That is why you see the lowest of the low in India holding the most exalted religious ideas. It is all through the work of these monks. But ask a man, "Who are the English?"—he does not know.... "Who governs you?" "We do not know." "What is the government?" They do not know. But they know philosophy. It is a practical want of intellectual education about life on this earth they suffer from. These millions and millions of people are ready for life beyond this world—is not that enough for them? Certainly not. They must have a better piece of bread and a better piece of rag on their bodies. The great question is: How to get that better bread and better rag for these sunken millions.

First, I must tell you, there is great hope for them, because, you see, they are the gentlest people on earth. Not that they are timid. When they want to fight, they fight like demons. The best soldiers the English have are recruited from the peasantry of India. Death is a thing of no importance to them.

Their attitude is, "Twenty times I have died before, and I shall die many times after this. What of that?" They never turn back. They are not given to much emotion, but they make very good fighters.

Their instinct, however, is to plough. If you rob them, murder them, tax them, do anything to them, they will be quiet and gentle, so long as you leave them free to practise their religion. They never interfere with the religion of others. "Leave us liberty to worship our gods, and take everything else!" That is their attitude. When the English touch them there, trouble starts. That was the real cause of the 1857 Mutiny—they would not bear religious repression. The great Mohammedan governments were simply blown up because they touched the Indians' religion....

Now there is no reason why they should suffer such distress—these people; oh, so pure and good!...

No national civilisation is perfect yet. Give that civilisation a push, and it will arrive at its own goal: do not strive to change it. Take away a nation's institutions, customs, and manners, and what will be left? They hold the nation together.

But here comes the very learned foreign man, and he says, "Look here; you give up all those institutions and customs of thousands of years, and take my tomfool tinpot and be happy." This is all nonsense.

We will have to help each other, but we have to go one step farther: the first thing is to become unselfish in help. "If you do just what I tell you to do, I will help you; otherwise not." Is that help?...

Well then, my plans are, therefore, to reach these masses of India....

Now, you see, we have brought the plan down nicely on paper; but I have taken it, at the same time, from the regions of idealism. So far the plan was loose and idealistic. As years

THE PLAN OF WORK

went on, it became more and more condensed and accurate; I began to see by actual working its defects, and all that.

What did I discover in its working on the material plane? First, there must be centres to educate these monks in the method of education.... In India, you will find every man is quite illiterate, and that teaching requires tremendous centres. And what does all that mean? Money. From the idealistic plane you come to everyday work. Well, I have worked hard, four years in your country [the U.S.A.], and two in England.... There are American friends and English friends who went over with me to India, and there has been a very rude beginning. Some English people came and joined the orders. One poor man worked hard and died in India. There are an Englishman and an Englishwoman who have retired; they have some means of their own, and they have started a centre in the Himalayas, educating the children. I have given them one of the papers I have started—a copy you will find there on the table—the Awakened India. And there they are instructing and working among the people. I have another centre in Calcutta....

I am glad to tell you I have made a rude beginning. But the same work I want to do, on parallel lines, for women....

That part has to be accomplished.[19]

My idea is to bring to the door of the meanest, the poorest, the noble ideas that the human race has developed both in and out of India, and let them think for themselves. Whether there should be caste or not, whether women should be perfectly free or not, does not concern me. "Liberty of thought and action is the only condition of life, of growth and wellbeing." Where it does not exist, the man, the race, the nation must go down....

My whole ambition in life is to set in motion a machinery

which will bring noble ideas to the door of everybody, and then let men and women settle their own fate.[20]

Look at that handful of young men called into existence by the divine touch of Ramakrishna's feet. They have preached the message from Assam to Sindh, from the Himalayas to Cape Comorin. They have crossed the Himalayas at a height of twenty thousand feet, over snow and ice on foot, and penetrated into the mysteries of Tibet. They have begged their bread, covered themselves with rags; they have been persecuted, followed by the police, kept in prison, and at last set free when the Government was convinced of their innocence.[21]

A movement which half a dozen penniless boys set on foot and which now bids fair to progress in such an accelerated motion—it is a humbug or the Lord's will?[22]

I have been criticised, from one end of the world to the other, as one who preaches the diabolical idea that there is no sin! Very good. The descendants of these very men will bless me as the preacher of virtue, and not of sin. I am the teacher of virtue, not of sin. I glory in being the preacher of light, and not of darkness.[23]

Travelling through many cities of Europe and observing in them the comforts and education of even the poor people, there was brought to my mind the state of our own poor people, and I used to shed tears. What made the difference? Education was the answer I got.[24]

In America the beds are very soft and cosy. You do not even see such things here [in India]. But there have been many nights when I could not sleep in those soft beds thinking of the extreme poverty of my own people. I have then passed nights on the floor tossing, without any sleep or rest.[25]

I don't feel tired even if I talk for two whole nights to an earnest inquirer; I can give up food and sleep and talk and talk. Well, if I have a mind, I can sit up in Samadhi in a Himalayan cave.... Why then don't I do so? And why am I here? Only the sight of the country's misery and the thought of its future do not let me remain quiet any more!—even Samadhi and all that appear as futile—even the sphere of Brahma with its enjoyments becomes insipid! My vow of life is to think of your welfare. The day that vow will be fulfilled, I shall leave this body and make a straight run up![26]

Going round the whole world, I find that people of this country are immersed in great Tamas [inactivity], compared with people of other countries. On the outside, there is a simulation of the Sattvika [calm and balanced] state, but inside, downright inertness like that of stocks and stones—what work will be done in the world by such people? How long can such an inactive, lazy, and sensual people live in the world?...

So my idea is first to make the people active by developing their Rajas, and thus make them fit for the struggle for existence. With no strength in the body, no enthusiasm at heart, and no originality in the brain, what will they do—these lumps of dead matter! By stimulating them I want to bring life into them—to this I have dedicated my life. I will rouse them through the infallible power of Vedic Mantras. I am born to proclaim to them that fearless message—"Arise! Awake!"[27]

I must frankly state that in my life-long experience in the work, I have always found "Occultism" injurious and weakening to humanity. What we want is strength. We Indians, more than any other race, want strong and vigorous thought. We have enough of the superfine in all concerns. For centuries we have been stuffed with the mysterious; the result is that our intellectual and spiritual digestion is almost hopelessly impaired, and the race has been dragged down to the depths of hopeless imbecility—never before or since experienced by any other civilised community. There must be freshness and vigour of thought behind to make a virile race. More than enough to strengthen the whole world exists in the Upanishads. The Advaita is the eternal mine of strength. But it requires to be applied. It must first be cleared of the incrustation of scholasticism, and then in all its simplicity, beauty and sublimity be taught over the length and breadth of the land, as applied even to the minutest detail of daily life. "This is a very large order"; but we must work towards it, nevertheless, as if it would be accomplished tomorrow. Of one thing I am sure—that whoever wants to help his fellow beings through genuine love and unselfishness will work wonders.[28]

I have never spoken of revenge, I have always spoken of strength. Do we dream of revenging ourselves on this drop of sea-spray? But it is a great thing to a mosquito![29]

Now my one desire is to rouse the country—the sleeping leviathan that has lost all faith in his power and makes no response. If I can wake it up to a sense of the Eternal Religion then I shall know that Sri Ramakrishna's advent and our birth are fruitful. That is the one desire in my heart: Mukti and all else appear of no consequence to me.[30]

Yes! The older I grow, the more everything seems to me to lie in manliness. This is my new gospel.[31]

I disagree with all those who are giving their superstitions back to my people. Like the Egyptologist's interest in Egypt, it is easy to feel an interest in India that is purely selfish. One may desire to see again the India of one's books, one's studies, one's dreams. My hope is to see again the strong points of that India, reinforced by the strong points of this age, only in a natural way. The new stage of things must be a *growth* from within.

So I preach only the Upanishads. If you look, you will find that I have never quoted anything but the Upanishads. And of the Upanishads, it is only that one idea, strength. The quintessence of the Vedas and Vedanta and all lies in that one word. Buddha's teaching was non-resistance, or non-injury. But I think this is a better way of teaching the same thing. For behind that non-injury lay a dreadful weakness. It is weakness that conceives the idea of resistance. I do not think of punishing or escaping from a drop of sea-spray. It is nothing to me. Yet to the mosquito it would be serious. Now I would make all injury like that. Strength and fearlessness. My own ideal is that saint whom they killed in the Mutiny and who broke his silence, when stabbed to the heart, to say, "And thou also art He!"

But you may ask, "What is the place of Ramakrishna in this scheme?"

He is the method, that wonderful unconscious method! He did not understand himself. He knew nothing of England or the English, save that they were queer folk from over the sea. But he lived that great life: and I read the meaning. Never a word of condemnation for any! Once I had been attacking one of our sects of diabolists. I had been raving on for three hours, and he had listened quietly. "Well, well!" said the old man as I finished, "perhaps every house may have a back door. Who knows?"[32]

[*Question: What is the function of your movement as regards India?*] To find the common bases of Hinduism and awaken the national consciousness to them. At present there are three parties in India included under the term "Hindu"—the orthodox, the reforming sects of the Mohammedan period, and the reforming sects of the present time. Hindus from North to South are only agreed on one point, namely on not eating beef. [*Not a common love for the Vedas?*] Certainly not. That is just what we want to re-awaken....

[*With which of these three parties do you identify yourself?*] With all of them. We are orthodox Hindus, but, we refuse entirely to identify ourselves with "Don't-touchism." That is not Hinduism: it is in none of our books; it is an unorthodox superstition which has interfered with national efficiency all along the line....

[*In what sense is Sri Ramakrishna a part of this awakened Hinduism?*] That is not for me to determine. I have never preached personalities. My own life is guided by the enthusiasm of this great soul; but others will decide for themselves how far they share in this attitude. Inspiration is not filtered out to the world through one channel, however great. Each generation should be inspired afresh. Are we not all God?...

Our method is very easily described. It simply consists in reasserting the national life. Buddha preached renunciation. India heard, and yet in six centuries she reached her greatest height. The secret lies there. The national ideals of India are *renunciation* and *service*. Intensify her in those channels, and the rest will take care of itself. The banner of the spiritual cannot be raised too high in this country. In it alone is salvation.[33]

The Vedanta ... [is] the one light that lightens the sects and creeds of the world ... the one principle of which all religions are only applications. And what was Ramakrishna Paramahamsa? The practical demonstration of this ancient principle, the embodiment of India that is past, and a foreshadowing of the India that is to be, the bearer of spiritual light unto nations.[34]

If the Lord wills, we shall make this Math a great centre of harmony. Our Lord [Sri Ramakrishna] is the visible embodiment of the harmony of all ideals. He will be established on earth if we keep alive that spirit of harmony here. We must see to it that people of all creeds and sects, from the Brahmana down to the Chandala, may come here and find their respective ideals manifested. The other day when I installed Sri Ramakrishna on the Math grounds, I felt as if his ideas shot forth from this place and flooded the whole universe, sentient and insentient. I, for one, am doing my best, and shall continue to do so—we must explain to people the liberal ideas of Sri Ramakrishna; what is the use of merely reading the Vedanta? We must prove the truth of pure Advaitism in practical life. Shankara left this Advaita philosophy in the hills and forests, while I have come to bring it out of those places and scatter it broadcast before the workaday world and society. The lion-roar of Advaita must resound in every hearth and home, in meadows and groves, over hills and plains.[35]

You will see only a little manifestation of what has been done. In time the whole world must accept the universal and catholic ideas of Sri Ramakrishna, and of this, only the beginning has been made. Before this flood everybody will be swept off.[36]

That activity and self-reliance must come in the people of the country in time—I see it clearly. There is no escape. The intelligent man can distinctly see the vision of the next three Yugas [ages] ahead. Ever since the advent of Sri Ramakrishna the eastern horizon has been aglow with the dawning rays of the sun which in course of time will illumine the country with the splendour of the midday sun.[37]

This boy born of poor Brahmin parents in an out-of-the-way village ... is literally being worshipped in lands which have been fulminating against heathen worship for centuries.

Whose power is it? Is it mine or yours? It is none else than the power which was manifested here as Ramakrishna Paramahamsa.... Here has been a manifestation of an immense power, just the very beginning of whose workings we are seeing, and before this generation passes away, you will see more wonderful workings of that power. It has come just in time for the regeneration of India.[38]

It seemed that we were going to change [the] theme in our national life, that we were going to exchange the backbone of our existence, as it were, that we were trying to replace a spiritual by a political backbone. And if we could have succeeded, the result would have been annihilation. But it was not to be. So this power became manifest. I do not care in what light you understand this great sage, it matters not how much respect you pay to him, but I challenge you face to face with the fact that here is a manifestation of the most marvellous power that has been for several centuries in India, and it is your duty ... to study this power, to find what has been done for the regeneration, for the good of India, and for the good of the whole human race through it. Ay, long before ideas of universal religion and brotherly feeling between different sects were mooted and discussed in any country in the world, here, in sight of this city, had been living a man whose whole life was a Parliament of Religions as it should be.[39]

Our heroes must be spiritual. Such a hero has been given to us in the person of Ramakrishna Paramahamsa. If this nation wants to rise, take my word for it, it will have to rally enthusiastically round this name.

It does not matter who preaches Ramakrishna Paramahamsa, whether I, or you, or anybody else. But him I place before you, and it is for you to judge, and for the good of our race, for the good of our nation, to judge now, what you shall do with this great ideal of life. One thing we are to remember that it was the purest of all lives that you have ever seen, or let me tell you distinctly, that you have ever read of. And before you is the fact that it is the most marvellous manifestation of soul-power that you can read of, much less expect to see. Within ten years of his passing away, this power has encircled the globe.... For the good of our race, for the good of our religion, I place this great spiritual ideal before you. Judge him not through me. I am only a weak instrument. Let not his character be judged by seeing me. It was so great that if I or any other of his disciples spent hundreds of lives, we could not do justice to a millionth part of what he really was.[40]

Jnana is all right; but there is the danger of its becoming dry intellectualism. Love is great and noble; but it may die away in meaningless sentimentalism. A harmony of all these is the thing required. Ramakrishna was such a harmony. Such beings are few and far between; but keeping him and his teachings as the ideal, we can move on....

God, though everywhere, can be known to us in and through human character. No character was ever so perfect as Ramakrishna's, and that should be the centre round which we ought to rally, at the same time allowing everybody to regard him in his own light, either as God, saviour, teacher, model, or great man, just as he pleases.[41]

My hope of the future lies in the youths of character—intelligent, renouncing all for the service of others, and obedient—who can sacrifice their lives in working out my ideas and thereby do good to themselves and the country at large.... If I get ten or twelve boys with the faith of Nachiketa, I can turn the thoughts and pursuits of this country in a new channel.[42]

Sometimes I feel a desire to sell the Math and everything, and distribute the money to the poor and destitute.... When I was in the Western countries, I prayed to the Divine Mother, "People here are sleeping on a bed of flowers, they eat all kinds of delicacies, and what do they not enjoy, while people in our country are dying of starvation. Mother, will there be no way for them!" One of the objects of my going to the West to preach religion was to see if I could find any means for feeding the people of this country.

Seeing the poor people of our country starving for food, a desire comes to me to overthrow all ceremonial worship and learning, and go round from village to village collecting money from the rich by convincing them through force of character and Sadhana, and to spend the whole life in serving the poor....

I sometimes feel the urge to break the barriers of "Don't-touchism," to go at once and call out, "Come, all who are poor, miserable, wretched, and down-trodden," and to bring them all together in the name of Sri Ramakrishna. Unless they rise, the Mother won't awaken. We could not make any provision for food and clothes for these—what have we done then? Alas! they know nothing of worldliness, and therefore even after working day and night cannot provide themselves with food and clothes. Let us open their eyes.

I see clear as daylight that there is the one Brahman in all, in them and in me—one Shakti dwells in all. The only difference is of manifestation....

After so much austerity, I have understood this as the real truth—God is present in every Jiva; there is no other God besides that. "Who serves Jiva, serves God indeed."[43]

You have not yet understood the wonderful significance of Mother's [Sri Sarada Devi's] life—none of you. But gradually you will know. Without Shakti [Power] there is no regeneration for the world. Why is it that our country is the weakest and the most backward of all countries?—because Shakti is held in dishonour there. Mother has been born to revive that wonderful Shakti in India ... Without the grace of Shakti nothing is to be accomplished.... I am coming to understand things clearer every day, my insight is opening out more and more.... To me, Mother's grace is a hundred thousand times more valuable than Father's. Mother's grace, Mother's blessings are all paramount to me.... Please pardon me. I am a little bigoted there, as regards Mother. If but Mother orders, her demons can work anything.... Faith is very difficult to achieve. Brother, I shall show how to worship the living Durga and then only shall I be worthy of my name.... Often enough, when I am reminded of the Mother, I ejaculate, "What after all is Rama?" Brother, that is where my fanaticism lies, I tell you. Of Ramakrishna, you may aver ... that he was an Incarnation or whatever else you may like, but fie on him who has no devotion for the Mother.[44]

I do not see into the future; nor do I care to see. But one vision I see clear as life before me: that the ancient Mother has awakened once more, sitting on Her throne rejuvenated, more glorious than ever.[45]

I have made a new path and opened it to all.[46]

This body is born and it will die. If I have been able to instil a few of my ideas into you all, then I shall know that my birth has not been in vain.[47]

During my Sadhana period when I was travelling round Bhāratavarsha [India], how many days had I spent in caves, how many a time had I even thought of giving up this body since liberation was not achieved, what strenuous efforts had

I made for my spiritual practices! But now I have not that thirst for liberation. My present mood is that so long as even one individual lives in this world without gaining liberation, I do not want my own liberation.[48]

You see, in my travels throughout India all these years, I have come across many a great soul, many a heart overflowing with loving kindness, sitting at whose feet I used to feel a mighty current of strength coursing into my heart, and the few words I speak to you are only through the force of that current gained by coming in contact with them. Do not think I am myself something great.[49]

Life is ever expanding, contraction is death. The self-seeking man who is looking after his personal comforts and leading a lazy life—there is no room for him even in hell. He alone is a child of Sri Ramakrishna who is moved to pity for all creatures and exerts himself for them even at the risk of incurring personal damnation, *itare kṛpaṇāḥ*—others are vulgar people.

Whoever, at this great spiritual juncture, will stand up with a courageous heart and go on spreading from door to door, from village to village, his message, is alone my brother, and a son of his. This is the test, he who is Ramakrishna's child does not seek his personal good. "*Prāṇātyaye'pi parakalyāṇacikīrṣavaḥ*—they wish to do good to others even when at the point of death." Those that care for their personal comforts and seek a lazy life, who are ready to sacrifice all before their personal whims, are none of us; let them pack off, while yet there is time. Propagate his character, his teaching, his religion. This is the only spiritual practice, the only worship, this verily is the means, and this the goal.[50]

CHAPTER NINE

SECOND VISIT TO THE WEST

The Journey

It took us two days to get out of the Hooghly....

In the night of the twenty-fourth June, our ship reached Madras. Getting up from bed in the morning, I found that we were within the enclosed space of the Madras harbour. Within the harbour the water was still, but without, towering waves were roaring, which occasionally dashing against the harbour-wall were shooting up fifteen or twenty feet high into the air and breaking in a mass of foam....

The ship left the harbour in the evening, when I heard a great shout, and peeping through the cabin-window, I found that about a thousand men, women, and children of Madras who had been sitting on the harbour-walls, gave this farewell shout when the ship started. On a joyous occasion the people of Madras also, like the Bengalis, make the peculiar sound with the tongue known as the Hulu.

It took us four days to go from Madras to Ceylon. That rising and heaving of waves which had commenced from the mouth of the Ganga began to increase as we advanced, and after we had left Madras it increased still more. The ship began to roll heavily, and the passengers felt terribly sea-sick....

The ship left Colombo on the morning of twenty-fifth June. Now we have to encounter full monsoon conditions. The more our ship is advancing, the more is the storm increasing and the louder is the wind howling—there is incessant rain, and enveloping darkness; huge waves are dashing on the ship's deck with a terrible noise, so that it is impossible to stay on the deck.... The ship is creaking, as if it were going to break to pieces. The Captain says, "Well, this year's monsoon seems to be unusually rough"....

In spite of our six days' journey being prolonged into fourteen days, and our buffeting terrible wind and rain night and day, we at last did reach Aden. The more we were ahead of Colombo, the more the storm and rain increased, the sky became a lake, and the wind and the waves grew fierce; and it was almost impossible for the ship to proceed, breasting such wind and wave, and her speed was halved. Near the island of Socotra, the monsoon was at its worst. The Captain remarked that this was the centre of the monsoon, and that if we could pass this, we should gradually reach calmer waters. And so we did. And this nightmare also ended....

On the fourteenth of July the steamer cleared the Red Sea and reached Suez.... This is a very beautiful natural harbour, surrounded almost on three sides by sandy mounds and hillocks, and the water also is very deep. There are innumerable fish and sharks swimming in it....

In the morning, even before breakfast, we came to learn that big sharks were moving about behind the ship. I had never before an opportunity to see live sharks ... As soon as we heard of the sharks, we hastened to the spot.... Crowds of men, women and children were leaning over the railings to see the sharks. But our friends, the sharks, had moved off a little when we appeared on the spot, which damped our spirit very much.... Half an hour—three quarters—we were almost tired of it, when somebody announced—there he was. About a dozen people shouted, "There he is coming!" Casting my eyes I found that at some distance a huge black thing was moving towards us, six or seven inches below the surface of

SECOND VISIT TO THE WEST

the water. Gradually the thing approached nearer and nearer. The huge flat head was visible; now massive his movement ... A gigantic fish.

The second class passengers have got their mettle highly roused. One of them is a military man and his enthusiasm knows no bounds. Rummaging the ship they found out a terrible hook ... To this they tightly fastened about two pounds of meat with a strong cord, and a stout cable was tied to it. About six feet from it, a big piece of wood was attached to act as a float. Then the hook with the float was dropped in the water.... We in eagerness stood on tiptoe, leaning over the railing, and anxiously waited for the shark ... There, he is moving near the hook, and examining the bait, putting it in his jaws! Let him do so. Hush—now he has turned on his side—look, he is swallowing it whole, silence—give him time to do it. Then, as "flat-head," turning on his side, had leisurely swallowed the bait, and was about to depart, immediately there was the pull behind! "Flat-head," astonished, jerked his head and wanted to throw the bait off, but it made matters worse! The hook pierced him, and from above, men, young and old, began to pull violently at the cable. Look, the head of the shark is above water—pull, brothers, pull!... Pull on, brothers! Oh, it is a fountain of blood! No, there is no use trying to save the clothes. Pull, he is almost within reach. Now, set him on the deck; take care, brother, be very careful, if he but charges on anybody, he will bite off a whole arm! And beware of that tail! Now, slacken the rope—thud! Lord! What a big shark! And with what a thud he fell on board the ship! Well, one cannot be too careful—strike his head with that beam—hallo, military man, you are a soldier, you are the man to do it. —"Quite so." The military passenger, with body and clothes splashed with blood, raised the beam and began to land heavy blows on the shark's head. And the women went on shrieking, "Oh dear! How cruel! Don't kill him!" and so forth, but never stopped seeing the spectacle. Let that gruesome scene end here. How the shark's belly was ripped open, how a torrent of blood flowed, how the monster continued to shake and move for a long time even after his entrails and heart had been taken off and his body dismembered, how from his stomach a heap of bones, skin, flesh, and wood, etc. came out—let all these topics go. Suffice it to say, that I had my meal almost spoilt that day—everything smelt of that shark....

Now comes the Mediterranean. There is no more memorable region than this, outside India. It marks the end of Asia, Africa, and of ancient civilisation. One type of manners and customs and modes of living ends here and another type of features and temperament, food and dress, customs and habits begins—we enter Europe....

The ship touched Naples—we reached Italy.... After leaving Naples the ship called at Marseilles, and thence straight at London.[1]

Suez, 14 July 1899 · You see this time I am really out, and hope to reach London in two weeks. I am sure to come to America this year and earnestly hope will have the opportunity of seeing you. I am so materialistic yet, you know! Want to see my friends in the gross body....

I was so, so bad in health in India. My heart went wrong all the way—what with mountain climbing, bathing in glacier water and nervous prostration! I used to get terrible fits [of asthma]—the last lasting about seven days and nights. All the time I was suffocating and had to stand up.

This trip has almost made a new man of me. I feel much better, and if this continues, hope to be quite strong before I reach America.[2]

England

Wimbledon, England, 3 August 1899 · We are in at last. Turiyananda and I have beautiful lodgings here.... I have recovered quite a bit by the voyage. It was brought about by the exercise on the dumb-bells and monsoon storms tumbling the steamer about the waves. Queer, isn't it? Hope it will remain.... It is nice and warm here; rather too much they say. I have become for the present a Shunyavādi, a believer in nothingness, or void. No plans, no afterthought, no attempt, for anything, *laissez-faire* to the fullest....

I look several years younger by this voyage. Only when the heart gives a lurch, I feel my age. What is this osteopathy, anyway? Will they cut off a rib or two to cure me? Not I, no manufacturing of cures from my ribs, sure. Whatever it be, it will be hard work for him to find my bones. My bones are destined to make corals in the Ganga.

Now I am going to study French ... but no grammar business.[3]

Wimbledon, 6 August 1899 · I don't know what I am to do next or anything to do at all. On board the steamer I was all right, but since landing [I am] feeling quite bad again. As to mental worry, there has been enough of late. The aunt whom you saw had a deep laid plan to cheat me, and she and her people contrived to sell me a house for 6,000 Rs., or £400, and I bought [it] for my mother in good faith. Then they would not give me possession, hoping that I would not go to court for the shame of taking forcible possession as a Sannyasin.

I do not think I have spent even one rupee from what you and others gave me for the work. Cap. Sevier gave me 8,000 Rs. with the express desire of helping my mother. This money, it seems, has gone to the dogs. Beyond this, nothing has been spent on my family or even on my own personal expenses—my food etc. being paid for by the Khetri Raja, and more than half of that went to the Math every month. Only, if Brahmananda spends some in the lawsuit [against the aunt], as I must not be robbed that way—if he does, I will make it good anyway, if I live to do it.

The money which I got in Europe and America by lecturing alone, I spent just as I like; but every cent I got for the work has been accounted for and is in the Math ...

I have no plans yet, nor care to make any. Neither do I wish to work. Let the Mother find other workers. I have my burden enough already.[4]

Wimbledon, August 1899 · I expect to be in New York in a few weeks, and don't know what next. I hope to come back to England next spring.

I fervently wish no misery ever came near anyone; yet it is that alone that gives us an insight into the depths of our lives, does it not?

In our moments of anguish, gates barred for ever seem to open and let in many a flood of light.

We learn as we grow. Alas! we cannot use our knowledge here. The moment we seem to learn, we are hurried off the stage. And this is Maya![5]

America

Ridgely Manor, 4 September 1899 · It is an awful spell of the bad turn of fortune with me last six months. Misfortune follows me ever wherever I go. In England, Sturdy seems to have got disgusted with the work; he does not see any asceticism in us from India.[6]

Ridgely Manor, 14 September 1899 · Mrs. Johnson is of opinion that no spiritual person ought to be ill. It also seems to her now that my smoking is sinful etc., etc. That was Miss Muller's reason for leaving me, my illness. They may be perfectly right, for aught I know ... but I am what I am. In India, the same defects plus eating with Europeans have been taken exception to by many. I was driven out of a private temple by the owners for eating with Europeans. I wish I were malleable enough to be moulded into whatever one desired, but unfortunately I never saw a man who could satisfy everyone. Nor can anyone who has to go to different places possibly satisfy all.

When I first came to America, they ill-treated me if I had not trousers on. Next I was forced to wear cuffs and collars, else they would not touch me etc., etc. They thought me awfully funny if I did not eat what they offered etc., etc....

In India the moment I landed they made me shave my head and wear "Kaupin" (loincloth), with the result that I got diabetes etc.... Of course, it is my Karma, and I am glad that it is so. For, though it smarts for the time, it is another great experience of life, which will be useful, either in this or in the next....

As for me, I am always in the midst of ebbs and flows. I knew it always and preached always that every bit of pleasure will bring its quota of pain, if not with compound interest. I have a good deal of love given to me by the world; I deserve a good deal of hatred therefore. I am glad it is so—as it proves my theory of "every wave having its corresponding dip" on my own person.

As for me, I stick to my nature and principle—once a friend, always a friend—also the true Indian principle of looking subjectively for the cause of the objective.

I am sure that the fault is mine, and mine only, for every wave of dislike and hatred that I get. It could not be otherwise.[7]

Ridgely Manor, 14 September 1899 · I have simply been taking rest at the Leggetts' and doing nothing. Abhedananda is here. He has been working hard.[8]

Ridgely Manor, 20 September 1899 · I am much better, thank you. Hitherto, excepting three days, there has not been any wet weather to speak of here. Miss Noble came yesterday, and we are having a jolly good time. I am very, very sorry to say I am growing fat again. That is bad. I will eat less and grow thin once more.[9]

Ridgely Manor, October 1899 · I don't think I ever posed for anything but what I am. Nor is it ever possible for me to do so, as an hour's contact is enough to make everybody see through my smoking, bad temper, etc. "Every meeting must have a separation"—this is the nature of things. I carry no feeling of disappointment even. I hope you will have no bitterness. It is Karma that brings us together, and Karma separates....

My method is never to ask but wait for voluntary help. I follow the same idea in all my work, as I am so conscious of my nature being positively displeasing to many, and wait till somebody wants me. I hold myself ready also to depart at a moment's notice. In the matter of departure thus, I never feel bad about it or think much of it, as, in the constant roving life I lead, I am constantly doing it. Only so sorry, I trouble others without wishing it.[10]

Ridgely Manor, 18 (?) October 1899 · There is one thing called love, and there is another thing called union. And union is greater than love.

I do not love religion. I have become identified with it. It is my life. So no man loves that thing in which his life has been spent, in which he really has accomplished something. That which we love is not yet ourself.... This is the difference between Bhakti and Jnana; and this is why Jnana is greater than Bhakti.[11]

Ridgely Manor, 23 October 1899 · I am sure my previous letter was coloured by the state of my body, as indeed is the whole of existence to us. Yet, Mother [Mrs. Hale], there is more pain than pleasure in life. If not, why do I remember you and your children almost every day of my life, and not many others? Happiness is liked so much because it is so rare, is it not? Fifty percent of our life is mere lethargy, ennui; of the rest, forty percent is pain, only ten happiness—and this for the exceptionally fortunate. We are oft times mixing up this state of ennui with pleasure. It is rather a negative state, whilst both pleasure and pain are nearer positive, though not positive.[12]

Ridgely Manor, 1 November 1899 · It seems there is a gloom over your mind. Never mind, nothing is to last for ever. Anyhow life is not eternal. I am so, so thankful for it. Suffering is the lot of the world's best and bravest—yet, for aeons yet—till things are righted, if possible, here—at least it is a discipline which breaks the dream. In my sane moments I rejoice for my sufferings. Some one must suffer here;—I am glad it is I, amongst others of nature's sacrifices.[13]

New York, 10 November 1899 · I am now in New York. Dr. Guernsey analysed my urine yesterday, and there was no sugar or albumen in it. So my kidneys are all right, at least at present. The heart is only nervous, requires calming!—some cheerful company and good, loving friends and quiet. The only difficulty is the *dyspepsia*, and that is the evil. For instance, I am all right in the morning and can walk miles, but in the evening it is impossible to walk after a meal—the gas—that depends entirely upon food, does it not? I ought to try the Battle Creek food [a kind of health food]. If I come to

Detroit, there will be quiet and Battle Creek food for me.

But if you come to Cambridge with all the instructions of the Battle Creek food, I will have it prepared there; or, between you and me, we will cook it. I am a good hand at that. You don't know a thing about cooking. Well, you may help in cleaning the plates etc. I always get money when I need it badly. "Mother" always sees to that. So, no danger on that head. I am not in the least danger of life, the Doctors agree—only if this dyspepsia goes away. And that is "food," "food," "food," and no worry. Oh, what a worry I have had![14]

New York, 21 November 1899 · Never mind my harshness. You know the heart always, whatever the lips say. All blessings on you. For the last year or so I have not been in my senses at all. I do not know why. I had to pass through this hell—and I have. I am much better—well, in fact. Lord help you all. I am going to the Himalayas soon to retire for ever. My work is done.[15]

Los Angeles, 6 December, 1899 · Some people are made that way, to love being miserable. If I did not break my heart over people I was born amongst, I would do it for somebody else. I am sure of that. This is the way of some, I am coming to see it. We are all after happiness, true, but that some are only happy in being unhappy—queer, is it not? There is no harm in it either, except that happiness and unhappiness are both infectious. Ingersoll said once that if he were God, he would make health catching, instead of disease, little dreaming that health is quite as catching as disease, if not more! That is the only danger. No harm in the world in my being happy, in being miserable, but others must not catch it. This is the great fact. No sooner a prophet feels miserable for the state of man than he sours his face, beats his breast, and calls upon everyone to drink tartaric acid, munch charcoal, sit upon a dung-heap covered with ashes, and speak only in groans and tears!—I find they all have been wanting. Yes, they have. If you are really ready to take the world's burden, take it by all means. But do not let us hear your groans and curses. Do not frighten us with your sufferings, so that we came to feel we were better off with our own burdens. The man who really takes the burden blesses the world and goes his own way. He has not a word of condemnation, a word of criticism, not because there was no evil but that he has taken it on his own shoulders willingly, voluntarily. It is the Saviour who should "go his way rejoicing," and not the saved.

This is the only light I have caught this morning. This is enough if it has come to live with me and permeate my life.

Come ye that are heavy laden and lay all your burden on me, and then do whatever you like and be happy and forget that I ever existed.[16]

Los Angeles, 9 December 1899 · After all, it is good for me, and good for those I love, that I should come here. Here at last in California! One of our poets says: "Where is Benares, where is Kashmir, where Khorasan, where Gujarat! O Tulsi! thus, man's past Karma drags him on." And I am here. After all it is best, isn't it?...

I had a lecture here last night. The hall was not crowded, as there was very little advertisement, but a fairly good sized audience though. I hope they were pleased. If I feel better, I am going to have classes in this city soon. I am on the business path this time, you know. Want a few dollars quick, if I can.[17]

Los Angeles, 12 December 1899 · I am brutal, very indeed. But about the tenderness etc., that is my fault. I wish I had less, much less of that—that is my weakness—and alas! all my sufferings have come from that.... I am very sorry I use harsh language to my boys; but they also know I love them more than anybody else on earth. I may have had Divine help—true; but oh, the pound of blood every bit of Divine help has been to me!! I would be gladder and a better man without that. The present looks very gloomy indeed; but I am a fighter and must die fighting, not give way—that is why I get crazy at the boys. I don't ask them to fight, but not to hinder my fight.

I don't grudge my fate. But oh! now I want a man, one of my boys, to stand by me and fight against all odds!...

If anything is to be done in India, my presence is necessary; and I am much better in health; possibly the sea will make me better. Anyway I did not do anything this time in America except bother my friends....

My mistakes have been great; but everyone of them was from too much love. How I hate *love*! Would I never had any Bhakti! Indeed, I wish I could be an Advaitist, calm and heartless. Well, this life is done. I will try in the next. I am sorry, especially now, that I have done more injury to my friends than there have been blessings on them. The peace, the quiet I am seeking, I never found. I went years ago to the Himalayas, never to come back; and my sister committed suicide, the news reached me there, and that weak heart flung me off from that prospect of peace! It is the weak heart that has driven me out of India to seek some help for those I love, and here I am! Peace have I sought, but the heart, that seat of Bhakti, would not allow me to find it. Struggle and torture, torture and struggle. Well, be it then, since it is my fate, and the quicker it is over, the better. They say I am impulsive, but look at the circumstances!...

Wah Guru ki Fateh! Victory unto the Guru!! Yes, let the world come, the hells come, the gods come, let Mother come, I fight and do not give in. Ravana got his release in three births by fighting the Lord Himself! It is glorious to fight Mother.[18]

Los Angeles, 22 December 1899 · I had a slight relapse of late, for which the healer has rubbed several inches of my skin off. Just now I am feeling it, the smart. I had a very hopeful note from Margo [Sister Nivedita]. I am grinding on in Pasadena; hope some result will come out of my work here. Some people here are very enthusiastic; the Raja-Yoga book did indeed great services on this coast. I am mentally very well; indeed I never really was so calm as of late. The lectures for one thing do not disturb my sleep, that is some gain. I am doing some writing too. The lectures here were taken down by a stenographer; the people here want to print them....

Slowly as usual plans are working; but Mother knows, as I say. May She give me release and find other workers for Her plans. By the by, I have made a discovery as to the mental method of really practising what the Gita teaches, of working without an eye to results. I have seen much light on concentration and attention and control of concentration, which if practised will take us out of all anxiety and worry. It is really the science of bottling up our minds whenever we like.... There is a pleasure in suffering even, when it is for others, is there not? Mrs. Leggett is doing well; so is Joe; I—they say—I too am. May be they are right. I work anyway and want to die in harness; if that be what Mother wants, I am quite content.[19]

Los Angeles, 23 December, 1899 · Yes, I am really getting well under the manipulations of magnetic healing! At any rate I am all right. There was never anything serious with my organs—it was nerves and dyspepsia.

Now I walk miles every day, at any time—before or after meals. I am perfectly well—and am going to remain so, I am sure.

The wheel is turning up, Mother is working it up. She

cannot let me go before Her work is done—and that is the secret....

Things are looking up. So get ready.[20]

Los Angeles, 27 December 1899 · I am making money fast—twenty five dollars a day now. Soon I will work more and get fifty dollars a day. In San Francisco I hope to do still better—where I go in two or three weeks. Good again—better, say I—as I am going to keep the money all to myself and not squander it any more. And then I will buy a little place in the Himalayas—a whole hill—about say, six thousand feet high with a grand view of the eternal snows. There must be springs and a tiny lake. Cedars—the Himalayan cedar forests—and flowers, flowers everywhere. I will have a little cottage; in the middle, my vegetable gardens, which I will work myself—and—and—and—my books—and see the face of man only once in a great while. And the world may go to ruin round about my ears, I would not care. I will have done with all my work—secular or spiritual—and retire. My! how restless I have been all my life! Born nomad. I don't know; this is the present vision. The future is to come yet. Curious—all my dreams about my own happiness are, as it were, bound to come to nothing; but about others' well being—they as a rule prove true.[21]

Los Angeles, 24 January 1900 · I am afraid that the rest and peace I seek for will never come. But Mother does good to others through me, at least some to my native land, and it is easier to be reconciled to one's fate as a sacrifice. We are all sacrifices—each in his own way. The great worship is going on—no one can see its meaning except that it is a great sacrifice. Those that are willing escape a lot of pain. Those who resist are broken into submission and suffer more. I am now determined to be a willing one.[22]

SECOND VISIT TO THE WEST

Los Angeles, 27 December 1899 · I am much better in health—able enough to work once more. I have started work already and have sent to Saradananda some money—Rs. 1,300 already—as expenses for the lawsuit. I shall send more, if they need it.... Poor boys! How hard I am on them at times. Well, they know, in spite of all that, I am their best friend....

I wired to the boys three weeks ago that I was perfectly cured. If I don't get any worse, this much health as I have now will do well enough. Do not worry at all on my account; I am up and working with a will....

I am very much more peaceful and find that the only way to keep my peace is to teach others. Work is my only safety valve....

I can only work when thrown completely on my own feet. I am at my best when I am alone. Mother seems to arrange so. Joe believes great things are brewing—in Mother's cup; hope it is so....

I can only say, every blow I had in this life, every pang, will only become joyful sacrifice if Mother becomes propitious to India once more....

I am going soon to work in California; when I leave I shall send for Turiyananda and make him work on the Pacific coast. I am sure here is a great field. The Raja-Yoga book seems to be very well known here....

Joe has unearthed a magnetic healing woman. We are both under her treatment. Joe thinks she is pulling me up splendidly. On her has been worked a miracle, she claims. Whether it is magnetic healing, California ozone, or the end of the present spell of bad Karma, I am improving. It is a great thing to be able to walk three miles, even after a heavy dinner.[23]

Los Angeles, 27 December 1899 · It is exactly like Northern Indian winter here, only some days a little warmer; the roses are here and the beautiful palms. Barley is in the fields, roses and many other flowers round about the cottage where I live. Mrs. Blodgett, my host, is a Chicago lady—fat, old, and extremely witty. She heard me in Chicago and is very motherly....

I am happy just now and hope to remain so for all the rest of my life....

I shall be very happy if I can make a lot of money. I am making some. Tell Margot, I am going to make a lot of money and go home by way of Japan, Honolulu, China, and Java. This is a nice place to make money quick in; and San Francisco is better, I hear.[24]

Pasadena, 17 January 1900 · I have been able to remit Rs. 2,000 to Saradananda, with the help of Miss MacLeod and Mrs. Leggett. Of course they contributed the best part. The rest was got by lectures. I do not expect anything much here or anywhere by lecturing. I can scarcely make expenses. No, not even that; whenever it comes to paying, the people are nowhere. The field of lecturing in this country has been overworked; the people have outgrown that.

I am decidedly better in health. The healer thinks I am now at liberty to go anywhere I choose, the process will go on, and I shall completely recover in a few months. She insists on this, that I am cured already; only nature will have to work out the rest.

Well, I came here principally for health. I have got it; in addition I got Rs. 2,000, to defray the law expenses. Good.

Now it occurs to me that my mission from the platform is finished, and I need not break my health again by that sort of work.

It is becoming clearer to me that I lay down all the concerns of the Math and for a time go back to my mother. She has suffered much through me. I must try to smooth her last days.

Do you know, this was just exactly what the great Shankaracharya himself had to do! He had to go back to his mother in the last few days of her life! I accept it, I am resigned. I am calmer than ever.... Then again, this is coming to me as the greatest of all sacrifices to make, the sacrifice of ambition, of leadership, of fame. I am resigned and must do the penance.... I want to make out a trust-deed of the Math in the names of Saradananda, Brahmananda, and yourself [Mrs. Ole Bull]. I will do it as soon as I get the papers from Saradananda. Then I am quits. I want rest, a meal, a few books, and I want to do some scholarly work. Mother shows this light vividly now.... It is now shown that—leaving my mother was a great renunciation in 1884—it is a greater renunciation to go back to my mother now. Probably Mother wants me to undergo the same that She made the great Acharya undergo in old days.... I am but a child; what work have I to do? My powers I passed over to you. I see it. I cannot any more tell from the platform. Don't tell it to anyone ... I am glad. I want rest; not that I am tired, but the next phase will be the miraculous touch and not the tongue—like Ramakrishna's.[25]

Los Angeles, 17 January 1900 · I have worked for this world ... all my life, and it does not give me a piece of bread without taking a pound of flesh.[26]

Los Angeles, 15 February 1900 · Well—but I am strong now ... stronger than ever I was mentally. I was mentally getting a sort of ironing over my heart. I am getting nearer a Sannyasin's life now....

I have got a few hundred dollars here. Going to San Francisco next week, and hope to do better there....

I am getting cool as a cucumber—let anything come, I am ready. The next move—any blow shall tell—not one miss—such is the next chapter.[27]

Pasadena, 20 February 1900 · Your letter [Mary Hale's] bearing the sad news of Mr. Hale's passing away reached me yesterday. I am sorry, because in spite of monastic training, the heart lives on; and then Mr. Hale was one of the best souls I met in life.... I have lost many, suffered much, and the most curious cause of suffering when somebody goes off is the feeling that I was not good enough to that person. When my father died, it was a pang for months, and I had been so disobedient....

We may read books, hear lectures, and talk miles, but experience is the one teacher, the one eye-opener. It is best as it is. We learn, through smiles and tears we learn. We don't know why, but we see it is so; and that is enough.... I wish we could all dream undisturbed good dreams....

You have had shelter all your life. I was in the glare, burning and panting all the time. Now for a moment you have caught a glimpse of the other side. My life is made up of continuous blows like that, and hundred times worse, because of poverty, treachery, and my own foolishness! Pessimism! You will understand it, how it comes. Well, well, what shall I say to you, Mary? You know all the talks; only I say this and it is true—if it were possible to exchange grief, and had I a cheerful mind, I would exchange mine for your grief ever and always. Mother knows best.[28]

California, 21 February 1900 · Wordy warfares, texts and scriptures, doctrines and dogmas—all these I am coming to loathe as poison in this my advanced age. Know this for certain that he who will work will be the crown on my head. Useless bandying of words and making noise is taking away our time, is consuming our life-energy, without pushing the cause of humanitarianism a step further.[29]

San Francisco, 2 March 1900 · I am busy making money; only

I do not make much. Well, I have to make enough to pay my passage home at any rate. Here is a new field, where I find ready listeners by hundreds, prepared beforehand by my books.

Of course money making is slow and tedious. If I could make a few hundreds, I would be only too glad.

My health is much better, but the old strength is not there yet. I hope it will come some day, but then, one had to work so hard to do the least little thing. I wish I had rest and peace for a few days at least ... Well, Mother knows best, as I say always. She knows best. The last two years have been specially bad. I have been living in mental hell. It is partially lifted now, and I hope for better days, better states.... I never know a moment's peaceful life. It has always been high pressure, mentally.[30]

San Francisco, 4 March 1900 · I don't want to work. I want to be quiet, and rest. I know the time and the place; but the fate or Karma, I think, drives me on—work, work. We are like cattle driven to the slaughter-house—hastily nibbling a bite of grass on the roadside as they are driven along under the whip. And all this is our work, our fear—fear, the beginning of misery, of disease, etc. By being nervous and fearful we injure others. By being so fearful to hurt we hurt more. By trying so much to avoid evil we fall into its jaws.

What a mass of namby-pamby nonsense we create round ourselves!! It does us no good, it leads us on to the very thing we try to avoid—misery....

Oh, to become fearless, to be daring, to be careless of everything![31]

San Francisco, 4 March 1900 · My health is about the same; don't find much difference; it is improving, perhaps, but very imperceptibly. I can use my voice, however, to make 3,000 people hear me, as I did twice in Oakland, and get good sleep too after two hours of speaking.[32]

San Francisco, 7 March 1900 · I am so so in health. No money. Hard work. No result. Worse than Los Angeles.

They come in crowds when the lecture is free—when there is payment, they don't. That's all.[33]

San Francisco, 17 March 1900 · Dr. and Mrs. Hiller returned to the city, much benefited, as they declare, by Mrs. Melton's rubbings. As for me, I have got several huge red patches on my chest. What materialises later on as to complete recovery, I will let you know....

I have been following the "Put up or shut up" plan here, and so far it has not proved bad. Mrs. Hansborough, the second of the three sisters, is here, and she is working, working, working—to help me. Lord bless their hearts. The three sisters are three angels ... Seeing such souls here and there repays for all the nonsense of this life.[34]

San Francisco, 22 March 1900 · You are correct that I have many other thoughts to think besides Indian people, but they have all to go to the background before the all-absorbing mission—my Master's work....

I would that this sacrifice were pleasant. It is not, and naturally makes one bitter at times; for know ... I am yet a man and cannot wholly forget myself; hope I shall some time....

As for me, I am tired on the other hand of eternal tramping; that is why I want to go back home and be quiet. I do not want to work any more. My nature is the retirement of a scholar. I never get it! I pray I will get it, now that I am all broken and worked out. Whenever I get a letter from Mrs. Sevier from her Himalayan home, I feel like flying off to the Himalayas. I am really sick of this platform work and eternal trudging and seeing new faces and lecturing.[35]

San Francisco, 25 March 1900 · I am much better and am growing very strong. I feel sometimes that freedom is near at hand, and the tortures of the last two years have been great lessons in many ways. Disease and misfortune come to do us good in the long run, although at the time we feel that we are submerged for ever.[36]

San Francisco, 28 March 1900 · I am working hard; and the harder I work, the better I feel. This ill health has done me a great good, sure. I am really understanding what non-attachment means. And I hope very soon to be perfectly non-attached.

We put all our energies to concentrate and get attached to one thing; but the other part, though equally difficult, we seldom pay any attention to—the faculty of detaching ourselves at a moment's notice from anything.

Both attachment and detachment perfectly developed make a man great and happy....

Things have got to come round—the seed must die underground to come up as the tree. The last two years were the underground rotting. I never had a struggle in the jaws of death, but it meant a tremendous upheaval of the whole life. One such brought me to Ramakrishna, another sent me to the U.S., this has been the greatest of all. It is gone—I am so calm that it astonishes me sometimes!! I work every day morning and evening, eat anything any hour—and go to bed at 12 PM in the night—but such fine sleep! I never had such power of sleeping before![37]

San Francisco, 7 April 1900 · I am on my own feet, working hard and with pleasure. To work I have the right. Mother knows the rest.

You see, I shall have to stay here, longer than I intended, and work. But don't be disturbed. I shall work out all my problems. I am on my own feet now, and I begin to see the light. Success would have led me astray, and I would have lost sight of the truth that I am a Sannyasin. That is why Mother is giving me this experience.[38]

Alameda, California, 20 April 1900 · I start for Chicago on Monday. A kind lady has given me a pass up to New York to be used within three months. The Mother will take care of me. She is not going to strand me now after guarding me all my life.[39]

Alameda, 23 April 1900 · I ought to have started today but circumstances so happened that I cannot forgo the temptation to be in a camp under the huge redwood trees of California before I leave. Therefore I postpone it for three or four days. Again after the incessant work I require a breath of God's free air before I start on this bone-breaking journey of four days.... I start tomorrow to the woods. Woof! get my lungs full of ozone before getting into Chicago.[40]

Alameda, 30 April 1900 · Sudden indisposition and fever prevent my starting for Chicago yet. I will start as soon as I am strong for the journey.[41]

Alameda, 2 May 1900 · I have been very ill—one more relapse brought about by months of hard work. Well, it has shown me that I have no kidney or heart disease whatsoever, only overworked nerves. I am, therefore, going today in the country for some days till I completely recover, which I am sure will be in a few days.[42]

San Francisco, 18 May 1900 · Going amongst different people with a message also does not belong to the Sannyasin; for a

Sannyasin, [there] is quiet and retirement, scarcely seeing the face of man.

I am now ripe for that, physically at least. If I don't go into retirement, nature will force me to it.[43]

New York, 13 June 1900 · There is no cause for any anxiety. As I wrote, I am healthier than ever; moreover, all the past fear of kidney troubles has passed away. "Worry" is the only disease I have, and I am conquering it fast.[44]

New York, 23 June 1900 · I am very well and happy and same as ever. Waves must come before a rise. So with me.... I am determined to get rid of all sentimentalism, and emotionalism, and hang me if you ever find me emotional. I am the Advaitist; our goal is knowledge—no feelings, no love, as all that belongs to matter and superstition and bondage. I am only existence and knowledge....

"Mother" looks after me. She is bringing me fast out of the hell of emotionalism, and bringing me into the light of pure reason....

Nobody has any power over me, for I am the spirit. I have no ambition; it is all Mother's work; I have no part.

Non-attachment has always been there. It has come in a minute. Very soon I stand where no sentiment, no feeling, can touch me.[45]

New York, 11 July 1900 · I have been much censured by everyone for cutting off my long hair....

I had been to Detroit and came back yesterday. Trying as soon as possible to go to France, thence to India.[46]

New York, 18 July 1900 · I stayed in Detroit for three days only. It is frightfully hot here in New York.... Kali [Swami Abhedananda] went away about a week ago to the mountains.

He cannot come back till September. I am all alone, and washing; I like it.[47]

New York, 24 July 1900 · I am to start on Thursday next, by the French steamer La Champagne.[48]

France

Excepting some parts of China, no other country in the world have I seen that is so beautiful as France.[49]

What is meant by bath in the West? Why, the washing of face, head, and hands, i.e. only those parts which are exposed. A millionaire friend of mine once invited me to come over to Paris: Paris, which is the capital of modern civilisation—Paris, the heaven of luxury, fashion, and merriment on earth—the centre of arts and sciences. My friend accommodated me in a huge palatial hotel, where arrangements for meals were in a right royal style, but, for bath—well, no name of it. Two days I suffered silently—till at last I could bear it no longer, and had to address my friend thus: "Dear brother, let this royal luxury be with you and yours! I am panting to get out of this situation. Such hot weather, and no facility of bathing; if it continues like this, I shall be in imminent danger of turning mad like a rabid dog." Hearing this, my friend became very sorry for me and annoyed with the hotel authorities, and said: "I won't let you stay here any more, let us go and find out a better place." Twelve of the chief hotels were seen, but no place for bathing was there in any of them. There are independent bathing-houses, where one can go and have a bath for four or five rupees. Good heavens! That very afternoon I read in a paper that an old lady entered into the bath-tub and died then and there! Whatever the doctors may say, I am inclined to think that perhaps that was the first occasion in her life to come into contact with so much water, and the frame collapsed by the sudden shock! This is no exaggeration.[50]

Paris, 23 August 1900 · The manuscript accounts of the Math just reached. It is delightful reading. I am so pleased with it.

I am going to print a thousand or more to be distributed in England, America and India. I will only add a begging paragraph in the end.[51]

Paris, 25 August 1900 · I gave a chance to Mrs. Bull to draw her money out of the Math; and as she did not say anything about it, and the trust deeds were waiting here to be executed, I got them executed duly at the British Consulate; and they are on their way to India now.

Now I am free, as I have kept no power or authority or position for me in the work. I also have resigned the presidentship of the Ramakrishna Mission.

The Math etc., belong now to the immediate disciples of Ramakrishna except myself. The presidentship is now Brahmananda's—next it will fall on Premananda etc., etc., in turn.

I am so glad a whole load is off me, now I am happy. I have served Ramakrishna through mistakes and success for twenty years now. I retire for good and devote the rest of my life to myself.

I no longer represent anybody, nor am I responsible to anybody. As to my friends, I had a morbid sense of obligation. I have thought well and find I owe nothing to anybody; if anything, I have given my best energies, unto death almost, and received only hectoring and mischief-making and botheration. I am done with everyone here and in India....

You must know once for all, I am born without jealousy, without avarice, without the desire to rule—whatever other vices I am born with.[52]

Paris, 28 August 1900 · Such is life—grind, grind; and yet what else are we to do? Grind, grind! Something will come—some way will be opened. If it does not, as it probably never will—then, then—what then? All our efforts are only to stave off, for a season, the great climax—death! Oh, what would the world do without you, Death! Thou great healer!

The world, as it is, is not real, is not eternal, thank the Lord!! How can the future be any better? That must be an effect of this one—at least like this, if not worse!

Dreams, oh dreams! Dream on! Dream, the magic of dream, is the cause of this life, it is also the remedy. Dream, dream, only dream! Kill dream by dream!

I am trying to learn French ... Some are very appreciative already. Talk to all the world—of the eternal riddle, the eternal spool of fate, whose thread-end no one finds and everyone seems to find, at least to his own satisfaction, at least for a time—to fool himself a moment, isn't it?

Well, now great things are to be done! Who cares for great things? Why not do small things as well? One is as good as the other. The greatness of little things, that is what the Gita teaches—bless the old book!...

I have not had much time to think of the body. So it must be well. Nothing is ever well here. We forget them at times, and that is being well and doing well....

We play our parts here—good or bad. When the dream is finished and we have left the stage, we will have a hearty laugh at all this—of this only I am sure.[53]

Paris, 1 September 1900 · I have no longer any desire to kill myself by touring. For the present I feel like settling down somewhere and spending my time among books. I have somewhat mastered the French language; but if I stay among the French for a month or two, I shall be able to carry on conversation well. If one can master this language and German sufficiently, one can virtually become well acquainted with European learning....

I keep sometimes well and sometimes bad. Of late I am again having that massage treatment by Mrs. Melton, who says, "You have already recovered!" This much I see—whatever the flatulence, I feel no difficulty in moving, walking, or even climbing. In the morning I take vigorous exercise, and then have a dip in cold water.

Yesterday I went to see the house of the gentleman with whom I shall stay. He is a poor scholar, has his room filled with books, and lives in a flat on the fifth floor. And as there are no lifts in this country as in America, one has to climb up and down. But it is no longer trying to me.

There is a beautiful public park round the house. The gentleman cannot speak English; that is a further reason for my going. I shall have to speak French perforce. It is all Mother's will. She knows best what She wants to have done. She never speaks out, "only keeps mum." But this much I notice that for a month or so I have been having intense meditation and repetition of the Lord's name.[54]

Paris, 15 September 1900 · I am getting enamoured of Paris. I now am living with a M. Jules Bois, a French savant, who has been a student and admirer of my works.

He talks very little English; in consequence, I have to trot out my jargon French and am succeeding well, he says. I can now understand if he will talk slowly.

Day after tomorrow I go to Bretagne [Brittany] where our American friends are enjoying the sea breeze—and the massage.

I go with M. Bois for a short visit; *après ça* [after that] I don't know where I go. I am getting quite Frenchy, *connaissez vous* [do you know]? I am also studying *grammaire* and hard at work.... In a few months I hope to be Frenchy, but by that time I will forget it by staying in England.

I am strong, well and content—no morbidity.[55]

Brittany, France, 20 (?) September, 1900 · Now I am staying on the sea-coast of France. The session of the Congress of History of Religions is over. It was not a big affair; some twenty scholars chattered a lot on the origin of the Shalagrama and the origin of Jehovah, and similar topics. I also said something on the occasion.[56]

And what your European Pandits say about the Aryan's swooping down from some foreign land, snatching away the lands of the aborigines and settling in India by exterminating them, is all pure nonsense, foolish talk! Strange, that our Indian scholars, too, say amen to them; and all these monstrous lies are being taught to our boys! This is very bad indeed.

I am an ignoramus myself; I do not pretend to any scholarship; but with the little that I understand, I strongly protested against these ideas at the Paris Congress. I have been talking with the Indian and European savants on the subject, and hope to raise many objections to this theory in detail, when time permits.[57]

Paris, 14 October 1900 [*Original in French*] · I am staying with a famous French writer, M. Jules Bois. I am his guest. As he is a man making his living with his pen, he is not rich; but we have many great ideas in common and feel happy together.

He discovered me a few years ago and has already translated some of my pamphlets into French....

I shall travel with Madame Calvé, Miss MacLeod, and M. Jules Bois. I shall be the guest of Madame Calvé, the famous singer. We shall go to Constantinople, the Near East, Greece, and Egypt. On our way back, we shall visit Venice.

It may be that I shall give a few lectures in Paris after my return, but they will be in English with an interpreter. I have no time any more, nor the power to study a new language at my age. I am an old man, isn't it?...

I am sending all the money I earned in America to India. Now I am free, the begging-monk as before. I have also resigned from the Presidentship of the Monastery. Thank God, I am free! It is no more for me to carry such a responsibility....

Thus it seems to me that a new chapter of my life is opening. It seems to me that Mother will now lead me slowly and softly. No more effort on roads full of obstacles, now it is the bed prepared with birds' down....

The experience of all my life, up to now, has taught me, thank God, that I always find what I am looking for with eagerness. Sometimes it is after much suffering, but it does not matter! All is forgotten in the softness of the reward.[58]

Paris, 22 October 1900 · Mr. Maxim of the gun fame is very much interested in me, and he wants to put in his book on China and the Chinese something about my work in America.... Canon Haweis [Reverend Hugh Reginald Haweis] also keeps track of my work in England.... It may be that Mother will now work up my original plan of international work....

It seems that after this fall in my health, physical and mental, it is going to open out that way—larger and more international work. Mother knows best.

My whole life has been divided into successive depressions and rises—and so, I believe, is the life of everyone. I am glad, rather than not, these falls come. I understand it all; still, I suffer and grumble and rage! Perhaps that is a part of the cause of the next upheaval.[59]

We have an adage among us that one that has a disc-like pattern on the soles of his feet becomes a vagabond. I fear, I have my soles inscribed all over with them.... The results are quite patent—it was my cherished desire to remain in Paris for some time and study the French language and civilisation; I left my old friends and acquaintances and put up with a new friend, a Frenchman of ordinary means, who knew no English, and my French—well, it was something quite extraordinary!

I had this in mind that the inability to live like a dumb man would naturally force me to talk French, and I would attain fluency in that language in no time—but on the contrary I am now on a tour through Vienna, Turkey, Greece, Egypt, and Jerusalem!...

I have three travelling companions—two of them French and the third an American. The American is Miss MacLeod... the French male companion is Monsieur Jules Bois, a famous philosopher and litterateur of France; and the French lady friend is the world-renowned singer, Mademoiselle Calvé....

She was born amidst very poor circumstances ... there is no better teacher than pain and poverty! That extreme penury and pain and hardship of childhood, a constant struggle against which has won for Calvé this victory, have engendered a remarkable sympathy and a profound seriousness in her life....

One special benefit I get from the company of these ladies and gentlemen is that, except the one American lady, no one knows English; talking in English is wholly eschewed, and consequently somehow or other I have to talk as well as hear French....

The tour programme was as follows—from Paris to Vienna,

and thence to Constantinople, by rail; then by steamer to Athens and Greece, then across the Mediterranean to Egypt, then Asia Minor, Jerusalem, and so on....

Formerly I had the notion that people of cold climates did not take hot chillies, which was merely a bad habit of warm climate people. But the habit of taking chillies, which we observed to begin with Hungary and which reached its climax in Rumania and Bulgaria etc., appeared to me to beat even your South Indians....

At 10 in the morning we left Constantinople, passing a night and a day on the sea, which was perfectly placid. By degrees we reached the Golden Horn and the Sea of Marmora. In one of the islands of the Marmora we saw a monastery of the Greek religion....

In the evening we reached Athens, and after passing a whole night under quarantine we obtained permission for landing in the morning. Port Peiraeus is a small town, but very beautiful....

At 10 AM on the fourth day we got on board the Russian steamer, Czar, bound for Egypt. After reaching the dock we came to learn that the steamer was to start at 4 AM—perhaps we were too early or there would be some extra delay in loading the cargo. So, having no other alternative, we went round and made a cursory acquaintance with the sculpture of Ageladas and his three pupils, Phidias, Myron, and Polycletus, who had flourished between 576 BC and 486 BC. Even here we began to feel the great heat.[60]

Port Tewfick, 26 November 1900 · The steamer was late; so I am waiting. Thank goodness, it entered the canal this morning at Port Said. That means it will arrive some time in the evening if everything goes right.

Of course it is like solitary imprisonment these two days, and I am holding my soul in patience.

But they say the change is thrice dear. Mr. Gaze's agent gave me all wrong directions. In the first place, there was nobody here to tell me a thing, not to speak of receiving me. Secondly, I was not told that I had to change my Gaze's ticket for a steamer one at the agent's office, and that was at Suez, not here. It was good one way, therefore, that the steamer was late; so I went to see the agent of the steamer and he told me to exchange Gaze's pass for a regular ticket.

I hope to board the steamer some time tonight. I am well and happy and am enjoying the fun immensely.[61]

CHAPTER TEN

"I BELIEVE..."

I BELIEVE IN GOD, and I believe in man. I believe in helping the miserable. I believe in going even to hell to save others.[1]

Of course I would commit a crime and go to hell forever if by that I could really help a human being![2]

I may have to be born again because I have fallen in love with man.[3]

I do not believe in a God or religion which cannot wipe the widow's tears or bring a piece of bread to the orphan's mouth.[4]

I have nothing whatever to do with ritual or dogma; my mission is to show that religion is everything and in everything.[5]

The glory of man is that he is a thinking being. It is the nature of man to think and therein he differs from animals. I believe in reason and follow reason having seen enough of the evils of authority, for I was born in a country where they have gone to the extreme of authority.[6]

If there ever is going to be an ideal religion, it must be broad and large enough to supply food for all these minds. It must supply the strength of philosophy to the philosopher, the devotee's heart to the worshipper; to the ritualist, it will give all that the most marvellous symbolism can convey; to the poet, it will give as much of heart as he can take in, and other things besides. To make such a broad religion, we shall have to go back to the time when religions began and take them all in.

Our watchword, then, will be acceptance, and not exclusion. Not only toleration, for so-called toleration is often blasphemy, and I do not believe in it. I believe in acceptance. Why should I tolerate? Toleration means that I think that you are wrong and I am just allowing you to live. Is it not a blasphemy to think that you and I are allowing others to live? I accept all religions that were in the past, and worship with them all; I worship God with every one of them, in whatever form they worship Him. I shall go to the mosque of the Mohammedan; I shall enter the Christian's church and kneel before the crucifix; I shall enter the Buddhistic temple, where I shall take refuge in Buddha and in his Law. I shall go into the forest and sit down in meditation with the Hindu, who is trying to see the Light which enlightens the heart of every one.

Not only shall I do all these, but I shall keep my heart open for all that may come in the future. Is God's book finished? Or is it still a continuous revelation going on? It is a marvellous book—these spiritual revelations of the world. The Bible, the Vedas, the Koran, and all other sacred books are but so many pages, and an infinite number of pages remain yet to be unfolded. I would leave it open for all of them. We stand in the present, but open ourselves to the infinite future. We take in all that has been in the past, enjoy the light of the present, and open every window of the heart for all that will come in the future. Salutation to all the prophets of the past, to all the great ones of the present, and to all that are to come in the future![7]

I have experienced even in my insignificant life that good motives, sincerity, and infinite love can conquer the world. One single soul possessed of these virtues can destroy the dark designs of millions of hypocrites and brutes.[8]

You see, I cannot but believe that there is somewhere a great Power that thinks of Herself as feminine, and called Kali and Mother.... And I believe in Brahman too.... But is it not always like that? Is it not the multitude of cells in the body that make up the personality, the many brain-centres, not the one, that produce consciousness?... Unity in complexity! Just so! And why should it be different with Brahman? It is Brahman. It is the One. And yet—and yet—it is the gods too![9]

Kali worship is not a necessary step in any religion. The Upanishads teach us all there is of religion. Kali worship is my special fad; you never heard me preach it, or read of my preaching it in India. I only preach what is good for universal humanity. If there is any curious method which applies entirely to me, I keep it a secret and there it ends. I must not explain to you what Kali worship is, as I never taught it to anybody....

Ceremonials and symbols etc. have no place in our religion which is the doctrine of the Upanishads, pure and simple. Many people think the ceremonial etc. help them in realising religion. I have no objection.

Religion is that which does not depend upon books or teachers or prophets or saviours, and that which does not make us dependent in this or in any other lives upon others. In this sense Advaitism of the Upanishads is the only religion. But saviours, books, prophets, ceremonials, etc. have their places. They may help many as Kali worship helps me in my secular work. They are welcome....[10]

I can do as I please, I am independent. Sometimes I live in the Himalaya Mountains, and sometimes in the streets of cities. I never know where I will get my next meal, I never keep money with me. I come here by subscription....

This is a good dress; when I am home I am in rags, and I go barefooted. Do I believe in caste? Caste is a social custom; religion has nothing to do with it; all castes will associate with me....

Why should I marry, when I see in every woman only the Divine Mother? Why do I make all these sacrifices? To emancipate myself from earthly ties and attachments so that there will be no rebirth for me. When I die I want to become at once absorbed in the divine, one with God. I would be a Buddha.[11]

It is of supreme importance to think what we ourselves believe. What we have realised, is the question. What Jesus, or Buddha, or Moses did is nothing to us, unless we too do it for ourselves. It would not satisfy our hunger to shut ourselves up in a room and think of what Moses ate, nor would what Moses thought save us. My ideas are very radical on these points. Sometimes I think that I am right when I agree with all the ancient teachers, at other times I think they are right when they agree with me. I believe in thinking independently. I believe in becoming entirely free from the holy teachers; pay all reverence to them, but look at religion as an independent research. I have to find my light, just as they found theirs.[12]

Be broad minded; always see two ways. When I am on the heights I say, "Shivo'ham, Shivo'ham: I am He, I am He!" and when I have the stomach-ache I say, "Mother have mercy on me!"[13]

I was born for the life of a scholar—retired, quiet, poring over my books. But the Mother dispenses otherwise—yet the tendency is there.[14]

Though I often say strange things and angry things, yet remember that in my heart I never seriously mean to preach anything but love! All these things will come right only when we realize that we love each other.[15]

It is selfishness that we must seek to eliminate. I find that whenever I have made a mistake in my life, it has always been because self entered into the calculation. Where self has not been involved, my judgment has gone straight to the mark.[16]

If I consider myself greater than the ant that crawls on the ground I am ignorant.[17]

In Girish Chandra Ghosh alone I have seen that true resignation—that true spirit of a servant of the Lord. And was it not because he was ever ready to sacrifice himself that Sri Ramakrishna took upon himself all his responsibility? What a unique spirit of resignation to the Lord! I have not met his parallel. From him have I learnt the lesson of self-surrender.[18]

The first obstruction to our following reason is our unwillingness to go to truth. We want truth to come to us. In all my travels, most people told me, "Oh, that is not a comfortable religion you talk about. Give us a comfortable religion!"

I do not understand what they mean by this "comfortable religion." I was never taught any comfortable religion in my life. I want truth for my religion. Whether it be comfortable or not, I do not care. Why should truth be comfortable always? Truth many times hits hard—as we all know by our experience. Gradually, after a long intercourse with such persons, I came to find out what they meant by their stereotypical phrase. These people have got into a rut, and they do not dare to get out of it. Truth must apologize to them.

I once met a lady who was very fond of her children and her money and her everything. When I began to preach to her that the only way to God is by giving up everything, she stopped coming the next day. One day she came and told me that the reason for her staying away was because the religion I preached was very uncomfortable. "What sort of religion would be comfortable to you?" I asked in order to test her. She said, "I want to see God in my children, in my money, in my diamonds."

"Very good, madam," I replied. "You have now got all these things. And you will have to see these things millions of years yet. Then you will be bumped somewhere and come to reason. Until that time comes, you will never come to God. In the meantime, go on seeing God in your children and in your money and your diamonds and your dances."[19]

In America there was a great agnostic, a very noble man, a very good man, and a very fine speaker. He lectured on religion, which he said was of no use; why bother our heads about other worlds? He employed this simile: we have an orange here, and we want to squeeze all the juice out of it. I met him once and said, "I agree with you entirely. I have some fruit, and I too want to squeeze out the juice. Our difference lies in the choice of the fruit. You want an orange, and I prefer a mango. You think it is enough to live here and eat and drink and have a little scientific knowledge; but you have no right to say that that will suit all tastes. Such a conception is nothing to me. If I had only to learn how an apple falls to the ground, or how an electric current shakes my nerves, I would commit suicide. I want to understand the heart of things, the very kernel itself. Your study is the manifestation of life, mine is the life itself. My philosophy says you must know that and drive out from your mind all thoughts of heaven and hell and all other superstitions, even though they exist in the same sense that this world exists. I must know the heart of this life, its

"I BELIEVE..."

very essence, what it is, not only how it works and what are its manifestations. I want the why of everything. I leave the how to children.[20]

I am not a Buddhist ... and yet I am.[21]

Of course I do not endorse all his philosophy. I want a good deal of metaphysics, for myself. I entirely differ in many respects, but, because I differ, is that any reason why I should not see the beauty of the man?... I wish I had one infinitesimal part of Buddha's heart. Buddha may or may not have believed in God; that does not matter to me. He reached the same state of perfection to which others come by Bhakti—love of God—Yoga, or Jnana.[22]

All my life I have been very fond of Buddha ... I have more veneration for that character than for any other—that boldness, that fearlessness, and that tremendous love! He was born for the good of men. Others may seek God, others may seek truth for themselves; he did not even care to know truth for himself. He sought truth because people were in misery. How to help them, that was his only concern. Throughout his life he never had a thought for himself.[23]

The Lord Buddha is my Ishta—my God. He preached no theory about Godhead—he was himself God, I fully believe it.[24]

I have a superstition—it is nothing, you know, but a personal superstition!—that the same soul who came once as Buddha came afterwards as Christ.[25]

[*Question: Did Buddha teach that the many was real and the ego unreal, while orthodox Hinduism regards the One as the real, and the many as unreal?*] Yes, and what Ramakrishna Paramahamsa and I have added to this is, that the Many and the One are the same Reality, perceived by the same mind at different times and in different attitudes.[26]

The Master said he would come again in about two hundred years—and I will come with him. When a Master comes, he brings his own people.[27]

> Nor angel I, nor man, nor brute,
> Nor body, mind, nor he or she,
> The books do stop in wonder mute
> To tell my nature; I am He.
>
> Before the sun, the moon, the earth,
> Before the stars or comets free,
> Before e'en time has had its birth,
> I was, I am, and I will be....
>
> Not two or many, 'tis but one,
> And thus in me all me's I have;
> I cannot hate, I cannot shun
> Myself from me, I can but love.
>
> From dreams awake, from bonds be free,
> Be not afraid. This mystery,
> My shadow, cannot frighten me,
> Know once for all that I am He.[28]

CHAPTER ELEVEN

THE LAST DAYS

Belur Math, 11 December 1900 · I arrived night before last. Alas! my hurrying was of no use.

Poor Captain Sevier passed away, a few days ago—thus two great Englishmen gave up their lives for us—us the Hindus. This is martyrdom if anything is.[1]

Belur Math, 15 December 1900 · Three days ago I reached here. It was quite unexpected—my visit, and everybody was so surprised.

Things here have gone better than I expected during my absence, only Mr. Sevier has passed away. It was a tremendous blow ... [2]

Belur Math, 19 December 1900 · Verily I am a bird of passage. Gay and busy Paris, grim old Constantinople, sparkling little Athens, and pyramidal Cairo are left behind, and here I am writing in my room on the Ganga, in the Math. It is so quiet and still! The broad river is dancing in the bright sunshine, only now and then an occasional cargo boat breaking the silence with the splashing of the oars. It is the cold season here, but the middle of the day is warm and bright every day.... Everything is green and gold, and the grass is like velvet; yet the air is cold and crisp and delightful.[3]

Belur Math, December, 1900 · My heart has become very weak. Change, I do not think, will do me any good, as for the last fourteen years I do not remember to have stopped at one place for three months at a stretch. On the other hand, if by some chance I can live for months in one place, I hope it will do me good. I do not mind this, however; I feel that my work in this life is done. Through good and evil, pain and pleasure, my lifeboat has been dragged on. The one great lesson I was taught is that life is misery, nothing but misery. Mother knows what is best. Each one of us is in the hands of Karma—it works out itself, and no nay. There is only one element in life which is worth having at any cost—and it is love. Love immense and infinite, broad as the sky and deep as the ocean. This is the one great gain in life. Blessed is he who gets it.[4]

Belur Math, 26 December 1900 · Dear Mr. Sevier passed away before I could arrive. He was cremated on the banks of the river that flows by his Ashrama, *à la* Hindu, covered with garlands, the Brahmins carrying the body and boys chanting the Vedas.

The cause has already two martyrs. It makes me love dear old England and its heroic breed. The Mother is watering the plant of future India with the best blood of England. Glory unto Her!...

I am calm and strong. Occasion never found me low yet; Mother will not make me now depressed.

It is very pleasant here, now the winter is on. The Himalayas will be still more beautiful with the uncovered snows.[5]

Belur Math, 26 December 1900 ·

> I look behind and after
> And find that all is right,
> In my deepest sorrows
> There is a soul of light.[6]

THE LAST DAYS

Belur Math, 26 December 1900 · I am going to Mayavati tomorrow. It is absolutely necessary that I should go there once.[7]

Mayavati, 6 January 1901 · This place is very, very beautiful, and they have made it simply exquisite. It is a huge place several acres in area, and is very well kept. I hope Mrs. Sevier will be in a position to keep it up in the future. She wishes it ever so much, of course....

The first day's touch of Calcutta brought the asthma back; and every night I used to get a fit during the two weeks I was there. I am, however, very well in the Himalayas.

It is snowing heavily here, and I was caught in a blizzard on the way; but it is not very cold, and all this exposure to the snows for two days on my way here seems to have done me a world of good.

Today I walked over the snow uphill about a mile, seeing Mrs. Sevier's lands; she has made beautiful roads all over. Plenty of gardens, fields, orchards, and large forests, all in her land. The living houses are so simple, so clean, and so pretty, and above all so suited for the purpose....

The snow is lying all round six inches deep, the sun is bright and glorious, and now in the middle of the day we are sitting outside, reading. And the snow all about us! The winter here is very mild in spite of the snow. The air is dry and balmy, and the water beyond all praise.[8]

Belur Math, 26 January 1901 · The moment I touch Bengal, especially the Math, the asthmatic fits return! The moment I leave, I recover!...

I am going to take my mother on pilgrimage next week. It may take months to make the complete round of pilgrimages. This is the one great wish of a Hindu widow. I have brought only misery to my people all my life. I am trying at least to fulfil this one wish of hers.[9]

Dacca, 20 March 1901 · At last I am in Eastern Bengal. This is the first time I am here, and never before knew Bengal was so beautiful. You ought to have seen the rivers here—regular rolling oceans of fresh water, and everything so green—continual production. The villages are the cleanest and prettiest in all India....

I am peaceful and calm—and am finding every day the old begging and trudging life is the best for me after all....

Things are going on, as is in the nature of things. To me has come resignation.[10]

Dacca, 29 March 1901 · My mother, aunt, and cousin came over five days ago to Dacca, as there was a great sacred bath in the Brahmaputra river. Whenever a particular conjunction of planets takes place, which is very rare, a huge concourse of people gather on the river on a particular spot. This year there has been more than a hundred thousand people; for miles the river was covered with boats.

The river, though nearly a mile broad at the place, was one mass of mud! But it was firm enough, so we had our bath and Puja [worship] and all that.

I am rather enjoying Dacca. I am going to take my mother and the other ladies to Chandranath, a holy place at the easternmost corner of Bengal.[11]

Dacca, 30 March 1901 · First of all, I must express my pleasure at the opportunity afforded me of coming to Eastern Bengal to acquire an intimate knowledge of this part of the country, which I hitherto lacked in spite of my wanderings through many civilised countries of the West, as well as my gratification at the sight of the majestic rivers, wide fertile plains, and picturesque villages in this, my own country of Bengal, which I had not the good fortune of seeing for myself before. I did not know that there was everywhere in my country of

Bengal—on land and water—so much beauty and charm. But this much has been my gain that after seeing the various countries of the world I can now much more appreciate the beauties of my own land.

In the same way also, in search of religion, I had travelled among various sects—sects which had taken up the ideals of foreign nations as their own, and I had begged at the door of others, not knowing then that in the religion of my country, in our national religion, there was so much beauty and grandeur. It is now many years since I found Hinduism to be the most perfectly satisfying religion in the world. Hence I feel sad at heart when I see existing among my own countrymen, professing a peerless faith, such a widespread indifference to our religion—though I am very well aware of the unfavourable materialistic conditions in which they pass their lives—owing to the diffusion of European modes of thought in this, our great motherland.[12]

I liked [East Bengal] on the whole. The fields, I saw, were rich in crops, the climate also is good, and the scenery on the hillside is charming. The Brahmaputra Valley is incomparable in its beauty. The people of East Bengal are a little stronger and more active than those of this part [West Bengal]. It may be due to their taking plenty of fish and meat. Whatever they do, they do with great persistence. They use a great deal of oil and fat in their food, which is not good, because taking too much of oily and fatty food produces fat in the body....

About religious ideas, I noticed the people are very conservative, and many have turned into fanatics in trying to be liberal in religion. One day a young man brought to me, in the house of Mohini Babu at Dacca, a photograph and said, "Sir, please tell me who he is. Is he an Avatara?" I told him gently many times that I know nothing of it. When even on my telling him three or four times the boy did not cease from his persistent questioning, I was constrained to say at last, "My boy, henceforth take a little nutritious food and then your brain will develop. Without nourishing food, I see your brain has become dried up." At these words the young man may have been much displeased. But what could I do? Unless I spoke like this to the boys, they would turn into madcaps by degrees....

People may call their Guru an Avatara; they may have any idea of him they like. But Incarnations of God are not born anywhere and everywhere and at all seasons. At Dacca itself I heard there were three or four Avataras!...

Going so far, should I not visit the birthplace of such a great soul, [Nag Mahashaya]? His wife fed me with many delicacies prepared by her own hand. The house is charming, like a peace retreat. There I took a swimming bath in a village pond. After that I had such a sound sleep that I woke at half past two in the afternoon. Of the few days I had sound sleep in my life, that in Nag Mahashaya's house was one. Rising from sleep I had a plentiful repast. Nag Mahashaya's wife presented me a cloth which I tied round my head as a turban and started for Dacca. I found that the photograph of Nag Mahashaya was being worshipped there. The place where his remains lie interred ought to be well kept. Even now it is not as it should be....

How can ordinary people appreciate a great man like him? Those who had his company are blessed indeed....

The Shillong hills are very beautiful. There I met Sir Henry Cotton, the Chief Commissioner of Assam. He asked me, "Swamiji, after travelling through Europe and America, what have you come to see here in these distant hills?" Such a good and kind-hearted man as Sir Henry Cotton is rarely found. Hearing of my illness, he sent the Civil Surgeon and inquired

THE LAST DAYS

after my health mornings and evenings. I could not do much lecturing there, because my health was very bad. On the way Nitai served and looked after me nicely....

[Kamakhya] is the land of the Tantras. I heard of one "Hankar Deva" who is worshipped there as an Avatara. I heard his sect is very widespread. I could not ascertain if "Hankar Deva" was but another form of the name Shankaracharya. They are monks—perhaps Tantrika Sannyasins, or perhaps one of the Shankara sects....

There they used to make much fuss about my food and say, "Why should you eat that food or eat from the hands of such and such?"—and so on. To which I had to reply, "I am a Sannyasin and a mendicant friar and what need have I to observe so much outward formality with regard to food etc.? Do not your scriptures say, "*Carenmādhukarīṁ vṛttimapi mlecchakulādapi*—one should beg one's food from door to door, ay even from the house of an outcast"?[13]

Shillong, April, 1901 [*During a severe attack of asthma*] · What does it matter! I have given them enough for fifteen hundred years![14]

Belur Math, 15 May 1901 · I have just returned from my tour through East Bengal and Assam. As usual I am quite tired and broken down.[15]

Belur Math, 3 June 1901 · True, my temper was ever bad, and nowadays owing to illness it occasionally becomes terrible—but know this for certain that my love can never cease.[16]

Belur Math, 14 June 1901 · I was thrown *hôrs de combat* [out of the fight] in Assam. The climate of the Math is just reviving me a bit. At Shillong—the hill sanatorium of Assam—I had fever, asthma, increase of albumen, and my body swelled to almost twice its normal size. These symptoms subsided, however, as soon as I reached the Math. It is dreadfully hot this year; but a bit of rain has commenced, and I hope we will soon have the monsoon in full force. I have no plans just now, except that the Bombay Presidency wants me so badly that I think of going there soon. We are thinking of starting touring through Bombay in a week or so....

We have seen enough of this life to care for any of its bubbles, have we not Joe? For months I have been practising to drive away all sentiments; therefore I stop here, and good-bye just now. It is ordained by Mother we work together; it has been already for the good of many; it shall be for the good of many more; so let it be. It is useless planning, useless high flights; Mother will find Her own way ... rest assured.[17]

Belur Math, end of June 1901 · I have manfully borne the terrific heat of my country in the plains, and now I am facing the deluging rains of my country. Do you know how I am taking rest? I have got a few goats and sheep and cows and dogs and cranes! And I am taking care of them the whole day! It is not trying to be happy; what for? Why should one not be unhappy as well—both being nonsense?—but just to kill time....

Don't worry, don't be anxious; for me the "Mother" is my protection and refuge; and everything must come round soon, better than my fondest dreams can paint.[18]

Belur Math, 1901 · This Kali is Brahman in manifestation. Haven't you heard Sri Ramakrishna's illustration of the "snake moving and the snake at rest"?... This time, when I get well, I shall worship the Mother with my heart's blood, then only will She be pleased.[19]

Belur Math, 1901 · Well, I was glad to see that there was yet a liberality of view at Kalighat. The temple authorities did not object in the least to my entering the temple, though they knew that I was a man who had returned from the West. On the contrary, they very cordially took me into the holy precincts and helped me to worship the Mother to my heart's content.[20]

When I returned to India after my visit to the West, several orthodox Hindus raised a howl against my association with the Western people and my breaking the rules of orthodoxy. They did not like me to teach the truths of the Vedas to the people of the West.[21]

Belur Math, 5 July 1901 · My health has been and is very bad. I recover for a few days only; then comes the inevitable collapse. Well, this is the nature of the disease anyway.

I have been touring of late in Eastern Bengal and Assam. Assam is, next to Kashmir, the most beautiful country in India, but very unhealthy. The huge Brahmaputra winding in and out of mountains and hills, studded with islands, is of course worth one's while to see.[22]

Belur Math, 6 August 1901 · "Mother knows," indeed; only I know that "Mother" not only knows, but does—and is going to do something very fine for me in the near future. What do you think will be very good for me on earth? Silver? Gold? Pooh! I have got something infinitely better; but a little gold will not be amiss to keep my jewel in proper surroundings, and it is coming, don't you think so?

I am a man who frets much, but waits all the same; and the apple comes to my mouth by itself. So, it is coming, coming, coming.[23]

Belur Math, 27 August 1901 · I would that my health were what you expected ... It is getting worse, in fact, every day, and so many complications and botherations without that. I have ceased to notice it at all....

I am a dying man; I have no time to fool in....

I am in a sense a retired man; I don't keep much note of what is going on about the Movement; then the Movement is getting bigger, and it is impossible for one man to know all about it minutely.

I now do nothing, except trying to eat and sleep and nurse my body the rest of the time.[24]

Belur Math, 2 September 1901 · As for me, I am very happy. Of course, Bengal brings the asthma now and then, but it is getting tame, and the terrible things—Bright's disease and diabetes—have disappeared altogether. Life in any dry climate will stop the asthma completely, I am sure. I get reduced, of course, during a fit, but then it takes me no time to lay on a few layers of fat. I have a lot of cows, goats, a few sheep, dogs, geese, ducks, one tame gazelle, and very soon I am going to have some milk buffaloes. These are not your American bison, but huge things—hairless, half aquatic in habits, and giving an enormous quantity of very rich milk.

Within the last few months, I got two fits [of asthma] by going to two of the dampest hill stations in Bengal—Shillong and Darjeeling. I am not going to try the Bengali mountains any more.[25]

Belur Math, 7 September 1901 · It is raining here day and night last three days. Two of our cows have calved.[26]

Belur Math, 7 September 1901 · Well, about the rains—they have come down now in right earnest, and it is a deluge, pouring, pouring, pouring night and day. The river is rising, flooding the banks; the ponds and tanks have overflowed. I have just now returned from lending a hand in cutting a deep drain to take off the water from the Math grounds. The rainwater stands at places some feet high. My huge stork is full of glee, and so are the ducks and geese. My tame antelope fled from the Math and gave us some days of anxiety in finding him out. One of my ducks unfortunately died yesterday. She had been gasping for breath more than a week. One of my waggish old monks says, "Sir, it is no use living in this Kali-Yuga when ducks catch cold from damp and rain, and frogs sneeze!"

One of the geese had her plumes falling off. Knowing no other method, I left her some minutes in a tub of water mixed with mild carbolic, so that it might either kill or heal; and she is all right now.[27]

Belur Math, 8 November 1901 · I have been ever since my trip to East Bengal almost bedridden. Now I am worse than ever with the additional disadvantage of impaired eyesight.[28]

Varanasi, 10 February 1902 · Mr. Okakura [of Japan] has started on his short tour.... A very well-educated rich young man of Varanasi, with whose father we had a long-standing friendship, came back to this city yesterday. He is especially interested in art, and spending purposely a lot of money in his attempts to revive dying Indian arts. He came to see me only a few hours after Mr. Okakura left. He is just the man to show him artistic India (i.e. what little is left), and I am sure he will be much benefited by Okakura's suggestions. Okakura just found a common terracotta water-vessel here used by the servants. The shape and the embossed work on it simply charmed him, but as it is common earthenware and would not bear the journey, he left a request with me to have it reproduced in brass. I was at my wit's end as to what to do. My young friend comes a few hours after, and not only undertakes to have it done, but offers to show a few hundreds of embossed designs in terracotta infinitely superior to the one Okakura fancied.

He also offers to show us old painting in that wonderful old style. Only one family is left in Varanasi who can paint after the old style yet. One of them has painted a whole hunting scene on a pea, perfect in detail and action!...

My plans are not settled; I may shift from this place very soon.[29]

Varanasi, 12 February 1902 · If in this hell of a world one can bring a little joy and peace even for a day into the heart of a single person, that much alone is true; this I have learnt after suffering all my life; all else is mere moonshine.[30]

Varanasi, 4 March 1902 · It is night now, and I can hardly sit up or write, yet still feel duty bound to write to you this letter, fearing lest it becomes my last, it may put others to trouble.

My condition is not at all serious, but it may become [so] any time; and I don't know what is meant by a low fever that almost never leaves me and the difficulty of breathing....

Ramakrishnananda came a few weeks before I came away, and the first thing he did was to lay down at my feet 400 Rs. he had collected in so many years of hard work!! It was the first time such a thing has happened in my life. I can scarcely suppress my tears. Oh, Mother! Mother! There is not all gratitude, all love, all manliness dead!! And, dear child, one is enough—one seed is enough to reforest the world.[31]

Belur Math, 21 April 1902 · It seems the plan of going to Japan seems to have come to nought....

I am getting on splendidly, they say, but yet very weak and no water to drink. Anyhow the chemical analysis shows a great improvement. The swelling about the feet and the complaints have all disappeared.[32]

Belur Math, 15 May 1902 · I am somewhat better, but of course far from what I expected. A great idea of quiet has come upon me. I am going to retire for good—no more work for me. If possible, I will revert to my old days of begging.[33]

Belur Math, 21 June 1902 · I am getting on anyhow and am quite strong. As to diet, I find I have to restrict myself and not follow the prescription of my doctor to eat anything I like. The pills continue, however. Will you ask the boys if they can get "Amalaki" fruits in the place [Mayavati] now? We cannot get them in the plains now. They are rather sour and puckery eaten raw; but make marmalade of whole [ones]—delicious. Then they are the best things for fermentation I ever get.[34]

This body will never be fit again. I shall have to leave it and bring another body to complete the work. There are many things that remain undone.[35]

I do not want Mukti. As long as there shall be one soul left, I have to come again and again.[36]

Belur Math, 1902 · I shall never see forty.... I delivered my message and I must go.... The shadow of a big tree will not let the smaller trees grow up. I must go to make room.[37]

Death has come to my bedside; I have been through enough of work and play; let the world realize what contribution I have made; it will take quite a long time to understand that.[38]

Belur Math, 2 July 1902 · I am making ready for death. A great tapasya and meditation has come upon me, and I am making ready for death.[39]

Belur Math, 4 July 1902 · If there were another Vivekananda, he would have understood what Vivekananda has done! And yet, how many Vivekanandas shall be born in time![40]

[*In Kashmir after an illness, Swami Vivekananda said as he lifted a couple of pebbles*] · Whenever death approaches me, all weakness vanishes. I have neither fear, nor doubt, nor thought of the external. I simply busy myself making ready to die. I am as hard as that [*the pebbles struck one another in his hand*]—for I have touched the feet of God![41]

If ever a man found the vanity of things, I have it now. This is the world, hideous, beastly corpse. Who thinks of helping it is a fool! But we have to work out our slavery by doing good or evil; I have worked it out, I hope. May the Lord take me to the other shore![42]

Whatever I had I have left in that country [America]. During the lectures a power used to emanate from this body and would infuse the audience....

If I put on the loin cloth and become absorbed in spiritual practice without thinking of ways and means of maintenance, then perhaps the power to grant Nirvikalpa Samadhi may come. It has become exhausted, or lost, by giving lectures in America.[43]

I have worked my best. If there is any seed of truth in it, it will come to life.... I am satisfied in my conscience that I did not remain an idle Swami. I have a note-book which has travelled with me all over the world. I find these words written seven years ago—"Now to seek a corner and lay myself there to die!" Yet all this Karma remained.[44]

As for myself I am quite content. I have roused a good many of our people, and that was all I wanted. Let things have their course and Karma its sway. I have no bonds here below. I have seen life, and it is all self—life is for self, love for self, honour for self, everything for self. I look back and scarcely find any action I have done for self—even my wicked deeds were not for the self. So I am content; not that I feel I have done anything specially good or great, but the world is so little, life so mean a thing, existence so, so servile—that I wonder and smile that human beings, rational souls, should be running after this self—so mean and detestable a prize.

This is the truth. We are caught in a trap, and the sooner one gets out, the better for one. I have seen the truth—let the body float up or down, who cares?[45]

From the very nature of things, it is difficult to understand anything of the world. And now after lifelong labour it seems that I have known a little and when I think of giving that knowledge to others, the call has come from Above: Come away, just come away—don't bother yourself about teaching others. It is not the will of the Granny that the play should be over.[46]

Oh, the grief! If I could get two or three like me, I could have left the world convulsed.[47]

Now I desire a little peace—it seems there is no more strength left to bear the burden of work and responsibility—rest and peace for the few days that I shall yet live! Victory to the Guru! Victory to the Guru!... No more lectures or anything of that sort. Peace![48]

Let me die a true Sannyasin as my Master did, heedless of money, of women, and of fame! And of these the most insidious is the love of fame![49]

Do you think that there will be no more Vivekanandas after I die!... There will be no lack of Vivekanandas, if the world needs them—thousands and millions of Vivekanandas will appear—from where, who knows! Know for certain that the work done by me is not the work of Vivekananda, it is His work—the Lord's own work! If one governor-general retires, another is sure to be sent in his place by the Emperor.[50]

"As the birds which have slept in the branches of a tree wake up, singing when the dawn comes, and soar up into the deep blue sky, so is the end of my life."

I have had many difficulties, and also some very great successes. But all my difficulties and suffering count for nothing, as I have succeeded. I have attained my aim. I have found the pearl for which I dived into the ocean of life. I have been rewarded. I am pleased....

I see the cloud lifting, vanishing, the cloud of my bad Karma. And the sun of my good Karma rises—shining, beautiful, and powerful.[51]

I am more calm and quiet now than I ever was.... My boat is nearing the calm harbour from which it is never more to be driven out. Glory, glory unto Mother! I have no wish, no ambition now. Blessed be Mother! I am the servant of Ramakrishna. I am merely a machine. I know nothing else. Nor do I want to know. Glory, glory unto Sri Guru![52]

Mother is becoming propitious once more. Things are looking up. They must.

Work always brings evil with it. I have paid for the accumulated evil with bad health. I am glad. My mind is all the better for it. There is a mellowness and a calmness in life now, which was never there before. I am learning now how to be detached as well as attached, and mentally becoming my own master....

Mother is doing Her own work; I do not worry much now. Moths like me die by the thousand every instant. Her work goes on all the same. Glory unto Mother!... Alone and drifting about in the will-current of the Mother has been my whole life. The moment I have tried to break this, that moment I have been hurt. Her will be done!...

I am happy, at peace with myself, and more of the Sannyasin than I ever was before. The love for my own kith and kin is growing less every day, and that for Mother increasing. Memories of long nights of vigil with Sri Ramakrishna under the Dakshineswar Banyan are waking up once more. And work? What is work? Whose work? Whom shall I work for?

I am free. I am Mother's child. She works, She plays. Why should I plan? What should I plan? Things came and went, just as She liked, without my planning. We are Her automata. She is the wirepuller.[53]

At those Blessed Feet is the perfection of Knowledge sought by the Jnanis! At those Blessed Feet also is the fulfilment of Love sought by the lovers! Oh, say, where else will men and women go for refuge but to those Blessed Feet! Alas! what folly for men in this world to spend their days fighting and quarrelling with one another as they do! But how long can they go on in that way? In the evening of life they must all come home, to the arms of the Mother.[54]

The battles are lost and won. I have bundled my things and am waiting for the great deliverer.

"Shiva, O Shiva, carry my boat to the other shore."

After all ... I am only the boy who used to listen with rapt wonderment to the wonderful words of Ramakrishna under the Banyan at Dakshineswar. That is my true nature; works and activities, doing good and so forth are all superimpositions. Now I again hear his voice; the same old voice thrilling my soul. Bonds are breaking—love dying, work becoming tasteless—the glamour is off life. Only the voice of the Master calling. —"I come Lord, I come." "Let the dead bury the dead, follow thou Me." —"I come, my beloved Lord, I come."

Yes, I come. Nirvana is before me. I feel it at times—the same infinite ocean of peace, without a ripple, a breath.

I am glad I was born, glad I suffered so, glad I did make big blunders, glad to enter peace. I leave none bound, I take no bonds. Whether this body will fall and release me or I enter into freedom in the body, the old man is gone, gone for ever, never to come back again! The guide, the Guru, the leader, the teacher has passed away; the boy, the student, the servant is left behind....

The sweetest moments of my life have been when I was drifting: I am drifting again—with the bright warm sun ahead and masses of vegetation around—and in the heat everything is so still, so calm—and I am drifting languidly—in the warm heart of the river! I dare not make a splash with my hands or feet—for fear of breaking the marvellous stillness, stillness that makes you feel sure it is an illusion!

Behind my work was ambition, behind my love was personality, behind my purity was fear, behind my guidance the thirst of power! Now they are vanishing, and I drift. I come! Mother, I come! In Thy warm bosom, floating wheresoever Thou takest me, in the voiceless, in the strange, in the wonderland, I come—a spectator, no more an actor.

Oh, it is so calm! My thoughts seem to come from a great, great distance in the interior of my own heart. They seem like faint, distant whispers, and peace is upon everything, sweet, sweet peace—like that one feels for a few moments just before falling into sleep, when things are seen and felt like shadows—without fear, without love, without emotion. Peace that one feels alone, surrounded with statues and pictures—I come! Lord, I come!

The world is, but not beautiful nor ugly, but as sensations

without exciting any emotion. Oh ... the blessedness of it! Everything is good and beautiful; for things are all losing their relative proportions to me—my body among the first. Om That Existence![55]

I am the infinite blue sky; the clouds may gather over me, but I am the same infinite blue ... These tin pots of bodies and foolish dreams of happiness and misery—what are they?

My dreams are breaking. Om Tat Sat![56]

Black and thick are the folds of sinister fate. But I am the master. I raise my hand, and lo, they vanish! All this is nonsense. And fear? I am the Fear of fear, the Terror of terror, I am the fearless secondless One, I am the Ruler of destiny, the Wiper-out of fact. Sri wah Guru![57]

Ha! ha! ... all is good! Nonsense. Some good, some evil. I enjoy the good and I enjoy the evil. I was Jesus and I was Judas Iscariot; both my play, my fun.... Be brave and face everything—come good, come evil, both welcome, both of you my play. I have no good to attain, no ideal to clench up to, no ambition to fulfil; I, the diamond mine, am playing with pebbles, good and evil; good for you—evil, come; good for you—good, you come too. If the universe tumbles round my ears, what is that to me? I am Peace that passeth understanding ... I am beyond, I am peace.[58]

I am being lifted up above the pestilential miasma of this world's joys and sorrows; they are losing their meaning. It is a land of dreams; it does not matter whether one enjoys or weeps; they are but dreams, and as such, must break sooner or later....

I cannot be sorry for anything any more. I am attaining peace that passeth understanding, which is neither joy nor sorrow, but something above them both.... Now I am nearing that Peace, the eternal silence. Now I mean to see things as they are, everything in that peace, perfect in its way. "He whose joy is only in himself, whose desires are only in himself, he has learned his lessons." This is the great lesson that we are here to learn through myriads of births and heavens and hells—that there is nothing to be asked for, desired for, beyond one's Self. "The greatest thing I can obtain is my Self." "I am free," therefore I require none else for my happiness. "Alone through eternity, because I was free, am free, and will remain free for ever." This is Vedantism. I preached the theory so long, but oh, joy!... I am realising it now every day. Yes, I am—"I am free." "Alone, alone, I am the one without a second."[59]

It may be that I shall find it good to get outside of my body—to cast it off like a disused garment. But I shall not cease to work! I shall inspire men everywhere, until the world shall know that it is one with God.[60]

ENDNOTES

References are abbreviated as follows:

CW — *The Complete Works of Swami Vivekananda*, 9 Volumes (Kolkata: Advaita Ashrama, 1992-1997)

DP — Swami Saradananda, *Sri Ramakrishna and His Divine Play* (Trans. Swami Chetanananda) (St. Louis: Vedanta Society of St. Louis, 2003)

GM — Swami Saradananda, *Sri Ramakrishna the Great Master* (Trans. Swami Jagadananda) (Chennai: Sri Ramakrishna Math, 2004)

Gospel — Mahendra Nath Gupta, *The Gospel of Sri Ramakrishna* (Chennai: Sri Ramakrishna Math, 1981)

Life — *The Life of Swami Vivekananda by His Eastern and Western Disciples*, 2 Volumes (Kolkata: Advaita Ashrama, 1989)

MS — Sister Nivedita, *The Master as I Saw Him*, 9th Edition (Kolkata: Udbodhan Office, 1962)

ND — Marie Louise Burke, *Swami Vivekananda in the West: New Discoveries*, 6 Volumes (Kolkata: Advaita Ashrama, 1999)

RM — *Reminiscences of Swami Vivekananda* (Kolkata: Advaita Ashrama, 2004)

ST — *Spiritual Talks by the First Disciples of Sri Ramakrishna* (Kolkata: Advaita Ashrama, 1936/2002)

NOTES TO PAGES 1–60

Chapter One
Birth and Boyhood
pages 1–8

1. Life 2.243
2. CW 8.59
3. CW 9.203
4. CW 9.203
5. CW 9.204
6. MS 164
7. CW 4.14
8. Life 1.40
9. CW 1.75
10. GM 829
11. CW 8.68–69
12. CW 9.205
13. CW 5.220
14. GM 850
15. Life 1.30
16. CW 7.123
17. Life 1.40–41
18. Life 1.45
19. CW 8.69–70
20. Life 1.45
21. GM 827
22. GM 834
23. CW 1.317–18
24. CW 3.345–46

Chapter Two
Discipleship
pages 9–44

1. CW 7.282
2. CW 5.186
3. CW 8.77–79
4. CW 4.178–79
5. Gospel 984–85
6. Life 1.76–77
7. Life 1.77–78
8. Gospel 985
9. Life 78–79
10. CW 5.392–93
11. Life 1.90
12. Gospel 981
13. Gospel 986
14. CW 1.326
15. Gospel 984
16. Gospel 980–81
17. Gospel 981
18. GM 684
19. GM 90
20. Life 96–97
21. CW 4.179–80
22. CW 7.414
23. CW 1.407
24. GM 873–74
25. GM 835
26. Gospel 980
27. GM 919
28. Life 131–33
29. Gospel 980
30. Life 123–28
31. Gospel 987
32. Life 130
33. MS 139–40, also CW 8.263–64
34. MS 10–11, also CW 9.411
35. CW 9.410
36. Gospel 904–06
37. Gospel 935
38. Gospel 935–36
39. Gospel 962
40. Gospel 972
41. Gospel 981
42. CW 7.139–40
43. CW 7.196–97
44. Gospel 985
45. CW 8.79–80
46. CW 7.413–14
47. CW 3.218
48. CW 3.460
49. CW 8.110–11
50. CW 7.206–07
51. CW 6.480
52. CW 6.232
53. CW 6.478
54. Life 1.145
55. CW 3.312
56. CW 7.264
57. CW 5.390
58. CW 5.389
59. CW 6.479
60. CW 6.345–46

Chapter Three
My Master
pages 45–72

1. DP 383–85; cf. CW 6.184–86, GM 369–71
2. CW 8.308–09
3. CW 3.267
4. CW 4.160–70
5. CW 7.220
6. CW 5.370
7. CW 4.170–73
8. CW 8.81–82
9. CW 4.173–77
10. CW 7.277
11. CW 5.261
12. MS 195, also CW 9.332
13. CW 3.99–100
14. CW 7.254
15. GM 435
16. CW 7.24–25
17. CW 4.184–86
18. MS 289, also CW 8.276
19. CW 5.404

– 354 –

NOTES TO PAGES 60–112

20. CW 7.194
21. CW 7.170–71
22. CW 5.227
23. CW 5.259
24. CW 4.477
25. CW 4.477–78
26. CW 6.311–12
27. CW 3.267–68
28. CW 6.464
29. CW 6.465
30. CW 6.266
31. CW 6.318
32. CW 7.205
33. CW 6.320
34. MS 140, also CW 8.264
35. MS 46, also CW 8.261
36. CW 7.261–62
37. CW 7.242–43
38. CW 7.219
39. CW 4.25
40. CW 7.496
41. CW 7.483–84
42. CW 7.414
43. CW 7.263
44. CW 4.417
45. CW 4.178
46. CW 3.233
47. CW 5.53–54
48. CW 5.186
49. CW 4.25
50. CW 4.29
51. CW 5.268–69
52. CW 7.199
53. CW 7.200
54. CW 4.279
55. CW 6.335
56. CW 4.183–84
57. ND 3.537–38
58. CW 6.330
59. CW 8.497

Chapter Four
Baranagore Math
pages 73–110

1. CW 8.80
2. CW 7.248–50
3. CW 6.342
4. CW 8.80–84
5. CW 7.250–51
6. CW 7.258
7. CW 8.300
8. CW 7.261
9. CW 7.185
10. CW 8.348
11. CW 4.186
12. CW 8.88
13. CW 8.297–98
14. CW 8.298–99
15. Gospel 981–82
16. Gospel 986–87
17. Gospel 987–88
18. MS 159–60, also CW 9.417
19. CW 6.202–03
20. CW 6.203–04
21. CW 6.204
22. CW 8.284
23. CW 6.206–07
24. CW 6.210
25. CW 6.214
26. CW 6.216
27. CW 6.216–17
28. CW 7.443–44
29. CW 6.220–21
30. CW 6.221–22
31. CW 7.242–43
32. CW 6.127
33. CW 2.1
34. CW 4.294–95
35. CW 7.446
36. CW 6.223–24
37. CW 6.234
38. CW 6.229–32
39. CW 7.449
40. CW 6.236–37
41. CW 6.239–42
42. CW 6.242–43
43. CW 8.186–87
44. CW 2.403
45. CW 1.338–39
46. CW 2.281–82
47. CW 7.251
48. CW 1.290–91
49. CW 7.137–38
50. CW 7.51–52
51. CW 6.515–517
52. CW 6.517–18
53. CW 2.10–11
54. CW 2.11–12
55. CW 2.22
56. CW 6.486
57. CW 1.327
58. CW 5.361
59. Life 1.351–52
60. RM 135
61. Life 1.354
62. Life 1.250
63. RM 355
64. CW 8.291–92
65. CW 8.294
66. CW 8.296
67. CW 6.246

Chapter Five
The Divine Call
pages 111–132

1. Life 1.248
2. MS 197
3. CW 5.15–16
4. CW 7.486–87
5. CW 6.289

– 355 –

NOTES TO PAGES 112–182

6. MS 207, also CW 8.31
7. CW 5.95
8. CW 5.96
9. CW 5.96
10. CW 5.92
11. CW 7.485
12. ND 1.67
13. CW 5.104
14. CW 5.104–105
15. CW 8.84–85
16. CW 3.223
17. CW 5.5–9
18. CW 5.11–19
19. CW 8.211
20. CW 3.208–09
21. CW 1.64–65
22. ND 1.20
23. CW 8.67
24. CW 8.58
25. CW 7.453–56
26. CW 7.456
27. CW 7.457
28. CW 5.20–25
29. CW 1.3–4
30. CW 1.20
31. CW 1.15
32. CW 9.433
33. ND 6.155, also CW 9.408
34. CW 8.326–28
35. CW 5.64
36. CW. 5.211
37. CW 6.249–50

Chapter Six
March of Events
pages 133–233

1. CW 3.310
2. CW 6.248–49
3. CW 6.252–53
4. CW 8.217
5. CW 8.104
6. CW 3.187
7. CW 2.27
8. CW 8.219
9. MS 233
10. CW 8.325–26
11. CW 8.329, 331
12. CW 9.8
13. CW 9.10–11
14. CW 8.300–01
15. CW 8.301–03
16. CW 9.14–15
17. CW 7.459
18. CW 8.303–04; cf ND 2.84
19. CW 6.250–56
20. CW 6.290–93
21. CW 5.358
22. CW 7.254–55
23. CW 4.344
24. CW 8.305
25. CW 5.31
26. CW 6.282–83
27. CW 9.18–19
28. CW 5.361
29. CW 7.462–63
30. CW 7.464–65; cf. ND 2.43–44
31. CW 7.466–67
32. CW 9.22
33. CW 7.467–68
34. CW 5.33–34
35. CW 7.469–70

36. CW 5.56
37. CW 8.306, 309; cf. ND 2.82
38. CW 8.310–14
39. CW 9.25
40. CW 5.36–37
41. CW 8.314–15
42. CW 9.26–27
43. CW 8.316–17
44. CW 6.259–61
45. CW 8.318–19
46. CW 9.32
47. CW 5.38–39
48. CW 9.33–35
49. CW 9.37
50. CW 5.42
51. CW 9.40–41
52. CW 8.321–22
53. CW 6.268
54. CW 5.43–44
55. CW 6.269–72
56. CW 5.46
57. CW 8.322
58. CW 8.316
59. CW 5.48
60. CW 8.324–25
61. CW 5.59
62. CW 4.367, 369
63. CW 9.49
64. CW 5.55
65. CW 6.283
66. CW 4.373
67. CW 5.63
68. CW 5.64–65
69. CW 5.67
70. CW 8.333
71. CW 5.70–73
72. CW 6.299
73. CW 6.299–300
74. CW 9.53–54
75. CW 3.185

NOTES TO PAGES 183–239

76. CW 7.124
77. CW 7.125–26
78. CW 5.418
79. CW 6.312
80. CW 3.190–91
81. CW 5.242–43
82. CW 5.244–45
83. CW 5.418
84. CW 5.76–77
85. CW 6.302–04
86. CW 6.309–10
87. CW 8.340–41
88. CW 8.335–36
89. CW 6.306–07
90. CW 8.337
91. CW 5.81–82
92. CW 7.489
93. CW 9.59
94. CW 8.338
95. CW 6.309
96. CW 5.84
97. CW 8.343–44
98. CW 8.345
99. CW 5.91
100. CW 9.65–66
101. CW 5.93–94
102. CW 5.92–93
103. CW 8.346
104. CW 8.349
105. CW 5.95
106. CW 3.310
107. CW 8.351
108. CW 2.27
109. ND 3.230, CW 6.343
110. CW 6.345, 347
111. CW 6.343–44
112. CW 8.352
113. CW 6.336–37
114. ND 3.326–28
115. CW 5.186–88

116. CW 9.71–72
117. CW 6.341
118. CW 5.97–98
119. CW 8.358–59
120. CW 5.314
121. CW 7.77
122. CW 5.360–61
123. CW 8.359
124. CW 8.360
125. CW 9.72
126. CW 9.73
127. CW 8.364–65
128. CW 8.365–67
129. CW 5.189–90
130. CW 8.361
131. CW 8.368–69
132. CW 8.370–71
133. CW 6.357–59
134. CW 9.80–81
135. CW 5.104–05
136. CW 8.373
137. CW 5.105–06
138. CW 5.259
139. CW 8.377
140. CW 7.499
141. CW 7.498–99
142. CW 8.378
143. CW 4.279–81
144. CW 6.495–96
145. CW 5.222
146. CW 5.212
147. CW 5.220–222
148. CW 7.501
149. CW 8.379
150. CW 6.365–67
151. CW 6.368
152. CW 8.380
153. CW 8.382
154. CW 9.89
155. CW 8.383–84
156. CW 8.388

157. CW 6.371–72
158. CW 5.113–14
159. CW 8.388
160. CW 4.274
161. CW 8.389–92
162. CW 6.373–75
163. CW 5.120
164. CW 5.123–25
165. CW 6.384–85
166. CW 8.392–93
167. CW 8.395
168. CW 5.348–49
169. CW 5.135–36
170. CW 5.211
171. CW 5.212–13
172. CW 7.320
173. CW 5.376
174. ND 3.128–29
175. RM 205–206
176. CW 7.301
177. CW 6.312–13
178. CW 6.463
179. CW 8.134

*Chapter Seven
Return to India
pages 234–270*

1. MS 96–97, also CW 8.262
2. CW 3.309
3. CW 6.293–95
4. CW 6.275
5. CW 5.114
6. ND 6.57–58, also CW 9.407
7. CW 3.139–40
8. CW 6.387–88
9. CW 7.337
10. CW 3.207–26
11. CW 8.396

12. CW 6.388–89
13. CW 5.350–51
14. CW 9.93
15. CW 5.128
16. CW 8.398
17. CW 6.389–91
18. CW 6.476–78
19. CW 6.483–84
20. Life 2.253
21. CW 7.505–06
22. CW 8.399–400
23. CW 8.401–02
24. CW 5.128–29
25. CW 8.404–05
26. CW 8.406
27. CW 6.402
28. CW 8.407
29. CW 5.134–37
30. CW 8.408–10
31. CW 8.410
32. CW 8.413–15
33. CW 8.416
34. CW 6.405–06
35. CW 8.417–18
36. CW 8.418
37. CW 8.419–21
38. CW 8.422–23
39. CW 8.426–27
40. CW 6.408
41. CW 8.429
42. CW 8.430–32
43. CW 8.435
44. CW 6.413
45. CW 8.436
46. CW 8.437
47. CW 8.443–44
48. CW 8.441–42
49. CW 8.446–47
50. CW 8.449
51. CW 8.450–51
52. CW 8.451–53

53. CW 9.106–07
54. CW 8.455
55. CW 9.388
56. CW 9.107
57. CW 6.416–17
58. CW 8.458
59. MS 109, also Life 2.39
60. MS 112–13
61. RM 18
62. CW 7.129–31
63. CW 9.108
64. CW 7.137
65. CW 8.461
66. CW 9.109
67. CW 7.114–17
68. CW 6.417
69. CW 9.112
70. RM 313
71. CW 6.418
72. CW 7.513–14
73. CW 9.115–16
74. CW 7.277
75. CW 7.271–73

Chapter Eight
The Plan of Work
pages 271–292

1. CW 4.312–14
2. CW 9.207
3. CW 4.365
4. CW 3.368
5. CW 3.381
6. CW 3.225–26
7. Life 2.232
8. CW 7.176
9. MS 29, also CW 9.412
10. ND 4.142
11. CW 3.316

12. CW 7.478
13. CW 6.281
14. CW 6.301–02
15. CW 3.322–24
16. MS 201
17. CW 6.519
18. CW 3.444–45
19. CW 8.85–91
20. CW 5.28–29
21. CW 4.352
22. CW 6.285
23. CW 3.240
24. CW 4.483
25. RM 356
26. CW 7.176–77
27. CW 7.181–82
28. CW 9.76–77
29. CW 5.413
30. CW 7.188
31. MS 145, also CW 8.264
32. CW 8.266–67
33. CW 5.226–28
34. CW 4.281
35. CW 7.162
36. CW 7.263
37. CW 7.183
38. CW 3.313–14
39. CW 3.314–15
40. CW 3.315–16
41. CW 4.356
42. CW 7.230–31
43. CW 7.245–47
44. CW 7.484–85
45. CW 4.353
46. ND 2.363
47. CW 7.239
48. RM 325–26
49. CW 5.331
50. CW 6.294

Chapter Nine
2nd Visit to the West
pages 293–324

1. CW 7.300–371
2. CW 9.116–17
3. CW 8.464–5
4. CW 9.118–19
5. CW 8.466–67
6. CW 8.470
7. CW 8.471–72
8. CW 8.470
9. CW 9.120
10. CW 8.478–79
11. CW 9.409
12. CW 9.122
13. CW 6.419
14. CW 9.124–5
15. CW 8.483
16. CW 7.520–21
17. CW 9.130–31
18. CW 6.419–21
19. CW 8.483–84
20. CW 6.421–22
21. CW 9.131–32
22. CW 6.422–23
23. CW 8.485–86
24. CW 8.488
25. CW 8.489–91
26. CW 8.524
27. CW 6.424–25
28. CW 8.492–93
29. CW 6.428
30. CW 8.493–94
31. CW 6.428–29
32. CW 8.495
33. CW 8.498
34. CW 7.521–22
35. CW 8.502–03
36. CW 6.429
37. CW 6.430–31
38. CW 8.513
39. CW 8.519
40. CW 8.519–20
41. CW 8.520
42. CW 8.521
43. CW 9.138
44. CW 9.141
45. CW 8.525–26
46. CW 8.526
47. CW 8.527
48. CW 8.528
49. CW 5.507
50. CW 5.471–72
51. CW 9.147
52. CW 6.434
53. CW 6.435–36
54. CW 8.533–35
55. CW 9.148–49
56. CW 8.532
57. CW 5.534–35
58. CW 8.537–38
59. CW 9.149
60. CW 7.372–402
61. CW 8.539

Chapter Ten
"I Believe..."
pages 325–332

1. CW 5.52
2. MS 26, also CW 9.412
3. ND 6.79, also CW 9.407
4. CW 5.50
5. CW 5.202
6. CW 2.336
7. CW 2.373–74
8. CW 5.127
9. MS 140–41, also CW 8.264
10. CW 8.522–23
11. CW 3.471–72
12. CW 4.45
13. ND 6.19, also CW 9.406
14. CW 6.399
15. CW 9.362
16. MS 150, also CW 8.266
17. ND 6.19, also CW 9.406
18. CW 7.271
19. CW 9.216–17
20. CW 2.186
21. CW 1.21
22. CW 4.135–36
23. CW 8.103–04
24. CW 6.227
25. MS 27, CW 9.412
26. CW 8.261
27. ND 6.17, also CW 9.406
28. CW 8.163-64

Chapter Eleven
The Last Days
pages 333–352

1. CW 6.439
2. CW 8.540
3. CW 6.440
4. CW 9.151–52
5. CW 6.440–41
6. CW 8.168
7. CW 5.150
8. CW 5.151–52
9. CW 5.154
10. CW 9.152–53
11. CW 5.158
12. CW 3.449–50

13. CW 7.207–10
14. Life 2.590
15. CW 5.159
16. CW 5.161
17. CW 5.162–63
18. CW 9.160
19. CW 7.229–30
20. CW 7.239
21. CW 8.136
22. CW 5.165–66
23. CW 9.160–61
24. CW 5.167–69
25. CW 9.163
26. CW 5.171
27. CW 6.442
28. CW 5.171
29. CW 5.174
30. CW 5.177
31. CW 9.180–81
32. CW 5.179
33. CW 5.179–80
34. CW 9.187–88
35. RM 354
36. RM 354
37. RM 242
38. ND 4.521, also CW 9.402
39. MS 328–29
40. Life 2.652
41. MS 329
42. CW 8.525
43. ND 4.520
44. CW 6.358
45. CW 6.398–99
46. ST 302
47. CW 6.356
48. CW 8.499
49. CW 5.413
50. CW 5.357–58
51. CW 8.538
52. CW 8.513
53. CW 8.517
54. CW 5.331
55. CW 6.431–33
56. CW 6.429
57. CW 8.522
58. CW 8.505
59. CW 8.503–05
60. CW 5.414